GRILLING BASICS

KNACK™

GRILLING
BASICS

A Step-by-Step Guide to Delicious Recipes

LINDA JOHNSON LARSEN

PHOTOGRAPHS BY DEBI HARBIN

Guilford, Connecticut
An imprint of The Globe Pequot Press

Copyright © 2009 by Morris Book Publishing, LLC

Editor-in-Chief: Maureen Graney
Editor: Katie Benoit
Cover Design: Paul Beatrice, Bret Kerr
Text Design: Paul Beatrice
Layout: Kevin Mak
Cover photos by Debi Harbin
All interior photos by Debi Harbin with the exception of All photos by Debi Harbin with the exception of p. 1 (left): Courtesy of Vermont Castings; p. 1 (right): www.frontgate.com; p. 2 (right): © 2006 Weber-Stephen Products Co. (Used with permission.); p. 3 © 2006 Weber-Stephen Products Co. (Used with permission.); p. 12 (right): Andrey Ushakov; p. 13 (right): © 2006 Weber-Stephen Products Co. (Used with permission.); p. 15 (right): Courtesy of Brookstone; p. 21 (left): Courtesy of Maverick Industries; p. 21 (right): © 2006 Weber-Stephen Products Co. (Used with permission.); p. 22 (right): Courtesy of Derrick Riches www.bbq.about.com; p. 23 (left): © 2006 Weber-Stephen Products Co. (Used with permission.); p. 23 (right): © Robert Byron | Dreamstime.com; p. 25 (left): © 2006 Weber-Stephen Products Co. (Used with permission.); p. 25 (right): Image by Sergio de Paula, Courtesy of Fogazzo Wood Fired Ovens and Barbecues:1-877-FOGAZZO, www.fogazzo.com; p. 33 Image by Sergio de Paula, Courtesy of Fogazzo Wood Fired Ovens and Barbecues:1-877-FOGAZZO, www.fogazzo.com; p. 34 (left): jocicalek/shutterstock; p. 35 (right): Courtesy of Solaire Infrared Grilling Systems www.vipgrills.com

Library of Congress Cataloging-in-Publication Data

Larsen, Linda, 1958-
 Knack grilling basics : a step-by-step guide to delicious recipes / Linda Johnson Larsen ; photographs by Debi Harbin.
   p. cm.
 ISBN 978-1-59921-508-2
 1. Barbecue cookery. I. Title.
 TX840.B3L39 2009
 641.7′6--dc22
                                        2008045956

Printed in China

10 9 8 7 6 5 4 3 2

To my dad, Duane, who always knew how to grill the best steak.

Acknowledgments

Thanks go to my dear husband, Doug, who helped keep the house running while I worked on this book; to my agent Barb Doyen for her help and support; and to my family for their love.

CONTENTS

INTRODUCTION

Grilling is one of the great American pastimes. Most of us look back on childhood scenes of a sunny backyard, with Dad enveloped in a cloud of fragrant smoke, wrapped in an apron and wielding a gigantic fork. Not everything that emerged from his grill tasted wonderful, but all was imbued with the excitement of cooking and eating outside, the smoky fragrance of burning charcoal, and the novelty of seeing Dad doing the cooking.

But in the 21st century, lots of men cook indoors and more women are starting to grill. More than 40 percent of women report using the outdoor grill, but many do not understand how the grill works or know about safe grilling practices. They are interested in feeding their families and guests healthy and safe food, with good flavors, inexpensive ingredients, and consistent results. Grilling outdoors isn't difficult, but you do have to follow some rules.

Grilling is a method of quick cooking. It is the oldest form of cooking. Food that is grilled is cooked on a rack or pan over a heat source, usually charcoal or wood, lately propane or natural gas. Barbecuing and smoking are not grilling. Barbecueing is cooking meats over low coal temperatures for hours. And smoking is cooking meats and some vegetables with smoke at lower temperatures for days at a time. Those methods require different equipment too.

Grill-frying and grill-roasting are two newer forms of grilling. The cooking times aren't as long as with barbecue. The food takes about as long to cook as stir-frying on the stove and roasting in the oven. You can cook quickly on a grill wok, which is usually perforated to add smoky flavor to the food, or roast larger cuts of meat, like roasts, turkeys, and hams in your outdoor grill.

There are basic rules to follow when grilling, just as in any other art or discipline. Take a little time to learn how to set up your grill, how long the coals will take to reach perfect grilling temperature, and how to control the temperature while cooking.

Grilling has come a long way since the 1950s. Now we grill indoors on special appliances, over fragrant woods like apple and mesquite, with charcoal and gas, and over campfires, too. Did you know that you can:

- Produce and adjust two different cooking temperatures at the same time on one simple charcoal grill?

- Test the temperature of your grill with your hand?

- Grill small items like chopped vegetables on any grill?

- Cook pizza on the grill?

- Use herbs in a marinade, in the fire, and as a cooking tool?

- Grill fruits for delicious side dishes and desserts?

- Reduce harmful chemicals that can be produced by cooking over fire by using a marinade?

You can grill just about anything. Grilled appetizers, meats, side dishes, desserts, and salads all have a special smoky flavor. And cleanup is a breeze! Just toss your grilling utensils into a soapy pan of water, and clean the grill with a brief scrub while it's still hot. That's it!

Getting Started

Choose your grill with care. If you are in the market for a new grill, you'll be amazed at the variety and selection. You can find everything from a Notebook grill, about the size of your laptop computer, to huge built-in grills with all the bells and whistles. I'll show you what to look for, and what you'll need to know when narrowing down the choices. Buy the sturdiest grill you can find in your price range. Quality of materials is more important than color or fancy gadgets.

Companies have come up with so many fun utensils, accessories, and toys for the outdoor grill that you can outfit an outdoor kitchen to compete with any indoor setup. Grill charms, special lights for the grill, cleaning tools, and specialized utensils make grilling fun.

You can decorate your outdoor kitchen just as you do your indoor kitchen. Aprons, hot pads, and towels can be coordinated to your outdoor furniture. Have fun with umbrella lights, solar lights, utensils, platters, and plates in different colors and styles. Think about comfortable seating for your guests, and have lots of side tables on which to place drinks and food.

Favorite Grilling Techniques

One of the easiest ways to cook is to wrap ingredients in foil and cook them on the grill. These "presentation packets" are a great way to entertain, and you can even let your guests assemble their own meals from food you lay out for a new twist on buffet entertaining. You are literally making a one-dish meal on the grill.

I discovered grilled meats served with fruit, fruit marinades, and fruity salsas a few years ago and I've never looked back. When you think about it, meats and fruits are natural partners. The acid in fruits acts as a natural tenderizer and the combination of sweet, juicy fruits with rich, savory, tender meats is really fabulous.

Many of us love eating rare hamburgers cooked on the grill. Food experts now recommend that we cook hamburgers until they are well done. While those thoroughly cooked burgers can be juicy if grilled very carefully, I've come up with a new method to let you have medium-rare hamburgers at home once more. Follow the directions to the letter and bite into a juicy, medium-rare burger dripping with flavor (see page 36).

The quick and easy recipes in this book are all made to be varied. In fact, changing a cooking recipe is one of the easiest ways to put your signature on the food you make and serve. Once you've mastered the basic recipe, it's time to add innovation! Substitute chicken breasts in a pork tenderloin recipe, grill salmon fillets in a recipe that calls for chicken, and use your favorite fruits, vegetables, seasonings, and cheeses to add a new twist.

When you're thinking about creating a new recipe, remember favorite dishes you've eaten at your local restaurant. Surf 'n' turf is a classic combination. Shrimp and steak is a natural, but what about salmon and chicken? Season the food with classic American ingredients like garlic and mustard, or choose ethnic flavors. Asian shrimp and sausage kabobs can be seasoned with hoisin sauce and lemongrass. Or take a Tex-Mex detour and grill flank steak and pair it with salmon brushed with salsa.

And don't forget condiments! One of the easiest ways to change the taste of any grilled meat is to serve unusual salsas and toppings. You can make a plain old steak or grilled tuna steak come alive with fiery chili salsa, peach

chutney, pineapple and avocado toppings, or smoky garlic salsa.

Food safety must always be considered whenever you're cooking or grilling. Follow the basic rules: don't leave perishable food out of refrigeration for longer than two hours (one hour if the weather is very hot), separate cooked and uncooked foods, use a fresh platter and utensils for cooked foods, and watch those internal temperatures whenever you're grilling meats. And always wash your hands, the work surface, utensils, and platters after coming in contact with raw meats and eggs. Just take some time and care with your food and you'll always serve fresh, wholesome, delicious meals to satisfy your family and friends.

Have fun with grilling and don't take it too seriously. If some of the food falls through the grate, or a few pieces of salmon burn, make light of it. Part of the fun of grilling is that the food isn't perfect and you are adding adventure and character to your dining experience. The more relaxed you are, the better your food will taste, and the more your guests will relax. If all else fails, chalk it up to experience and order in pizza!

So get your grill ready and mix and match these recipes for the best grilling season of your life. Choose from any of my quick and easy, tried and true recipes, or pick your own favorite recipes and start grilling.

AROUND THE GRILL
You must have all equipment ready before you start to cook

Organizing your grill space is just as important as organizing your kitchen. You must have a clean and sturdy outdoor workspace that is large enough to hold platters, food, and utensils without crowding.

Everything has to be ready and waiting for you before you add food to the grill. Prepare all of the ingredients, collect the utensils and equipment you'll need, and read through the recipe. Then you're ready to grill the food to perfection.

Whether you use gas, charcoal, or electricity to grill your food, some basic rules apply. Be sure you understand how your grill works before you fire it up for the first time. Read through the instruction booklets and owner's manuals that the manufacturer provides. Those manuals contain a lot of important information about the safe use of your grill and

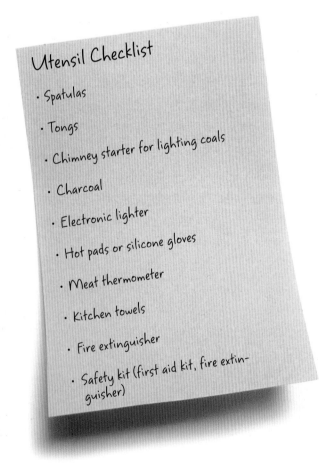

Utensil Checklist

- Spatulas
- Tongs
- Chimney starter for lighting coals
- Charcoal
- Electronic lighter
- Hot pads or silicone gloves
- Meat thermometer
- Kitchen towels
- Fire extinguisher
- Safety kit (first aid kit, fire extinguisher)

Equipment for Charcoal Grill

- Clean the grill right after you finish grilling, then again before you start. A hot grill is easier to clean.

- Store charcoal in a metal bucket, not in the paper bag it came in.

- Position your charcoal grill so it faces away from wind and weather, which can affect how quickly the coals burn.

- A sturdy metal shovel and bucket to move and hold ash is necessary for charcoal grill maintenance and safety.

recommendations for optimum performance. And be sure you understand each and every switch, button, and lever on the grill.

Follow safety rules and apply common sense whenever you use your grill. Keep kids and pets away from the grill area; they can distract you or get hurt coming into contact with the hot surfaces. And never leave the grill while it is lit. For a charcoal grill, dispose of coals carefully and according to fire safety standards. And have fun!

YELLOW LIGHT

One of the most important rules for grilling is to be sure you have enough fuel. Never skimp on fuel. Charcoal will lose heat after 30 minutes, and you'll need to add more briquettes to maintain heat. Most propane tanks have enough gas to cook for 3 to 4 hours. Buy an extra bag of charcoal or an extra propane tank just to be sure.

Equipment for Gas Grill

- Gas grills don't need much extra equipment, except for cooking utensils and a cleaning brush.

- Check all of your equipment before you turn on the grill. Be sure that the propane tank is free from rust and dents.

- The tank for a propane grill is stored under or next to the grill. Some grills have a built-in shelf to hold it securely.

- A gas gauge is helpful to keep track of propane so you don't run out of fuel while cooking.

Grill Location

- Locate your grill carefully. It must be on a solid and level non-flammable surface.

- Grill mats to place under the grill are a good choice for safety. These mats are non-flammable and will extinguish sparks immediately.

- Keep the grill away from your house and away from greenery, especially trees and brush.

- Never move a grill that has been lit. And be sure there are no flammable materials around the grill before you begin.

YOUR OUTDOOR KITCHEN
Organizing your workspace is essential to good grilling practices

Think of your grill and the space around it like an outdoor kitchen. The same safety and health practices you use in your indoor kitchen should be used when cooking outdoors.

Have a source of water nearby, both to aid in cooking and as a safety measure. You should have a way to keep food cool, either with a small refrigerator or chest full of ice. Equipment to clean your hands and utensils should always be part of your outdoor kitchen. Food safety has to be followed to the letter. It's more important than ever in an outdoor kitchen. Some rules include: keep cooked and uncooked food separate, never put cooked food on a platter that held uncooked food, and refrigerate perishable foods after two hours. For the outdoor kitchen, this rule has an addendum: if the ambient temperature is over 80 degrees F, refrigerate foods after one hour.

How to Set Up Workspace

• Separate and designate space for cooked and uncooked food

• Separate tongs and spatulas for cooked and uncooked food

• Set out nonperishable condiments, spices, and herbs and clean platters for cooked food

• Have on hand heavy duty foil, a sharp knife, and a cutting board

Simple Charcoal Grill Kitchen

Bring along a magnet when you look for a steel grill. Cheaper grades of steel attract magnets, while sturdy grades don't.

- Even an inexpensive charcoal grill should be sturdy, with a deep fire bed and steel or iron grates.

- An electric lighter is easier to use and more reliable than matches.

- Look for grills that have a hinged cooking rack, so you can easily add more coals without removing the rack.

- A small, sturdy table is necessary, not only for convenience, but for safety. Balancing a large platter of hot food near a fired-up grill is dangerous.

Read through recipes before you begin, and be sure that you have all of the ingredients and equipment on hand. The food won't stop cooking to wait for you.

Gather all the food and utensils together on your kitchen counter before you take it out to the grill. Then arrange everything around the cooking surface and begin.

Charcoal Grill Kitchen

- A more complicated charcoal grill is more expensive than a kettle grill, but the built-in work space offers a huge advantage.

- Keep the counters clean and dry, and wipe them down with soap and water before you start cooking.

- More expensive charcoal grills often have built-in propane or electric ignition sources to make fire starting easier.

- Store charcoal briquettes well away from the grill area in a solid fireproof container with a lid.

Gas Grill Kitchen

- Side burners are a nice addition to larger gas grills, so consider paying a bit extra for one or two.

- You can use pots and pans on the side burners to cook sauces and pasta and precook vegetables.

- Warming trays and two-level grates are good options for the more complicated gas grills. This helps you control flare-ups and cooking speeds.

- Some kitchens even come with built-in sinks and refrigerators. Clean and maintain them as you would indoor equipment.

INSIDE PREP OPTIONS
These are the types of preparation that must be done inside

While the main cooking event takes place outside, there are some preparation steps that must be completed inside, for ease and convenience as well as food safety.

Weather is always a consideration when preparing food outdoors. If it's very hot or very cold outside, think about doing all of the preparation work inside where you will be more comfortable. When you're working with sharp knives and ex-tremely hot cooking surfaces, if your hands are too cold or are slippery with sweat, you risk an accident.

Weather also has an impact on food safety. Heat speeds up deterioration of food, and sunlight warms food up even faster. Always be careful with perishable foods and work with them as quickly as you can.

Meats and mixtures containing raw egg and dairy products

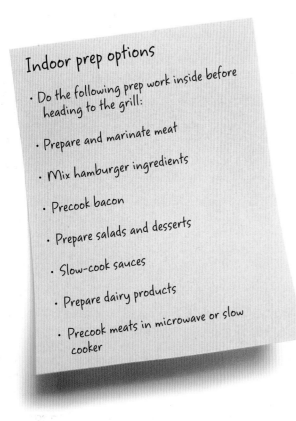

Indoor prep options

- Do the following prep work inside before heading to the grill:

- Prepare and marinate meat

- Mix hamburger ingredients

- Precook bacon

- Prepare salads and desserts

- Slow-cook sauces

- Prepare dairy products

- Precook meats in microwave or slow cooker

Meats Must Stay Cool

- Meats, especially ground meats, must be kept below 40°F at all times until they are cooked.

- Refrigerate meats as soon as you come home from the grocery store. And don't make extra stops on the way; come directly home with perishable foods.

- Never defrost meats at room temperature. Defrost overnight in the refrig-erator, Or thaw meat in the microwave, then cook immediately.

- Wash your hands and all work surfaces with soap and water before and after you handle raw meat.

should be prepared indoors, since these foods should be kept at a cool temperature until it's time to grill. You should also marinate meat indoors; in fact, meat should always be marinated in the refrigerator, not on the counter for any time longer than ten minutes.

If it's really hot outside, do most of your preparation indoors. Delicate herbs, fruits, and vegetables will quickly lose flavor and quality in the heat. And remember that perishable foods, cooked or uncooked, should be handled carefully and served immediately or refrigerated.

GREEN ● LIGHT

Purchase several large platters or use full-sized cookie sheets to help you ferry food and utensils from your inside kitchen to the outside kitchen. Be sure you can lift the platters when they are loaded with equipment. Also look into using old-fashioned utensil and drink caddies and carts that will make coordinating your two kitchens a breeze.

Marinate Meats in the Refrigerator

- Marinades add flavor and make meats tender. Marinades are composed of oil, seasonings, and an acid.

- Never marinate meats on the counter or outside. All meats should marinate in the refrigerator to avoid the danger zone of 40° to 140°F.

- To avoid cross-contamination with other utensils and foods, prepare chicken, pork, and steak indoors on a cutting board before adding to the marinade.

- Don't marinate meats longer than the suggested time or they can become mushy.

Use a Microwave or Slow Cooker to Precook Food

- Precooking foods, especially meats, in the microwave or slow cooker is better done inside. These appliances are made for indoor use.

- In the microwave, be sure to drain off fats as the meat cooks for best flavor and for a finished product that will develop a nice char on the grill.

- For the slow cooker, trim excess visible fat from meats before you cook them.

- Be sure that precooked meats are grilled immediately, for food safety reasons.

OUTSIDE PREP OPTIONS

You can do some preparation of certain foods outside on your grill work surfaces

You can do some types of preparation outdoors, especially if you have several sturdy work surfaces set up near the grill. Work with nonperishable foods, like vegetables and fruits, while you enjoy the nice weather and converse with friends.

Use your work surface like you would a kitchen island or table. You can strip herbs, chop vegetables, skewer kabobs, and even precook vegetables outside.

Invite guests to participate in these activities. Someone can husk corn to be spread with butter and grilled, while another person can prepare bell peppers for charring.

Pasta can be boiled in a sturdy pot on the grill or side burner, and you can fry onion rings or French fries on the grill as

Kabobs on Chilled Tray

- Chill a tray or two in the freezer for several hours and use it to assemble meat kabobs outdoors.

- While the tray is chilling, soak wooden kabobs in water so they won't burn on the grill.

- There are trays available with gel inserts that you can chill or heat up; they'll hold temperature for three hours.

- Be sure that you work with and cook perishable foods quickly, and serve them as soon as they are done.

Messy Preparation

- Some messy preparations like shucking corn and pitting cherries are perfect for outside duty.

- All you need is the produce and a pail for the waste. You can add peels, corncobs, and leaves to a charcoal fire.

- Remove cooked corn from the cob by placing it in the center hole of a Bundt pan.

- Cut down the cob so the kernels release into the pan. Place the cob in the compost pile or add it to charcoal.

well. Whether or not you stir-fry complete meals on the grill, you can use a cast iron skillet to pre cook ingredients like potatoes and other root vegetables for skewers and for making foil packages.

You can also cook breakfast foods on the grill; pancakes and bacon on a griddle, and eggs in a heavy saucepan right over the coals for a wonderful smoky flavor.

Cleanup outside is also a possibility. You can place a couple of large containers full of soapy water near the grill to hold utensils and platters as you work. Then cleanup will be easy.

Slice and Cube Vegetables and Fruits

- Peeling and slicing fruits and vegetables is another preparation step to complete outdoors.

- It's easy and convenient to prepare vegetables and fruits outside, and much more pleasant than working in the kitchen.

- Use a plastic or wood cutting board placed on top of steel countertops so they aren't marred by the sharp knife.

- Use a food screen, plastic wrap, or foil to cover prepared food to keep it safe from insects and animals.

Precook Vegetables Outside

- Even if you don't have a side burner, you can precook root vegetables in boiling water in a pot on the cooking grate.

- Prepare the vegetables on your work table or attached countertop while the water comes to a boil.

- Use a pasta insert with holes that fits into the pot. Then all you have to do is lift the insert to drain the vegetables.

- Let the pot holding the boiling water cool on a solid, heatproof surface.

TYPES OF SMOKE

Lump charcoal, woods, vines, herbs, and wood chips provide lots of smoke flavor

Smoke is one key to grilling flavor. Some people say that food isn't on the grill long enough to impart true wood flavor, but there is a taste difference between food cooked over smoke and food that is simply broiled, sauteed, or pan fried. And then there's the ephemeral feeling of being enveloped in flavorful smoke as you work that only happens when you cook over a grill. The aroma in the air adds to the party feeling and contributes to the overall flavor of the food.

Milder foods like vegetables or fish will pick up more smoke flavor than strongly-flavored foods like ribs or beef steak. Choose from charcoal briquettes, lump charcoal, and hardwoods to fire your charcoal grill, and you can add other

Lump Charcoal

- Real charcoal is made of wood that has been burned in an oxygen-starved environment, removing everything but carbon and ash.

- Lump charcoal is an efficient source of heat that burns evenly.

- Lump charcoal is made from

real solid wood—unlike briquettes, which are often made from sawdust and fillers—so you don't have to worry about additives or chemicals in your fire.

- Actual charcoal burns slightly hotter than briquettes and will be ready for food in about 20 minutes.

Hardwood Logs

- You can use hardwood logs in your charcoal grill for a true grilling experience.

- Never use treated woods or softwoods like pine, which contain resins that give food an off-flavor. Be sure the woods are not moldy.

- It takes more skill to cook over actual wood, since the temperature of the fire varies according to the moisture in the wood.

- Build a hardwood fire as you would a campfire, starting with kindling and stacking small logs on top.

smoke producers like herbs, spices, vines, and wood chips.

Never use briquettes soaked in lighter fluid, soft woods, or chemically treated woods for grilling. The briquettes soaked in lighter fluid may impart off-flavors. Soft woods like pine give off a strong resinous flavor that isn't very palatable. And chemically treated woods are definitely hazardous.

Have fun choosing different types of wood and other flavor providers. You can find this equipment at kitchenware stores, at many hardware stores, and at some lumberyards.

Wood flavors are subtle, but do make a difference. Apple and cherry add some sweetness and fruity flavor, while ash is a light flavor. Cherry and hickory have a heavy, assertive flavor. Maple smoke is mellow, warm, and slightly sweet, while mesquite and oak are woodsy and earthy. Grapevines are rich and fruity, while pecan is sweet and slightly nutty.

Vines, Herbs, Wood Chips, Chunks, and Pellets

- Vines, herbs, wood chips, and wood chunks can be placed directly on charcoal. Chips and chunks must be soaked, but flavored wood pellets can be used dry.

- Grapevines are the most common vines used for smoke flavor.

- Any herb or spice, dried or fresh, can be added directly to a burning charcoal fire. Herb stalks can be used as kabob skewers.

- Soak wood chips and chunks in water for 1 hour before adding to the fire so they'll smoke.

Gas Grill Flavor Additions

- Herbs, vines, and wood chips and chunks can't be placed directly on the gas grill burners. They should be enclosed in foil packets or smoke boxes.

- To form a foil packet, use heavy duty foil and wrap the items, using a double fold.

- Make several cuts in the top of the packet so smoke can escape.

- A smoke box should be made from stainless steel. It has a cover with slits in it to release smoke.

KEY GRILLING FLAVORS

Rubs, brines, pastes, marinades, planks, and spice blends all add to the smoky grill flavor

We love grilled food because of all of that flavor. The caramelization, crust, and smokiness are all delicious. But there are other ways to add flavor to grilled food. Cedar planks or wood paper, rubs, marinades, sauces, glazes, and spice blends are all fun and easy ways to flavor food.

But did you know that rubs and marinades do more than just add flavor? When you grill, two kinds of carcinogens are created. One, poly-cyclic aromatic hydrocarbons, occur when food burns. And the second, called heterocyclic amine, or HCA, is created from the high heat of the fire. Marinades reduce the amount of HCAs on your food by acting as a barrier, or the acids and herbs themselves may be preventative.

Lemon-Garlic Marinade

¼ cup olive oil

¼ cup lemon juice

1 tablespoon honey

2 cloves garlic, minced

1 tablespoon minced fresh rosemary

½ teaspoon grated lemon zest

⅛ teaspoon lemon pepper

Salt and pepper to taste

Mix all ingredients and marinate meat for 8–24 hours.

Cedar Planks

- Add flavor to food by cooking directly on a piece of solid wood that has been soaked in water. You can add, spices, juices, or wine to this liquid for even more flavor.

- Use fresh, raw, untreated wood. You can find planks in hardware stores. Or buy flavored, seasoned planks at hardware or kitchenware stores.

- Soak the plank for 1 hour, then place on the grill. Cover and heat until smoke begins to come through the vents.

- Place the food on the plank, cover, and cook as directed.

For food safety, always "cook off" the marinade by turning the sides brushed with marinade toward the heat for at least 1 minute.

Dry rubs

Marinades

- Dry rubs are an easy way to add intense flavor to foods, and to help develop a crust and caramelization.

- These rubs can be made in quantity and stored in an airtight container in a cool, dry place.

- Remove the amount you want from the container and place on small plate, then use. Don't dip foods directly into the container.

- It's easy to vary a rub recipe; just use your favorite ingredients. Write down the recipe and label the container.

- Most marinades use too much oil, which can cause flare-ups. Reduce the oil by ½ in most other recipes (not including this book).

- Marinades tenderize meat with acid. Acidic ingredients like citrus juices, vinegar, and wine break down fibers in meat.

- If you combine a rub and a marinade, you get a paste. Rub paste on food and refrigerate for 1 hour.

- Try placing meats on other foods while grilling. A bed of rosemary, lemon slices, or onion slices adds great flavor to chicken or fish.

GAS OR CHARCOAL?

Here's how to choose between the two basic types of outdoor grills

Most grills are powered with gas or charcoal. The end result of smoky, caramelized food with a nice crust is the same. Choose the grill you want based on price, convenience, and style.

Charcoal grills are less expensive and offer fewer features, but more challenges in terms of creating and maintaining the fire. Here's where you can satisfy your primitive urge to cook over fire. Building and maintaining a fire will take just as much or more time as grilling the food. Most charcoal aficionados love this part of outdoor cooking.

Gas grills are more expensive. Because they are necessarily more complicated than charcoal, and have more parts and mechanics, they cost about twice as much as charcoal grills. They are easier to use because there's no need to build

Pros and cons of charcoal

- Less expensive
- Attains higher heat
- Best for grill-roasting and slow barbecue
- More smoke flavor
- More challenge in fire lighting
- More difficult to control temperature
- Needs more equipment
- Messier to use
- Takes longer to begin cooking

Charcoal Grill

- There are several ways to start a charcoal fire. Briquettes soaked in lighter fluid are easy, but they can add chemical taste to the food.

- Electric fire starters are easy to use; just plug them in and place in the charcoal.

- A chimney starter is easy, too. Place it in the fire bed, add newspaper, and top with charcoal. Light the newspaper and let the coals burn until covered with ash.

- Or build a pyramid of coals over kindling and light.

a fire; you just flip a switch. The fuel is natural gas or propane, which is clean burning and quick to heat. You can start cooking much sooner, and you buy propane tank refills less often than charcoal and fire starting equipment.

Charcoal burns drier than gas because it only produces carbon dioxide when it burns. Gas produces carbon dioxide and 30 percent water vapor. That's why many foods, especially steaks, char and sear better over charcoal than over gas. But other than this searing difference, both grills cook food the same.

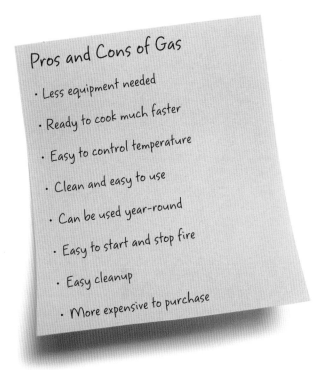

Pros and Cons of Gas

- Less equipment needed
- Ready to cook much faster
- Easy to control temperature
- Clean and easy to use
- Can be used year-round
- Easy to start and stop fire
- Easy cleanup
- More expensive to purchase

MAKE IT EASY

Most charcoal grills have about 400 square inches of cooking space, while gas grills have up to 700 square inches, with more on warming grates. A larger grill will let you cook more food more quickly and gives you the option of cooking more than one type of food at the same time, especially if those foods require different temperatures.

Gas Grill

- A gas grill consists of a gas supply, which is mixed with air, then lit and used to heat flavor bars or ceramic briquettes.

- The grate sits on top of the bars or briquettes and holds the food.

- The flame should be mostly blue. If the flame is yellow, the venturi tubes that connect the burners to the valve and add air to the gas may need cleaning.

- Close the lid and heat for 10 minutes. Then open the grill, scrape the grate, and start cooking.

NECESSARY COOKING UTENSILS
With these basic cooking utensils, you can safely fire up the grill

Utensils act as an extension of your hands when you're grilling. Remember, even kabob handles can get screaming hot over the fire, so always protect your hands by using hot pads, long-handled tongs, spatulas, and brushes.

Many tools are made for the grill with heat-resistant handles. These materials shouldn't transmit heat; still, be careful handling tools over the hot fire.

Buy the sturdiest and best utensils you can afford. Tongs should be made from stainless steel and have very long handles; and they should be spring-loaded, so the only action needed is to close them. Get several sizes and shapes of spatulas. And it's always helpful to have more than one thermometer.

Also think about purchasing one set of utensils to use on

Necessary Utensils
- Long-handled spring-loaded stainless steel tongs
- Long-handled regular spatula
- Long-handled fish spatula
- Long-handled fork
- Instant-read thermometer
- Silicone brushes
- Chef's knife
- Paring knife
- Cutting board
- Heat-proof thermometer

Spring-loaded Tongs

- Spring-loaded tongs are, hands down, the most important tools for grilling.

- Spring-loaded means that they open automatically, and you squeeze to close them on the food. If you don't have spring-loaded tongs, you have to open and close the tongs, which

is cumbersome.

- Color-coordinated tongs are good for using on cooked and uncooked food.

- Designate specific tongs to use on meat, fish, or vegetables, as the tongs can transfer residue and char from one food to another.

uncooked meats and meats on the grill, and another to use on the completely cooked meats. Cross-contamination occurs easily between utensils. Either wash them thoroughly in hot soapy water in between uses, or have separate sets.

Clean utensils right away when you're done grilling, because food and sauces can burn onto their surfaces and make a mess. They can soak in a container or sink of soapy water until you're ready to dry them and put them away. And keep them clean and dry, so they're ready to go when you are.

Brushes

- There are many kinds of brushes and mops available, from herb brushes you assemble yourself to high-tech tools.

- Use a new, natural-bristle paintbrush or basting brush to add sauces, pastes, and marinades to the food.

- Silicone brushes and mops have the advantage of being easy to clean. They are dishwasher-safe and won't rust or corrode.

- Fresh herbs, gathered in a bunch and tied with cotton twine, add even more flavor to your food when used as a brush.

Thermometers

- Instant-read and heat-resistant thermometers are important tools for food safety.

- Heat-resistant thermometers are used for long-cooked large cuts of meat. Insert one into the meat before placing it on the grill.

- These tools are the fastest and most accurate way to check doneness of meat, poultry, and seafood. Digital readouts are faster than a dial.

- Some thermometers are available in the form of a fork, which combines two tools in one.

MORE COOKING AIDS

Equipment specially made for the grill, from grill baskets to woks, will make grilling more fun and satisfying

There are hundreds, if not thousands, of grilling utensils, cooking aids, gadgets, and toys that you can use to make your grilling experience easier and more fun. Your local hardware store has many cooking aids, kitchenware stores have some too, and even grocery stores have a good selection of tools. But for the greatest selection of grilling gadgets, turn to the Internet and grilling catalogs.

In Resources, you'll find a list of websites and catalogs that will provide you with tools and toys. Just browsing through them can give you ideas about how to use your grill and entertain. Many of these toys are useful, too, assisting you in cooking foods more easily and playing a role in food safety.

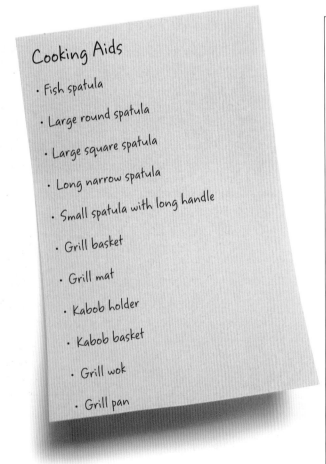

Cooking Aids

- Fish spatula
- Large round spatula
- Large square spatula
- Long narrow spatula
- Small spatula with long handle
- Grill basket
- Grill mat
- Kabob holder
- Kabob basket
- Grill wok
- Grill pan

Spatulas

- Spatulas are the second-most important grilling tool; used to turn fragile foods.

- Spatulas must be sturdy and heavy, and have a long wood or silicone handle that won't transfer heat.

- Have several different shapes and sizes of spatulas for turning food. The unusually shaped spatula shown above, for turning fish, is a great aid for any large food. Small spatulas help loosen food and turn kabobs.

- Spray the spatula with nonstick cooking spray so it won't stick, even to glazed foods.

The tools you use will depend on the food you cook. Every now and then, try something new. Many of these tools and toys are quite inexpensive, so you can experiment with them without making a big investment.

As you continue grilling, you'll find that you reach again and again for the same tools. When you love a utensil, try to buy more than one. Cooking equipment comes and goes in the marketplace, so when you find a good tool, it's best to buy several.

Grill Basket

- Grill baskets help you cook smaller foods that would otherwise fall through the grate.

- Look for a hinged grill basket to easily add and remove the food. The basket should have a long handle.

- Like spatulas, baskets come in all shapes and sizes. There's even a basket shaped like a whole fish, and another that holds corn on the cob!

- Spray the basket with non-stick spray or brush with oil before you add the food for perfect results.

Grilling Wok

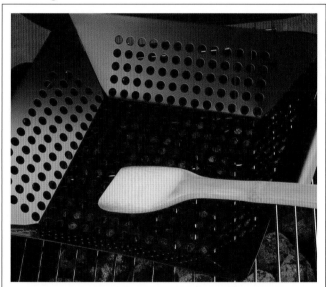

- Woks and pans for the grill are different from traditional versions; they have holes!

- The holes mean that you can't add a sauce, but they add an incomparable smoky flavor to the food.

- Marinate the food in a sauce, put the wok in the sink, and pour the food into it. Then you're set to grill.

- You can use a silicone heat-proof spatula, a wooden spoon, or a metal spatula to stir the food on the wok.

GRILLING TOYS
Motorized brushes, charms, and spice holders make grilling fun

Grilling toys not only make grilling more fun, they also make great presents. You can find everything from grilling charms, like wine glass charms, which mark individual steaks or chicken breasts, to a marshmallow roasting stick that lets you know when the marshmallow is done. (The prongs separate when it's perfectly grilled.)

Other toys, which actually have a purpose include popcorn poppers, hot dog racks, and timers and spice racks that are functional and cute. Be sure that you're buying quality too; even the toys should be sturdy and well made, with no loose parts or cheap materials. Even though you're having fun grilling, you still have to keep safety in mind.

You can find grilling toys just about anywhere, from the grocery store to the hardware store to specialty tourist shops.

Toys and Accessories

- Grill charms
- Spice rack
- Motorized grill brush
- Pizza stone and pizza peel
- Marshmallow fork
- Grill popcorn popper
- Hot dog roller
- Drumstick holder
- Thermapen
- Grill light
- Rotisserie

Grill Charms

- Grill charms are unbelievably cute and useful. If one of your guests wants a well done steak, while another wants it medium rare, charms are an easy way to distinguish the food.

- Have your guests pick the charm they want to mark their food on the grill.

- Write a note on a notepad about which charm belongs to which guest.

- Remember to warn your guests that the metal charms are going to be very hot when they come off the grill.

Just like utensils, you have to take care of your grilling toys. Wash them in soapy water and dry them well after each use, and store in safe places. Follow manufacturer's directions for using and maintaining these toys and tools, and don't use them for unintended purposes.

Remember where you bought your toys, because when others see what you have, they'll want some too!

Spice Rack

- Spices, whether straight from the grocery store or blends you make yourself, add great flavor to grilled food.

- A spice rack that hangs on the side of the grill is a very convenient way to organize your outdoor kitchen.

- Other racks attach to the insides of grill cabinet doors and can hold condiment bottles, too.

- Don't leave spices outdoors for a long time. They have to stay in a cool and dry place to keep their potency.

Motorized Grill Brush

Since it's important to keep the grill clean, there are lots of fun tools available, including a brush that uses steam to scrape the grate.

- A metal or brass brush is a must for cleaning your grill. But you can have fun with even that prosaic activity.

- A motorized brush makes cleaning super fast and easy. A clean grill is very important for flavor and food safety.

- It's a great choice for older grillers or those with arthritis since you don't need to press down hard.

- Use the motorized brush only on a cool grill. The brushes are softer and can melt in the heat.

MORE FUN ACCESSORIES

Lots of utensils and goodies are both fun and helpful for grilling

Outdoor cooking just seems more lighthearted than traditional cooking indoors. And there are so many fun accessories and toys to add a whimsical touch to your cookout. Some toys are very useful as well!

The types of toys and accessories you buy will depend on what you grill. If you like to grill pizzas, a pizza stone and a pizza peel will make the experience much more satisfying.

For cooking large cuts of meat, a sturdy rack will shield the meat from direct heat so it cooks more evenly. And grill mats and woks help you cook vegetables with ease.

With these accessories, you're looking for fun, but the equipment should also have a function. The tools and toys should be made for use with the grill; be sure to read labels and directions.

KNACK GRILLING BASICS

Pizza Stone

- Pizza stones are similar to planks, but they are reusable and provide lots of direct heat.

- Pizza dough cooks smoky and crisp on the grill. You can place the dough directly on the rack, but the stone makes it easier.

- The pizza stone can heat up to 500°F, so be very careful handling it.

- A pizza peel, or large circular wooden spatula with a long handle, will easily and safely take the pizza off the stone.

Grill Light on Spatula

A grill light is not only a fun accessory but a safety must when grilling at night. If the grill area is well lit, you'll avoid accidents.

- The multipurpose grill light attaches to the handle of any utensil to focus light on the food.

- There are some spatulas and tongs that have a built-in light. Be sure to follow cleaning instructions on those utensils.

- You can also find LED lights that attach to the side of the grill to light up the entire surface.

- These lights are specially made to stand up to the heat of the grill. Don't use an ordinary clip-on light.

If you like to grill at night or in the fall and winter when the days are short, there are several types of grill lights to buy. Some attach directly to the grill; others are made to be fastened onto tongs or forks so you can direct the light at the food.

Rotisseries cook large cuts of meat with ease, and new-fangled thermometers make food safety and checking meat doneness a breeze.

Thermapen

- New thermometers not only read an exact internal can temperature in seconds, but some don't even touch the food!

- The Thermapen is a professional-grade thermometer with a fold-out probe that registers temperature in 4 seconds.

- Infrared thermometers don't touch the food. They can judge doneness of baked goods or vegetables. Don't use this thermometer for meat doneness.

- Some infrared thermometers come equipped with an internal temperature probe.

Grill Rotisserie

- You can make your own rotisserie chicken or turkey better than that from the deli, and the grill does all the work.

- Some grills come with a rotisserie attachment, but you can buy a separate aftermarket rotisserie, even for charcoal grills.

- Meats self-baste on the rotisserie because the fat melts and moves around the meat as it cooks.

- Read instructions carefully. Buy one with a powerful motor, and don't try to jerry-rig a rotisserie yourself.

GRILL SAFETY KIT
Grilling can be a dangerous occupation. Here are tools to keep you safe

As with any activity that involves high heat and fire, you must have a safety kit on hand at all times. And be sure that you know how to use it.

The kit should contain a well-stocked and up-to-date first aid kit. Be sure you include medicines and salves to treat burns. There should also be a fire extinguisher that you know

how to use, along with boxes of salt and baking soda that can be used to put out fires.

Access to a hose or running water is also important. This can be used to treat burns and to put out a charcoal fire that gets out of control. Assemble the kit when you buy your grill, and check the contents, looking for expiration dates. Buy new

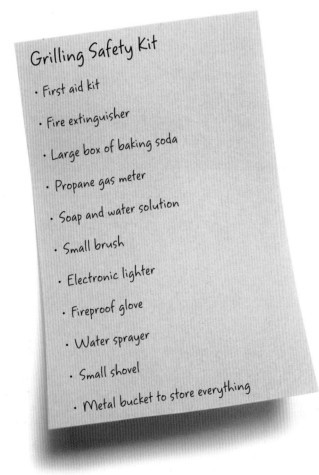

Grilling Safety Kit

- First aid kit

- Fire extinguisher

- Large box of baking soda

- Propane gas meter

- Soap and water solution

- Small brush

- Electronic lighter

- Fireproof glove

- Water sprayer

- Small shovel

- Metal bucket to store everything

Checking for Gas Leak

- Be sure the tank is turned off and the burners are off. Check the connections.

- Mix up a solution of 1 part liquid soap to 1 part water. Brush the solution on all the gas connections using a clean brush or soft rag, then open the valves.

- If bubbles form, especially bubbles that grow, there is a leak. Perform a second test.

- If a second test confirms a leak, do not use the grill; call a qualified serviceperson for repair.

equipment for every new season. You can buy complete kits, or make your own. Store the equipment in a metal bucket with a secure lid.

If you smell gas, turn the grill off immediately and call for a repair. The gas should be enclosed in the tubes and burners and should not smell. If the odor persists, call the fire department.

And be sure that the coals in your charcoal grill are completely cool before you retire the grill for the night. Too many house fires have been started by a spark from hot coals.

• • • • • • • • • • • RED ● LIGHT • • • • • • • • • • • •

The easiest and safest way to put out a fire is to smother it. Just close the lid and the vents if you can. If you can't, baking soda or salt dumped on the fire will smother it. Be careful about using water to put out a charcoal fire; it can cause an explosion. And never use water to extinguish a gas fire.

Silicone Gloves

- There are many types of hot pads and gloves on the market. Buy several pairs, all of the highest quality you can afford.

- Leather gloves are the classic accessory. Buy gloves that extend over your wrists for the most protection.

- The newer silicone gloves withstand more heat. You can even touch the grilling surface when you're wearing these gloves.

- But don't tempt fate. Don't handle coals, flavor rods, or burning wood with the gloves.

Grilling Safety Kit

- Learn how to use a fire extinguisher before you need it. When you need to use it, you won't have time to read the instructions.

- Be sure to check the expiration date on the extinguisher and other kit items.

- Never reduce flare-ups on a gas grill with a water sprayer. Move the food around or turn burners off.

- Treat your safety kit like any other grill tool or accessory. Keep it clean and dry, and within reach at all times.

CHARCOAL GRILL TYPES

There are several types of charcoal grills from which to choose

Charcoal grills range from a small portable tabletop model to a fancy large grill set into a countertop that's part of a complete outdoor kitchen. Price ranges vary from a few dollars to hundreds of dollars.

These grills are less expensive than gas grills simply because they are less complicated. All you need to grill is a container to hold charcoal and a rack to place over the charcoal.

But you do need to keep buying charcoal or another fuel throughout the life of the grill. This is comparable to purchasing propane gas refills. Hardwoods, flavored woods, and fuel like vines or lump charcoal are more expensive. Other maintenance and running costs are minimal.

You may want to buy several different sizes and types of charcoal grills. A small Notebook grill can be taken on a picnic

Costs and Upkeep

- Small grill costs under $100
- Larger grills cost $200 or more
- Charcoal costs about $9 a pound
- Portable workstations cost $50
- Aftermarket tables and counters are available
- Clean grill before and after each use
- Remove ash after each use
- Keep vents clear of ash buildup
- Cover grill when cool and not in use

Notebook Grill

- Small, portable grills are great choices for campers, RV travelers, tailgaters, and picnic fans.

- The new Notebook grill folds up like a laptop computer for easy storage, and even has handles to make it super portable.

- Be sure that the small grill has stainless steel grates, a deep firepan, and sturdy construction.

- Treat these small grills with the same care as larger ones. Keep them clean and be sure they are cool and dry before storing.

or used to cook appetizers when grill-roasting a large cut of meat. A couple of basic kettle grills will let you cook a whole meal for company. And a large built-in charcoal grill will let you feed a crowd or entertain a large group.

Even if you have just a basic square or kettle grill, you can add to it with products ranging from countertops to whole kitchens. Many of these products are designed specifically for charcoal grills.

GREEN ● LIGHT

Another type of charcoal grill is a kamado grill, which uses pressure and heat to cook food. One common brand of kamado is The Big Green Egg. These expensive grills are made of heavy cast iron. They use very little fuel. The lid locks onto the grill, creating an environment like a pressure cooker so food is ready in a flash.

Kettle Grill

- Look for a sturdy kettle grill with a deep grill pan and a high cover for most versatility.

- The grill should be made of sturdy stainless steel and have a large cooking surface of at least 200 square inches.

- You can buy shelves that attach to the side of the grill and fold down; use a wooden or metal cutting board on top.

- Look for sturdy, well-made aftermarket products to really enhance the usability of the grill.

Charcoal Grill Kitchen

- The charcoal grill can be incorporated into a kitchen just like a gas grill.

- Have an outdoor kitchen built and set a charcoal grill into it, or purchase a grill with counters and cabinets attached.

- Consider adding a charcoal grill to your outdoor gas kitchen. Charcoal does a better job of searing meat but can be more challenging to cook with.

- If you want to build a large kitchen, consult with a designer and carefully consider placement of appliances.

FIRE IT UP

Learn the easiest and fastest ways to light the fire in your charcoal grill

To start a charcoal fire, you need some special equipment: An ignition source can be lighter fluid, an electric coil, a chimney starter, or newspaper or paraffin coils and a match. The coals, whether briquettes, wood, or lump charcoal, will cook down to ash on their own once they have been started.

There are several ways to start the charcoal in your grill. All work well, but some are quicker and more convenient than others. And some are safer to use than others. On windy days, an electric coil is probably the safest. Using newspaper without a chimney starter can be risky. Whatever method you use, don't leave the grill until the coals have caught and safely started to burn.

Coal-Starting Method and Times

- Chimney starter: about 20 minutes
- Charcoal pyramid: about 30 minutes
- Lighter fluid: about 30 minutes
- Paraffin fire starter: about 30 minutes
- Electric coil: about 20 minutes
- Charcoal briquettes: about 30 minutes
- Wood chips or chunks: about 30 minutes
- Logs: about 1 hour

Charcoal Pyramid

- Starting coals using a pyramid is the simplest method. Stack about 50 briquettes in a pyramid shape in the grill pan.

- Pour a ½ cup of lighter fluid over the briquettes, or tuck a paraffin fire starter under the coals.

- Let the fluid soak in for 5 minutes. Then carefully light the coals with a long match or electric lighter. Never add more lighter fluid after starting the fire.

- Let the coals burn for 25 minutes or until they are covered with ash, spread in an even layer, and cook.

Once the fire is started, it will maintain cooking temperatures for about an hour. If you are cooking longer than that, you'll need to add more charcoal or wood to the grill.

In general, one pound of meat needs thirty charcoal briquettes to cook. Use one hundred coals for the typical meal. If you cook longer than one hour, add more charcoal to the grill for a constant temperature. You can add ten to twelve briquettes directly to the fire, or start more in a chimney starter and add them to the coals as needed.

YELLOW LIGHT

There is an appliance that claims to start charcoal grills in sixty seconds, available from Hammacher Schlemmer (see Resources). It looks like a flame-thrower and may be just as risky to use. It's better to light your grill using more traditional methods.

Electric Starter

- An electric starter is made of a metal coil attached to a fireproof handle, with an electric cord.

- The coil heats up when the starter is plugged into an outlet. Place the coil in the center of the briquettes.

- A heavy duty extension cord can be used if the cord is too short to reach from the grill to an outlet.

- Remove the coil once the coals have caught fire. Let it cool completely on a heatproof surface.

Chimney Starter

- A chimney starter is convenient. It looks like a round metal can with a handle attached.

- Place the chimney in the grill pan and fill the chimney with coals. Tip the chimney slightly and tuck newspaper or paraffin starters in the bottom. Light the paper through the holes at the bottom.

- Let the charcoal burn until covered with ash. Using a fireproof glove, tip the coals into the grill pan and arrange.

- Let the chimney cool completely before storing.

COAL TEMPERATURES

Judging the temperature of the coals is critical to getting the best results

One of the biggest mistakes new grillers make is to start cooking before the coals are actually ready. Charcoal, whether briquette or lump, takes time to get to the proper temperature. If you start cooking before the coals are correctly burned, you risk burning the food without cooking the interior. And, if you use briquettes soaked in lighter fluid, also called matchlight

charcoal, there's a chance the food will taste of chemicals.

Coals are ready when they are evenly covered with a gray ash and there are no visible flames. There can be some red glowing areas, but there should be no black coals. Spread the coals around if they aren't burning evenly. Use a coal rake or fireplace poker, and a silicone mitt to protect your hands.

Gauging Temperature with your Hand

- If you can hold your hand 2 inches above the grate for:

- 2 seconds, the fire is high, about 500 degrees F.

- 3 seconds, the fire is medium-high, about 400 degrees F.

- 5 seconds, the fire is medium, about 350 degrees F.

- 6 seconds, the fire is medium-low, about 300 degrees F.

- 7 seconds, the fire is low, about 250 degrees F.

Coals Too Cool

- The coals shown above are only about one-third ready at this stage. The food will not sear properly if you add it to the grill at this time.

- At this point, lighter fluid will not be burned off and will affect the food's flavor.

- If the coals stay at this stage for more than 15 minutes, you'll need to add more hot coals.

- Light more in a chimney; do not add more coals to the grill and relight them.

If you use a chimney starter, wait until the coals are covered with ash before adding them to the grill pan. The coals are then immediately ready for cooking. This is also a good way to add coals when the food is cooking.

But with the other methods, you must watch and wait until the coals are ash-covered before you add the food.

If you use lump charcoal, it will burn faster than briquettes or wood, and you'll need to add more sooner than you think.

CHARCOAL VS. GAS

Red Hot Coals

- The coals in this picture are too hot and are not ready for cooking.

- The food will burn and be raw on the inside if you try to cook over coals at this stage.

- The leaping flames will cause flare-ups and will burn and char the food. They can also burn you while you manipulate the food.

- Just let the coals keep burning and they will come to the proper cooking temperature in about 10–15 minutes.

Coals are Ready

- When the coals are evenly covered with a gray or white ash, they are ready for cooking. At night, the coals will be glowing red.

- New briquettes, with a grooved exterior, will light faster and be ready in about 15 minutes.

- The food will cook evenly and quickly, with nice grill marks and a moist interior.

- Now you can move the coals around for higher or lower heat and for indirect or direct grilling, using your long-handled tongs.

CONTROLLING TEMPERATURE

Believe it or not, you can control temperature, even on a charcoal grill

Just like a stovetop or oven, the temperature of a grill must be adjusted and maintained for perfect results. This is accomplished in several ways: moving the coals around, opening and closing the vents, and moving the food away from or closer to the coals.

Before you even light the coals, you can arrange hotter and cooler areas on the grill, or set up for indirect grilling. A two-level fire is created by piling coals thicker on one side of the grill than the other. And by leaving part of the grill pan free from coals, you create a more gentle heat.

The food can then be moved around from the hotter to cooler parts of the grill as needed. Sear food over the hot

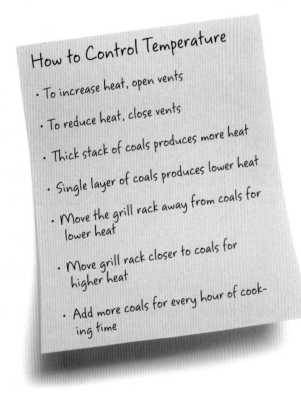

How to Control Temperature

- To increase heat, open vents

- To reduce heat, close vents

- Thick stack of coals produces more heat

- Single layer of coals produces lower heat

- Move the grill rack away from coals for lower heat

- Move grill rack closer to coals for higher heat

- Add more coals for every hour of cooking time

Indirect Heat

- For charcoal, arrange coals so they cover one half of the grill pan, or arrange them on both sides, with an empty space in the middle.

- Place an aluminum drip pan on the empty area. This will reduce flare-ups, catch drippings, and add flavor in the form of smoke.

- Your gas grill must have at least two burners for indirect heat.

- Turn one burner off and place the drip pan over the unused burner on the flavor bars or lava rocks.

parts, then move to cooler areas to cook through.

For the most control on a charcoal fire, build a gradual fire. Create an even slope with the coals from four to five thick on one side, down to an empty area on the other. This will give you an even gradient of temperature across the grill.

Gas grills are controlled by turning burners on and off, and by choosing low, medium, and high heat. You can then move the food around, just like over charcoal, to hotter and cooler parts of the grill.

ZOOM

Indirect heat is used to cook larger cuts of meat that cook longer. With the cover down, this turns your grill into an oven, since the heat circulates up and around the food. For the most flavor, place the cover so the vents are on the side opposite the coals. You'll need to add more coals each hour.

Two-level Fire

- The two-level fire is one of the best ways to control grill temperatures.

- The hot side of the fire should have coals four deep, and the cool side should have a single layer of coals.

- Move the food around as it cooks. Sear over the hot area, and then move to the cooler area to cook the food through.

- Control flare-ups with this type of fire by moving the food away from the flame to the cooler area.

Direct Heat

- For a direct fire, the coals not only have to be at the proper temperature, but they need to be evenly arranged.

- Be sure that the coals are in a layer three–four thick.

- With the vents open 100 percent, the fire will be hot.

- Vents open 75 percent will result in medium heat, and vents that are half closed will create a low fire.

- When you add more coals, mix the hot and dying coals to keep the heat consistent.

GAS GRILL TYPES

Gas grills range from simple propane-powered machines to complicated kitchens

Gas grills offer unparalleled convenience. But there's more to do than turning on a burner and cooking the food. You have to perform safety checks every time, when you change the propane tank, and at the beginning of each grilling season.

Be sure that the drip pan or grease catcher is cleaned or changed regularly. If grease builds up here, it can start a fire that will cause a lot of damage. Some grills have a grease catcher that you clean; others have disposable catchers.

To start the grill, perform a gas leak test, then open the lid and turn on the burners. When the burners light, close the lid and preheat for ten minutes. Don't add food during this time; the temperature has to stabilize before you start cooking.

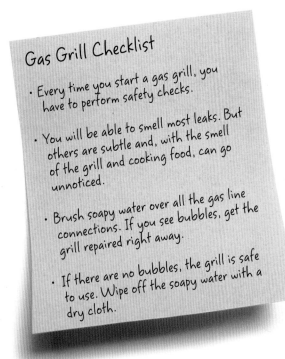

Gas Grill Checklist

• Every time you start a gas grill, you have to perform safety checks.

• You will be able to smell most leaks. But others are subtle and, with the smell of the grill and cooking food, can go unnoticed.

• Brush soapy water over all the gas line connections. If you see bubbles, get the grill repaired right away.

• If there are no bubbles, the grill is safe to use. Wipe off the soapy water with a dry cloth.

Propane Gas Grill

• Propane grills are more popular than grills fueled with natural gas.

• Look for welded, not riveted steel in a gas grill. Those connections are stronger, and the grill will last longer.

• Every time you add a new propane tank, you must check every connection: From the tank to the grill, around all the hoses, and the connection to the burners.

• Store propane tanks outside, on a fireproof level surface. Never store tanks in your garage or house.

The grill must be cleaned both before and after cooking. Before cooking, open the grill and clean with a wire brush. Lightly oil the rack using a towel gripped with your longs. There are also pads presoaked in the perfect amount of oil that you can use. Then adjust the burners to high, medium, and low, or turn off one or more burners for indirect grilling.

If you smell gas, turn off the grill and immediately call for repairs.

CHARCOAL VS. GAS

Natural Gas Grill

- For a natural gas grill, a technician must install a line from a natural gas source, usually from your house to the grill.

- Some grills can be converted from propane to natural gas. The information will be in your owner's manual.

- With natural gas grills, you'll never run out of gas. The gas is piped from the system to the grill.

- Unless you are a certified technician, don't install a permanent gas grill or try to repair grills.

Fancy Gas Kitchen

- Fancy outdoor kitchens can cost tens of thousands of dollars.

- Once you get into these complicated grills and kitchens, expect material and quality to be superior.

- At this level, food grates should always be heavy

duty stainless steel or cast iron, and the grill should be made of double sheets of stainless.

- These grills won't cook better than more inexpensive grills; the quality of the food that comes off them depends on the skill of the cook.

ELECTRIC GRILLS AND OTHERS

If you live in an apartment or don't want to fuss with charcoal or gas, electric grills can be the answer

Beyond charcoal and gas grills, there are some other choices. Many regulations for apartments and condos prohibit the use of a gas or charcoal grill on a balcony or terrace. An electric grill can be the answer.

Electric grills are just plugged into an outlet. You still have to be careful with these grills because they will get almost as

hot as charcoal or gas grills. Note that qualifier: 'almost'. You won't be able to get the type of char or sear on electric grills that you can on gas or charcoal grills.

Some of these electric grills have interesting controls. One type from Fire Stone lets you choose the doneness for your meats. You then insert a probe and the grill will let you know

Dual Contact Indoor Grill

- Dual contact indoor grills, which George Foreman made famous, replicate some of the flavor and look of food cooked on a charcoal or gas grill.

- The cooking area has raised bars, which add grill marks to the food.

- Because the food cooks on both sides at the same time, remember to cut cooking time in half.

- Grease drains out of these grills into a small removable pan in front. Always use this pan when using the grill.

Backyard Smoker

- Smokers are made to cook food for a long time over low heat and produce maximum smoke.

- The temperature for smoking is around 200°F. You can smoke on a charcoal grill with a low fire. Add soaked wood chips or chunks to the charcoal.

- The smoke doesn't penetrate the flesh of the meat, but concentrates on the outside.

- The long, slow heat helps break down fibers and tissue in the meat to make it very tender.

when the meat is done.

Infrared grills are the hot new choice for serious grillers. This technology uses standard gas burners but concentrates the flame onto special tiles that change the heat to infrared energy, which is like the energy from the sun.

Smoking is entirely different from grilling, although indirect grilling can mimic the smoking effect. Smokers cook food slowly at a low temperature, infusing it with smoke flavor. A stand-alone vertical or horizontal smoker is a good addition to your outdoor kitchen if you prefer this type of cooking.

ZOOM

The smoker is made for inexpensive cuts of meat. In fact, that's how the art of smoking started. Ranch hands and cowboys were given "poor" cuts of meat like brisket as part of their pay, which they smoked over a low heat for a long period of time. Now barbecue joints in the south take pride in long-smoked meats.

Electric Outdoor Grill

Infrared Grill

- An electric outdoor grill is the most convenient grill of all, but the heat of these grills doesn't get as high as charcoal or gas.

- Just plug in the grill and turn it on to cook, then turn it off and unplug when you're finished.

- As with all grills, never leave an electric grill unattended.

- These grills still need cleaning just like any appliance. The grates will probably be ceramic or porcelain coated.

- The infrared grill is a dry heat method, which doesn't produce moisture vapor like a gas grill does. It's better for searing foods.

- The heat is much higher on infrared grills, reaching temperatures well above 700°F.

- Manufacturers claim the grills can cook foods in half the time of traditional gas or charcoal grills.

- Some of the higher end propane or natural gas grills have an infrared burner too, to quickly sear steaks just like a charcoal grill.

CLASSIC BEEF BURGERS

The all-beef burger is easy to make and can be very juicy and tender if you follow these directions

Burgers cook quickly over direct heat. For the best burgers, choose coarsely ground chuck with 20 percent fat. Combine all of the flavoring and binding ingredients, then add the ground meat and mix just until combined.

Choose very fresh beef, add a few ingredients to season and add moisture, and work the mixture as little as possible.

When the burgers are cooking on the grill, never press down on them with a spatula. That will squeeze the juice right out of the meat as it cooks. The burgers are ready to turn when they release from the grill. If they stick, keep cooking. For fewer HCAs (see page 10), flip burgers every minute so the surface has a chance to cool a bit. *Yield: 4 burgers*

Ingredients

2 tablespoons condensed beef broth
1 slice white bread, crumbled
¼ cup minced onion
2 cloves garlic, minced
2 tablespoons butter
1 teaspoon grill seasoning
⅛ teaspoon pepper
¼ teaspoon salt
2 tablespoons water
1¼ pounds ground chuck
4 (½-inch-thick) slices onion
4 slices cheddar cheese
4 hamburger buns, split
4 thick slices tomato
4 slices butter lettuce
Condiments

Classic Beef Burger

- Combine broth and bread in small bowl; stir and set aside.

- Cook onions and garlic in butter; add grill seasoning, pepper, salt, water, and bread mixture and mix, then add ground chuck. Form into patties.

- Grill burgers over direct heat

- for 5 minutes. Turn onto indirect heat and add onion to direct heat. Grill meat for 5–7 minutes until 160°F, onions for 4–6 minutes.

- Add cheese to burgers; place split buns on grill; cover for 60–70 seconds. Assemble hamburgers as desired.

For perfectly shaped burgers, consider purchasing a hamburger press. This tool makes perfect rounds, with a slight indentation pressed into the center of the burger so it doesn't curl as it's grilling. The press compresses the meat lightly so the burgers aren't tough, and the finished result is a juicy, professional-looking burger. It also helps you make the burgers faster.

All-American Burger: Add 2 tablespoons ketchup to the ground meat instead of water. Use American cheese in place of cheddar cheese.

Cajun Burger: Add 1 minced jalapeño pepper, 2 teaspoons grill seasoning, and 1 tablespoon adobo sauce to the onion mixture along with water. Use Pepper Jack cheese instead of the cheddar cheese.

Mix Ingredients Gently

Shape the Burgers Evenly

- Cook onion and garlic completely until translucent before adding to the meat. The time on the grill isn't long enough to cook the vegetables.

- The bread and broth help keep the meat moist while it's cooked to well done.

- Gentle handling ensures the hamburgers will be tender.

- You can add most anything to the beef, but be sure the total additions do not add up to more than ⅔ cup per pound, or the burgers won't hold together as they cook.

- To form the burgers, divide the mixture into 4 equal sections using a knife or your hand.

- Pick up 1 section and loosely shape it into a round or oval shape to match the bun.

- Turn the mixture gently in your hand, forming a smooth, solid edge.

- Use a spoon to gently make a dent in the middle of the burger. This will prevent rounding of the beef as it cooks, so the finished burger will be flat.

BEEF BURGERS

ETHNIC BURGERS

There are so many ways to flavor and top a beef burger, from every ethnic cuisine

If you have a favorite cuisine, whether it's French, Mexican, or Greek, you can add ingredients and seasonings to your beef burgers to reflect those flavors. The basic rules for adding ingredients to meat still apply.

Use your imagination to add everything from cooked vegetables to specialty sauces to unusual herbs and spices and different breads to make your burgers special. Be sure that the ingredients will blend with the ground meat. Additions should be chopped fine so the finished burger stays together and cooks completely on the grill. Think about your favorite flavor combinations, and when you come up with a winner, be sure to write it down so you can make it again. *Yield: 4 burgers*

Ingredients

⅓ cup sauerkraut

2 tablespoons finely chopped green onion

2 tablespoons beer

⅛ teaspoon pepper

2 tablespoons mustard

8 slices bacon

1 ½ pounds coarsely ground chuck

4 slices Muenster cheese

4 rye or Kaiser sandwich buns

¼ cup grainy mustard

1 cup baby spinach leaves

German Burger

- Finely chop sauerkraut and drain in a strainer or colander.

- In large bowl, combine sauerkraut, green onion, beer, pepper, and mustard. Partially cook bacon until translucent and set aside.

- Add ground chuck to sauerkraut mixture; mix gently until combined. Form into 4 patties and wrap with bacon, then grill 5 minutes over direct heat. Turn burgers to indirect heat and cook 3 minutes; top with cheese.

- Grill the buns, cut side down, and spread with grainy mustard. Assemble burgers.

Sauerkraut is a traditional German side dish that adds a spicy and salty flavor to burgers. You can find sauerkraut canned in the vegetable aisle of the supermarket and sometimes fresh in the produce aisle. Sauerkraut is fermented cabbage that has been preserved with salt. The bacteria that add the sharp flavor to sauerkraut is naturally present on the cabbage.

• • • • RECIPE VARIATION • • • •

Left Bank Burgers: Add 2 minced shallots, 1 teaspoon dried herbes de Provence, and ½ teaspoon salt for sauerkraut, mustard, and beer. Substitute Grùyere cheese for Muenster and Kaiser roll for rye bun.

English Burgers: Add 2 tablespoons each brown mustard and Worcestershire sauce instead of sauerkraut, beer, and bacon. Substitute English muffins.

Preparing Sauerkraut

Wrap Burger with Bacon

- Drain sauerkraut by placing it in a colander; press down. Do not drain it in paper towels; you want some of the moisture in the burgers.

- It's not difficult to chop sauerkraut; just be sure that all of the long strands are chopped.

- Use a chef's knife and place the drained sauerkraut on the chopping board. Chop the sauerkraut by moving the knife through it in several directions.

- Be sure that the sauerkraut is evenly distributed in the meat.

- Partially cook bacon by placing it in a cold skillet. Turn heat to medium and cook bacon until it can be moved.

- Turn bacon and cook on second side until some fat is rendered and the bacon is translucent but still pliable.

- Wrap bacon around the edge of the hamburger, or wrap around middle of the burger like you would wrap a package.

- The bacon will finish cooking on the grill, where the fat and juices will flavor the burger.

SLIDERS

Tiny "two-bite" burgers are the latest rage, and kids love them

Small hamburgers are the newest trend in incarnations of the grilled hamburger. These burgers are 2 inches in diameter and are served on cocktail or small sandwich buns.

The burgers are prepared just like larger variations, but they have to be handled more carefully. It's easiest to place the burgers in a grill basket or on a smaller rack placed over the main grill rack so they don't fall through and burn up in the coals.

Top these little burgers with sliced plum tomatoes, cheese, pickled jalapeños, shredded lettuce, tiny pickles, or anything else you'd like. One of the best things about sliders is that you can eat 2 or 3 hamburgers, each flavored and topped in a different way. *Yield: 12 mini burgers*

Ingredients

⅓ cup minced onions

2 tablespoons butter

1 teaspoon onion salt

⅛ teaspoon pepper

2 tablespoons condensed beef broth

1½ pounds 80 percent lean ground beef

12 dinner rolls or mini English muffins

12 2-inch slices cheddar or Muenster cheese

4 plum tomatoes, sliced

Ketchup or mustard

Sliders

- In small saucepan, cook onion in butter until very tender, about 6–7 minutes.

- Place onion mixture in large bowl and mix in onion salt, pepper, and broth. Add ground beef and mix gently.

- Form into 2½-inch-thick small burgers using an ice cream scoop or small cup.

- Place in grill basket; cook over medium direct coals for 4 minutes. Flip basket to indirect heat, open, top burgers with bottom half of rolls, and cook for 3–5 minutes until done. Assemble burgers with cheese, tomatoes, and condiments.

Form the Tiny Burgers

Cook the Burgers

- Press the scoop or measuring cup into the meat mixture, then scrape off excess on the side of the bowl.

- Release the meat into the palm of your hand and gently flatten the meat so it's ½ inch thick. The burgers should be 2½ inches wide.

- Spray the scoop or measuring cup with nonstick cooking spray so the meat releases easily.

- You can make larger sliders, depending on the size of the buns you buy. Cook larger sliders for 1–2 minutes longer.

- After the first flip, open the basket and place the bottom half of the bun on each burger. The juice will soak into the meat as it cooks.

- For well-done burgers, rely on accurate cooking time. Break a burger open to check doneness; it should not be pink.

- Coal temperature must be consistent and even for best results.

- Place a layer of sliced onions in the basket to add more flavor to the burgers as they cook.

BEEF BURGERS

MEDIUM RARE BURGERS

Yes, you can safely serve a medium rare burger with these special instructions

Most people stopped eating rare burgers when the FDA recommended they be cooked to a final internal temperature of 165 degrees F. The bacteria on the surface of the meat are mixed through the meat when it is ground.

The following method kills the bacteria on the surface before the meat is ground so you can serve medium rare burgers. Since steaks should be cooked to 140 degrees F, which is medium rare, these burgers are cooked to that temperature. The burgers will be pink and juicy inside.

You don't need to add much to these burgers, as the quality of the meat is the focus. So buy sirloin or chuck, with about 20 percent fat and good marbling. *Yield: 4 burgers*

Ingredients

1¼ pounds beef chuck steak

½ teaspoon salt

½ teaspoon steak seasoning

4 slices cheddar cheese

4 onion buns, split

2 tablespoons butter, softened

4 leaves red lettuce

Ketchup or mustard

Medium-Rare Burger

- Prepare and preheat grill and all other ingredients. Chill steak and equipment.

- Bring a large pot of water to a boil. Drop steak into water. Leave it in water for 20 seconds and remove.

- Cut steak into 1-inch cubes and place on ice. Grind in batches to a coarse grind, then grind all together again to medium grind; add salt and steak seasoning.

- Form into burgers; grill over direct heat to 135°F. Add cheese and cover for 60 seconds. Assemble burgers with buttered, grilled rolls, and remaining ingredients.

MAKE IT EASY

Use a food processor, a hand grinder, or a grinding attachment for a stand mixer to grind the meat. Or use the pulse feature on the food processor. The meat should be cold; do not overprocess. Carefully follow manufacturer directions for the hand grinder or stand mixer attachment. And be sure that all your equipment is impeccably clean.

RED ● LIGHT

There are two caveats to this cooking method. You must immediately cook the burgers after the meat has been ground. Never partially cook meat and save it to cook later. Even freezing partially cooked meat is a no-no. So have everything ready and waiting for the meat. And don't use this method with chicken or turkey, since bacteria is present all through the meat in those cuts.

Blanch the Steak

- Chuck steak, sirloin steak, or a combination of both is the best choice for the proper amount of fat.

- Trim any large areas of visible fat before blanching the steak.

- Chill the steak, along with the blade and bowl, or grinder parts, in the freezer for 30 minutes before blanching.

- Be sure the water is boiling hard before you add the steak. Start counting the seconds as soon as the steak is in the water.

Grind the Meat

- Grind the meat in small batches until coarsely ground, then combine it all and briefly grind again until medium for even consistency.

- Don't overprocess the meat and don't grind until fine, or the burgers will be mushy.

- Add any extra ingredients you'd like when grinding the meat. Chopped onion, garlic, shallots, or scallions are delicious.

- Gently form the meat into patties. Do not press or compact the meat, but be sure edges are solid.

BEEF BURGERS

STUFFED BURGERS

Stuffed burgers are extra flavorful and delicious and easy to make with some special care

Stuff your burger with different ingredients to add a personal touch to your grilling. You can add everything from salsa to finely chopped cooked vegetables to cheese and other meats.

To stuff a burger, simply make 2 patties in place of 1, add the filling, and press to seal the edges together. These burgers will be slightly tougher than Classic Burgers (see page 36)

because they have to hold the filling securely inside.

Adding too much filling is a common mistake when making stuffed burgers. The proportion of filling to burger must be precise. About 3 to 4 tablespoons are enough filling to taste delicious, but not so much that it leaks out of the burger or blows it apart. *Yield: 4 burgers*

Ingredients

⅓ cup finely chopped onion

2 cloves garlic, minced

1 tablespoon butter

1¼ pounds ground chuck

1 tablespoon Worcestershire sauce

1 teaspoon dried Italian seasoning

16 pepperoni slices

½ cup shredded part-skim mozzarella cheese

4 slices Colby cheese

1 focaccia bread, sliced horizontally

½ cup pizza sauce

¾ cup chopped green bell pepper

Pizza Burgers

- Sauté onion and garlic in butter until tender. Remove from heat and cool.

- Combine ground chuck, Worcestershire sauce, and Italian seasoning. Divide into 8 pieces; form into ¼-inch-thick patties. Top half of the patties with onion mixture, pepperoni, and shredded

mozzarella. Top with remaining patties and seal.

- Grill over direct heat, turning once, until cooked, about 8–10 minutes; add Colby during last minute.

- Cut focaccia into quarters and add burgers. Top with sauce and bell peppers.

Monte Cristo

Stuffed Burgers: Cook onion and garlic in butter; add ¼ cup chopped ham. Add Worcestershire sauce, ⅛ teaspoon white pepper, and 2 tablespoons Dijon mustard to meat. Omit Italian seasoning, pepperoni, mozzarella, and Colby cheeses. Use Muenster cheese shredded in filling and sliced on burgers. Use toasted English muffins for focaccia; use mustard and sour cream for pizza sauce and bell pepper.

Blue Cheese Bacon Burgers

For filling, combine ½ cup blue cheese, 2 tablespoons butter, and 5 slices crisply cooked, crumbled bacon. Omit butter, onion, garlic, Italian seasoning, pepperoni, mozzarella, and Colby. Top the burgers with sliced Havarti cheese. Use Kaiser rolls in place of focaccia, and use sliced tomato, mustard, and mayonnaise in place of pizza sauce and green pepper.

Fill the Burgers

Grill Carefully

- Handle the meat a bit more firmly than with unstuffed burgers.

- Don't add additional ingredients to the meat, since it must be fairly strong to hold together and keep the filling inside.

- Press the edges of the 2 thin burgers together firmly but gently and be sure all of the filling is completely covered with meat.

- Keep the fillings and toppings fairly simple, but use flavorful ingredients so the taste and texture contrast is strong.

- Use 3 to 4 tablespoons of filling for each burger. Don't use hot filling; let it cool first.

- Spread the filling evenly over the burger, but leave ½-inch edges without filling so the burger can be securely sealed.

- On the grill, turn only once to keep the filling inside. Use a large spatula and handle the burgers gently.

- Add cheese and other toppings to the top of the burger during the last minute of cooking time.

BEEF BURGERS

DELUXE BURGERS

More expensive and exotic ingredients make a beef burger special

When you eat out in a fancy restaurant, you can spend a lot of money on a hamburger. Some restaurants in New York and California use Kobe beef, a beef from Japan that costs around $80 a pound. But for a really deluxe, delicious burger you don't need to spend that much money.

Just choose fresh beef, handle the meat gently, and add some special ingredients to make one of the best burgers you have ever tasted. Brie cheese is very rich and smooth,

with a strong flavor. Mixing bits of it into the meat adds an incomparable taste.

And caramelized onions, which have cooked for a long time in butter, add a special sweet and smoky flavor to these burgers. Yum! *Yield: 4 burgers*

Ingredients

2 tablespoons butter

1 tablespoon olive oil

2 onions, chopped

2 tablespoons condensed beef broth

1 slice white bread, crumbled

½ cup Brie cheese

1¼ pounds freshly ground chuck

½ teaspoon salt

½ teaspoon grill seasoning

⅛ teaspoon pepper

4 hoagie buns, split

3 tablespoons butter

Brie Burger

- Melt butter and olive oil in medium pan. Add onions; cook over medium heat until translucent. Reduce heat to low and cook onions, stirring frequently, until brown, 30–40 minutes.

- Combine broth and bread in small bowl. Freeze Brie for 30 minutes, trim off rind, freeze again, then remove and dice.

- Place ground chuck in large bowl; add seasonings, bread mixture, and Brie; mix.

- Form into 4 oval patties and grill over direct heat for 4–5 minutes on each side until done. Top with onions; place on toasted, buttered buns.

Prepare the Brie

- A very sharp knife is necessary to trim the rind from the Brie and cut it into an even dice.

- Diced cheese is about ¼-inch square. If the pieces of cheese are any larger, they will make large holes in the burgers as they melt.

- Freeze the cheese for 30 minutes so it's firm, then remove the rind, or soft white coating, with the knife.

- Return the cheese to the freezer for another 10 minutes, then remove and dice.

Finish the Burgers

- Spray the grate with non-stick cooking spray before you begin.

- Cook the burgers on the first side until they release from the grate, flip and cook again until they release. Then flip once a minute until they're done.

- Other very rich cheeses will work too, like a triple crème cheese, Camembert, or a ripe soft goat cheese.

- Add sour cream or mayonnaise to the caramelized onions before you add them to the grilled burgers for even more flavor.

BEEF BURGERS

TURKEY BURGER

White or dark meat turkey can be ground to use in juicy, low fat turkey burgers

Turkey burgers became popular in the 1990s as an alternative to higher-fat beef burgers. And they're delicious! Because turkey is lower in fat than beef, you need to take some special steps for the juiciest and most tender burger.

The key to the best burger is to handle the meat as little as possible. That applies to turkey burgers too. Because the meat is delicate, it does need more filler. A burger made of just ground turkey would be tough and dry.

A combination of light and dark meat, ground together, is your best choice for a turkey burger. Then with about ½ cup of fillers per pound, let your imagination run wild and create your own special turkey burgers. *Yield: 4 burgers*

Ingredients

1 tablespoon butter
¼ cup minced onion
2 cloves garlic, minced
2 tablespoons grated apple
¼ cup dried breadcrumbs
1 egg, beaten
1 tablespoon Worcestershire sauce
2 teaspoons low-sodium soy sauce
1¼ pounds ground turkey
3 tablespoons mayonnaise
3 tablespoons Dijon mustard
1 tablespoon olive oil
4 onion buns
2 tablespoons butter
1 avocado, peeled and sliced

Classic Turkey Burger

- In small saucepan, melt butter. Cook onion, garlic until tender, about 6 minutes. Remove to large bowl.

- Add apple, breadcrumbs, egg, Worcestershire sauce, and soy sauce; mix. Add turkey; mix.

- Chill mixture for 1 hour.

Preheat grill. Mix mayo and mustard. Form into 4 patties.

- Brush burgers with olive oil; grill over direct heat for 5 minutes. Flip over indirect heat and cook for 5–7 minutes until 165°F. Grill buttered buns in last 2 minutes. Assemble burgers with mayo mixture and avocado.

Tex-Mex Turkey Burger
Add 1 minced jalapeño to the onion and garlic mixture and cook until tender. Substitute ⅓ cup crushed nacho chips for the breadcrumbs. Omit Worcestershire sauce. Top burgers with slice of Pepper Jack cheese just before they are done. Substitute taco sauce and sour cream for mayonnaise and mustard mixture, and serve the burgers on a toasted French bun.

Spinach Feta Turkey Burger
Cook ½ cup shredded baby spinach with the onion and garlic mixture. Omit breadcrumbs and soy sauce. Add ¼ cup crumbled feta cheese and 2 tablespoons crushed buttery round cracker crumbs to the turkey meat. Top finished burgers with ¼ cup feta and roasted red peppers in place of avocado.

Turkey Breast v. Dark Meat

Mixed Meat

Breast Only

- You can find ground turkey breast and ground mixed dark and light turkey meat at most supermarkets.

- You may have to ask the butcher to grind some for you. The ground meat is highly perishable.

- Or you can grind it yourself, chilling the meat first and using a food processor.

- Perform your own taste test to decide for yourself: make some burgers with breast meat and some with a combination.

Chill the Burgers

- Turkey meat is more delicate than hamburger, so it must be kept cold.

- If the meat is too soft, refrigerate it for 1 hour. If it still isn't workable, add 2 tablespoons more breadcrumbs.

- Don't try to flip the burgers until they release easily from the grill.

- A light coating of olive oil on the grill and on the burgers will help them release and keep them together.

ALL OTHER BURGERS

SALMON OR TUNA BURGER

Tender burgers made from canned or fresh salmon or tuna are delicious and easy

Salmon and tuna are excellent choices for burgers. You can use well-drained canned or pouch salmon or tuna, or you can grind fresh salmon or tuna in your food processor.

To use fresh meat, remove any small pin bones by using tweezers or small tongs. Cut into 1-inch chunks and process briefly in the food processor.

You can also finely chop the raw salmon or tuna with a chef's knife. Proceed as directed with recipe, but be sure to cook the patties to 145 degrees F.

Salmon and tuna are more strongly flavored than turkey, so they can handle more assertive seasonings. Good herb choices include thyme, rosemary, and dill. *Yield: 4 burgers*

Ingredients

1 tablespoon butter
3 tablespoons finely minced onion
1 egg
1 egg yolk
¼ cup dry breadcrumbs
2 tablespoons orange juice
½ teaspoon dried thyme leaves
⅛ teaspoon pepper
1 (14-ounce) can sockeye salmon
¼ cup sour cream
1 tablespoon orange juice
2 tablespoons mustard
4 sesame seed buns
2 tablespoons butter

Salmon Burgers

- In small bowl, microwave butter and onion on high for 2–3 minutes until tender. Remove to large bowl; let cool.

- Stir in egg, egg yolk, breadcrumbs, orange juice, thyme, and pepper; mix well. Stir in salmon until mixed. Cover and chill for 1–4 hours in refrigerator.

- Combine sour cream, remaining orange juice, and mustard for topping. Shape into 4 patties.; chill meat.

- Grill on indirect heat for 5–6 minutes on each side, until firm. Toast buttered buns; assemble burgers.

Asian Tuna Burgers

Start with a 12-ounce can of tuna. Add 3 cloves minced garlic, 1 tablespoon grated ginger root, and 2 tablespoons hoisin sauce. Omit butter, onion, orange juice, thyme, mustard, and sour cream. Serve on sourdough buns with lettuce and fresh bean sprouts. For condiment, combine 2 tablespoons hoisin sauce with ⅓ cup sour cream.

Greek Salmon Burgers

Add 3 cloves minced garlic to the onion mixture. Add ¼ cup feta cheese, 3 tablespoons chopped olives, and ½ teaspoon dried oregano to salmon. Omit orange juice, thyme, mustard, and sour cream. Top finished burgers with another ¼ cup of feta cheese. Serve on Kaiser rolls in place of sesame rolls, with honey mustard, tomato, and lettuce.

Preparing Salmon

- When canned, salmon bones are edible and are a good source of calcium. You can crush them with your fingers to mix into the meat.

- There are bones and skin in canned salmon. These can be mixed into the burgers, but you can also remove them for aesthetic reasons.

- Drain the salmon or tuna very well before adding to the other ingredients.

- Salmon processed in pouches doesn't contain skin or bones, but does need to be thoroughly drained.

Mix Ingredients and Chill

- Unlike other ground meats, you can work salmon and tuna more with your fingers and the burgers won't be tough.

- Press the burger mixture together firmly and make sure edges are well rounded so they don't fall apart on the grill.

- Let the salmon mixture sit in the refrigerator for 1–4 hours so the flavors blend before cooking.

- Brushing the burgers with olive oil and rubbing the cooking grate with oil will help prevent sticking.

CHICKEN BURGER

You can grind your own chicken to make savory chicken burgers, flavored many ways

Ground chicken makes delicate burgers that are ideally suited to many cuisines and flavors. Ground chicken is becoming more readily available in the supermarket, but again, you can grind your own at home.

If you use just the chicken breast, the burgers will be quite low in fat. If you use half breast and half thigh, the burgers will be lower in fat than a beef burger. But all-dark-meat ground chicken has just as much fat as a beef burger.

As with turkey burgers, ground chicken has to be handled gently, and may need refrigeration after mixing ingredients and forming the patties. *Yield: 4 burgers*

Ingredients

1 tablespoon olive oil
2 tablespoons minced green onion
2 tablespoons minced celery
¼ cup minced ham
¼ cup shredded Swiss cheese
1 egg
Salt and pepper to taste
1¼ pounds ground chicken
1 tablespoon olive oil
4 slices Swiss cheese
¼ cup mayonnaise
2 tablespoons mustard
Romaine lettuce leaves
4 slices tomato
4 sourdough rolls
2 tablespoons butter

Chicken Monte Cristo Burger

- Cook olive oil, onion, and celery until tender. Remove from heat and place in large bowl; cool completely.

- Add ham, shredded cheese, egg, salt, and pepper; mix well. Add chicken; mix until combined. Chill 1–2 hours.

- Form into 4 patties, cover, and chill for another hour. Prepare and preheat grill.

- Brush burgers with olive oil and grill over indirect heat for 5–6 minutes on each side, turning once, until 165°F. Top with sliced cheese, and assemble burgers with remaining ingredients.

Add ¼ cup barbecue sauce, 1 tablespoon Worcestershire sauce, and 1 minced jalapeño to egg and breadcrumbs, then mix in chicken. Omit olive oil, green onion, celery, ham, and Swiss cheese. Serve burgers on buttered, grilled hamburger buns with more barbecue sauce, tomato, sliced red onion, and lettuce.

Instead of using plain ketchup or mustard on your special burgers, match the topping to the seasonings. For Greek burgers, mix thick yogurt with lemon juice and olives. For Tex-Mex burgers, guacamole is perfect. For Asian burgers, mix ketchup with hoisin sauce for a flavor boost. And for classic burgers, use everything from mayonnaise to mustard to pickle relish.

Grind Chicken

- Chicken should be well chilled before and after being ground.

- A food processor is the best appliance to use to grind the chicken.

- You can add chopped onion or garlic to the food processor to grind along with the chicken for more moisture and flavor.

- Ground chicken is very perishable. Use it the same day you grind it or freeze it up to one month. After it's thawed, use immediately.

Mix Burger Ingredients

- Be sure that the vegetables are tender and cool before adding the rest of the ingredients.

- You don't want the cheese to melt or get too soft or the burgers will be too soft to handle.

- Refrigerate the chicken after it's been combined with the other ingredients, and again after the patties are formed.

- Because these patties are so tender and delicate, you may want to cook them on a grill mat or perforated heavy duty foil.

MIXED SEAFOOD BURGER
Fresh seafood creates unusual and flavorful burgers

Combine several different types of seafood for a fabulously fresh burger with a taste of Florida. You can use any combination of seafood that strikes your fancy.

Fish puree may sound strange, but it's the binder that holds everything together. You can also puree scallops to hold the mixture together.

A grill basket is key to making these tender burgers. If you don't have one, you could cook the burgers on lightly greased heavy duty foil. For a smoky flavor, cut several small slashes on the foil to let the smoke through.

The crab is cooked, but the shrimp is not. The raw shrimp and fish help cushion the crab so it doesn't overcook while the burgers grill. *Yield: 4 burgers*

Ingredients

2 cloves garlic, minced
1 shallot, minced
1 tablespoon butter
1/3 cup Saltine cracker crumbs
1/2 teaspoon Old Bay seasoning
1/8 teaspoon pepper
1/4 pound orange roughy fillet
1/2 pound lump crabmeat
1/2 pound medium raw shrimp
1/4 cup mayonnaise
2 tablespoons chopped fresh basil
2 tablespoons grainy mustard
4 leaves lettuce
4 hot dog buns

Mixed Seafood Burger

- Cook garlic and shallot in butter. Remove to large bowl and cool. Add crumbs, seasoning, and pepper.

- Place raw fish fillet in a food processor; process until smooth. Add bowl.

- Chop crab and shrimp and add; mix gently. Chill 1 hour. Mix mayonnaise, basil, and mustard.

- Form oval patties and place in grill basket. Grill on indirect heat for 3–5 minutes on each side, turning once, until done. Serve with lettuce and mayonnaise mixture on hot dog buns.

Shrimp Burgers: Cook ¼ cup minced onion with garlic. Use 1 pound shrimp and ¼ pound scallops for puree; form into round patties. Use toasted sourdough buns with seafood sauce and lettuce.

Creole Crab Burgers: Cook 2 tablespoons each minced celery, green pepper with garlic. Omit shallot, shrimp, and fish. Add ⅓ cup mayo. Use 1 pound crabmeat.

ZOOM

It's important to think about the texture of the burger when you pick the bun to serve it in. Very tender burgers like this Mixed Seafood Burger should be served with a soft bun. Hot dog buns are traditional for lobster salad sandwiches. Look for unsliced hot dog buns, and slice them through the top instead of the side to hold the burger.

Prepare Seafood

- To pick over the crab, look for small bits of shell and cartilage; they will feel hard and sharp.

- Peel and devein the shrimp before chopping. Use a small knife to cut the shell along the back of the shrimp and pull it off.

- Cut a thin slit on the back of the shrimp and pull out or rinse out the dark vein.

- Puree the fish just until smooth. Don't over-puree it or it may fall apart.

Grill Burgers in Basket

- Chill the delicate mixture before and after shaping it into burgers. Make the burgers almost as long as the hot dog buns, and about 1 inch thick.

- Spray grill basket with nonstick cooking or grilling spray before adding the burgers.

- Brush burgers lightly with olive oil. The burgers don't touch the grill, so it doesn't need to be oiled.

- Watch the patties on the grill. Brown them over high heat, then move to indirect or lower heat to finish cooking.

ALL OTHER BURGERS

DRESSED-UP VEGGIE BURGER

These vegetarian burgers are delicious

There are two kinds of veggie burgers: those you make yourself, and the frozen premade type that you dress up with lots of fun ingredients.

A made-from-scratch burger must have enough strength to hold together on the grill, but enough moisture so it's tender. Ingredients like mashed or refried beans, cooked grains or rice, and chopped cooked vegetables are basic ingredients.

Preformed vegetarian patties are usually made of soy or wheat gluten. If you're allergic to those products, your own homemade burger is the best choice.

You can't change the flavor or ingredients in the preformed patties, so use your imagination when topping them. Set out a topping bar to give your guests choices. *Yield: 4 burgers*

Ingredients

1/3 cup minced onion

3 cloves garlic, minced

1 tablespoon olive oil

1 (15-ounce) can pinto beans

1/2 cup cooked cold brown rice

1/3 cup soft whole wheat breadcrumbs

1 egg

1 tablespoon low-sodium soy sauce

2 teaspoons grill seasoning

1/4 cup sour cream

1/4 cup salsa

1 tablespoon lime juice

4 slices Muenster cheese

4 English muffins, split

Veggie Burgers

- Cook onion and garlic in olive oil until vegetables start to caramelize and pan is almost dry.

- Drain beans, rinse, and dry on paper towel.

- Combine beans in food processor with onion mixture, rice, crumbs, egg, soy sauce, and seasoning; process until smooth. Refrigerate for 2–3 hours. Combine sour cream, salsa, and lime juice.

- Shape bean mixture into patties; chill 2–3 hours, or freeze. Grill patties on foil on direct heat until crisp, 5 minutes per side. Add cheese, sauce; serve on muffins.

Spicy Black Bean Burgers:
Add 1 minced jalapeño to onion mixture. Add ⅓ cup minced red bell pepper, 2 eggs, and ¼ cup ground oatmeal. Omit rice, breadcrumbs, pinto beans, and soy sauce. Use 15-ounce can black beans. Serve on hamburger buns with the same salsa and sour cream topping, but use cheddar cheese instead of Muenster.

Light Vegetarian Burgers
Use 15-ounce can lima beans, ¼ cup cooked cold lentils, 1 teaspoon Italian seasoning, and ½ cup white breadcrumbs. Omit pinto beans, rice, soy sauce, and grill seasoning. Omit salsa topping and Muenster. Top the burgers with plain salsa and serve wrapped in corn tortillas, which have been softened by wrapping in foil and heating on the grill.

Mix Burger Ingredients

- As long as you keep the proportions about the same, you can use just about any vegetarian ingredients in these burgers.

- You may need to vary the dry or wet ingredients, depending on the moisture in the cooked grains or legumes.

- The mixture should be fairly firm. For a crunchy exterior, coat the burgers in wheat germ, cornmeal, or breadcrumbs before grilling.

- A grill rack or perforated aluminum foil is a good choice for cooking these burgers.

Dress up Premade Burgers

- There are many varieties of premade vegetarian burgers on the market. Morningstar Farms, Gardenburger, and Boca are companies that produce these products.

- Make premade burgers special with the toppings. Try topping the burgers with cheese; use soy cheese if you want to make them vegan.

- Salsa, cooked pasta sauces, pesto, and flavored mayonnaise, along with ketchup and mustard, are great topping choices.

- Some of these burgers come already flavored, with cheese added or on top. Read labels!

ALL OTHER BURGERS

MUSHROOM BURGER
Large mushroom caps are delicious grilled and stuffed

Large portobello mushrooms are the perfect choice for another vegetarian "burger." These big mushrooms are 2–3 inches across and have a rich flavor, which makes them a great choice for a meat substitute.

You can find large mushrooms at the regular grocery store. If you can't find the really large mushrooms, you can substitute 2–3 smaller ones. Grill and fill them as directed, then put 3 on 1 bun.

The gill area of the mushroom makes a natural bowl to fill with all kinds of wonderful ingredients, from caramelized onions and sun-dried tomatoes to tapenade or Brie.

To remove stems, gently pull the stem from the mushroom cap. It should separate easily. Chop and use it in the filling, or discard. *Yield: 4 burgers*

Ingredients

4 large (4–5 inches) portobello mushrooms

1 tablespoon olive oil

½ teaspoon salt

⅛ teaspoon pepper

4 (½-inch-thick) red onion slices

1⅓ cups shredded Havarti cheese

2 teaspoons minced fresh thyme leaves

4 whole-wheat buns, split

2 tablespoons butter

4 red lettuce leaves

Havarti Mushroom Burger

- Remove stems from mushrooms. Scrape out gills. Brush with olive oil; sprinkle with salt and pepper.

- Place onion slices on grill. After 5 minutes, turn onions; cook mushrooms, stem side down, over indirect heat 5–7 minutes. Turn onto direct heat; grill 4 minutes.

- Place grilled onion in mushroom cap; sprinkle with cheese and thyme; return to grill.

- Place buttered buns on grill. Cover and cook 1–2 minutes until cheese melts. Serve mushrooms on toasted buns with lettuce.

Swiss Mushroom Burgers
Cook 1 chopped red bell pepper and 2 cloves garlic in 1 tablespoon olive oil. Cool and add ½ cup sour cream and 1 cup shredded Swiss cheese. Omit buns, thyme, red lettuce, and red onion. Place this mixture in grilled caps. Serve on grilled Kaiser rolls with butter lettuce.

French Portobello Burgers
Cook 1 cup chopped onion in 1 tablespoon butter and olive oil until caramelized, about 20 minutes. Cool and combine with ⅓ cup crumbled blue cheese and ⅓ cup cubed Brie cheese. Use this mixture to top the mushrooms. Omit buns, Havarti, and red onion. Serve on grilled French bread slices with sour cream.

Prepare Mushrooms

- Don't rinse mushrooms or soak them in water to clean; they'll absorb it and will be watery.

- Wipe the mushrooms with a damp cloth to clean. Mushrooms are grown in fertilized soil, so don't worry about germs.

- The gills are the dark, fine web of delicate material around the stem. They are edible, but can be bitter when cooked.

- Gently scrape the gills away with a spoon so there will be more room for filling. Discard the gills.

Grill and Finish Burgers

- Be sure the onion slices are small enough to fit into the mushroom caps. Pull off outer rings if necessary.

- You can also chop the onions and caramelize them in a pan with butter on the grill or in the kitchen.

- Thread a soaked wooden skewer through the onion slices to hold them together on the grill.

- Top the hot grilled burgers with a cold topping for contrast. Combine fresh chopped vegetables with salad dressing or sour cream.

ALL OTHER BURGERS

BEEF KABOBS

From chunks of sirloin to meatball "lollipops," beef is a great choice for kabobs

Kabobs are a fun way to cook and serve food. Food is cut into cubes, wedges, and slices and threaded onto wood or metal skewers. They're like a one-dish meal on a stick!

Always place kabobs perpendicular to the rungs of the grill rack. It's important to oil the rack and the food when you're cooking small pieces.

There are two rules for kabob food size. Rule one: If the foods have the same cooking time, like mushrooms and bell peppers, be sure the pieces of food are about the same size. Rule two: If foods have different cooking times, they have to be cut proportionately, larger or smaller. Foods that cook quicker are cut larger, while slower cooking foods are smaller. *Yield: 6 kabobs*

Ingredients

1 tablespoon butter

¼ cup minced onion

4 cloves garlic, minced

2 tablespoons apple cider vinegar

¼ cup cola beverage

2 tablespoons brown sugar

1 teaspoon grill seasoning

¼ teaspoon garlic pepper

1½ pounds sirloin steak, cubed

12 1-inch red potatoes

2 red bell peppers, cut into 2-inch pieces

1 onion, cut into 16 wedges

2 tablespoons vegetable oil

Classic Beef Kabobs

- Cook onion and garlic in butter until beginning to brown, about 10–12 minutes.

- Remove from heat; add vinegar, cola, sugar seasoning, and pepper. Cut ½-inch slit in center of each beef cube. Add to marinade; refrigerate for 8–24 hours.

- Drain beef, save marinade. Cook potatoes in boiling water for 6–8 minutes until almost tender. Thread all ingredients on skewers. Brush with oil.

- Grill on direct heat for 5–7 minutes; turn and brush frequently with marinade until beef is medium rare.

Hawaiian Beef Kabobs: Add ¼ cup pineapple juice and ½ teaspoon ginger to marinade. Omit vinegar, brown sugar, cola, and potatoes. Add pineapple cubes to skewers and substitute green peppers for red peppers.

ZOOM

To be sure that the beef is flavored all the way through and that it cooks in the same time as the vegetables, cut a slit into the meat before it goes into the marinade. This lets the marinade, and the heat, penetrate to the center of the beef. When you skewer the meat, push the skewer through the 2 halves so it holds them together.

Soak Wooden Skewers

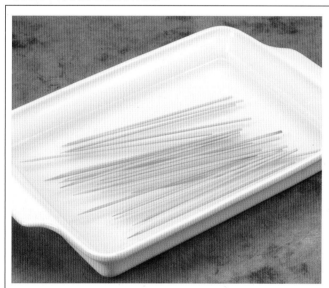

- Wooden skewers must be soaked in water for at least 30 minutes so they won't burn up and disintegrate on the grill.

- The skewers will still burn, but will hold together after soaking. You can wrap the ends with foil to protect them.

- Leave a space of about ¼ inch between the pieces of food so they cook evenly.

- Buy kabob holders or racks, which will help make cooking easier. The ends will still get hot, so use a hot pad to handle.

Thread Food on Skewers

- Metal skewers are reusable and won't burn on the grill. They will get very hot, so use care handling them.

- Look for flat or twisted skewers so the food won't twirl when the kabobs are turned.

- Beef and vegetables should be cut to the same size. Cut onions in wedges so they will stay on the skewer.

- Meat grain matters when making beef kabobs. For easier skewering, thread wooden skewers with the grain of the meat, metal against.

CHICKEN KABOBS

Chunks of chicken grill quickly, so they can pair with more delicate veggies and fruits

Chicken is a delicate meat, so it's delicious paired with delicate foods. This versatile meat can be flavored so many ways. Chicken with curry is delicious grilled with fruit, or seasoned with Italian spices and paired with peppers and onion.

Because chicken is a low-fat food, it will be moister and have better taste if marinated for a few hours in the refrigerator before being grilled.

Don't marinate chicken longer than 24 hours, or the acid in the marinade will start "cooking" the protein. This will make the chicken tough and mushy at the same time.

Chicken breasts or thighs can be used on kabobs. Cook the dark meat for 7–8 minutes. *Yield: 6 kabobs*

Ingredients

2 cloves garlic, minced

1 tablespoon curry powder

1 tablespoon olive oil

¼ cup apple juice

2 tablespoons honey

1 tablespoon lime juice

½ teaspoon salt

⅛ teaspoon pepper

1½ pounds boneless, skinless chicken breast

1 cup large red grapes

1 cup strawberries

1 cup pineapple chunks

4 green onions, cut into 1-inch pieces

Curried Chicken and Fruit Kabobs

- Cook garlic and curry powder in oil for 3 minutes. Add apple juice, honey, lime juice, salt, and pepper; remove from heat.

- Cut chicken into 1-inch cubes and add to marinade. Refrigerate for 8–24 hours. Add fruit and onions to marinade for last hour.

- Drain food, reserving marinade. Thread chicken onto 6 skewers. Thread fruit and onions on 6 skewers.

- Grill kabobs over direct heat, brushing with marinade; cook chicken for 5–8 minutes until well done; fruit just until marks appear, 2–3 minutes.

Classic Chicken Kabobs: For marinade, use ⅓ cup zesty Italian salad dressing with 2 tablespoons Dijon mustard. Cut 1 onion into wedges; separate sections. Thread onto 6 skewers, alternating onion and chicken; Thread 1 pint cherry tomatoes, 8 ounces button mushrooms, and 2 yellow bell peppers, sliced, on 6 more skewers.

Have a kabob party! Place meats, vegetables, and fruits on cold trays next to skewers and let your guests assemble their own. Use grill charms to tell them apart. Be sure to cook the meat within 2 hours, 1 hour if the ambient temperature is more than 80 degrees F. And supply hand wipes so your guests can clean up after creating their kabob masterpieces.

Marinate Chicken Fruit and Onion

Grill Kabobs

- The curry powder is cooked briefly in oil to enhance and strengthen the flavors.

- The fruit and onion should be approximately the same size so they cook evenly on the grill.

- You can make your own curry powder, or buy premixed blends at any grocery store or food co-op.

- For curry powder, combine cinnamon, cloves, cardamom, turmeric, mace, red and black pepper, and ground chiles.

- Kabob holders and baskets make grilling skewers much easier.

- Be sure to oil the holder or basket or spray it with grilling spray before you add the food.

- Place the chicken and fruit on separate kabobs because it is so important to cook chicken to well done. Remove the fruit as it finishes.

- Make extra marinade and boil it for 2 minutes, then add to sour cream and serve as a dipping sauce.

PORK KABOBS

Pork tenderloin, pork chops, and roasts make delicious kabobs

The best cuts for pork kabobs include chops, tenderloin, and loin roast. These meats will cook for different times, so you can't directly substitute one for the other.

Pork is a low-fat meat, so marinades enhance texture and add flavor. A dry rub is perfect for this tender meat. Sometimes there is a membrane over the tenderloin called the silver skin; pull this off before cubing. Add olive oil and citrus juice for extra flavor and to help prevent sticking on the grill.

Pork tenderloin will cook the quickest, about 5–6 minutes total. The chops will take 7–8 minutes, and the roast, which should be marinated by itself for a few hours, will take 9–10 minutes, even when cubed. *Yield: 6 kabobs*

Ingredients

½ teaspoon cumin seeds

½ teaspoon coriander seeds

2 tablespoons brown sugar

½ teaspoon salt

⅛ teaspoon black pepper

⅛ teaspoon cayenne pepper

1 pound pork tenderloin, cubed

2 mangoes, peeled and cubed

2 green bell peppers, cut into squares

1 tablespoon olive oil

1 tablespoon lime juice

3 cups hot cooked rice

Pork and Mango Skewers

- Grind seeds in a coffee grinder or mortar and pestle. Mix in small bowl with brown sugar, salt, and peppers.

- Cut pork into 1-inch cubes. Prepare mango and bell peppers and combine all in large bowl. Sprinkle with spices and toss.

- Drizzle with olive oil and lime juice; toss again. Cover; chill for 2–3 hours.

- Thread food onto skewers, starting and ending with green peppers. Grill over direct heat for 7–9 minutes until pork is tender and slightly pink. Serve with rice.

MAKE IT EASY

Use your imagination when creating kabob varieties. Learn about the foods of a cuisine and incorporate those into kabobs. Mexican kabobs could be made from pork, different chile peppers, and corn on the cob cut into 2-inch pieces. Spanish kabobs would use a paprika marinade and pearl onions. Caribbean kabobs would use mangoes, papaya, and a Creole rub.

• • • • RECIPE VARIATION • • • •

German Kabobs: For brine, mix 1/3 cup beer, 1/4 cup water, and 2 tablespoons brown mustard. Cut pork into 1½-inch cubes; skewer with onion wedges and pre-cooked baby potatoes. Baste with beer mixture.

Ham Kabobs: Add 1 tablespoon grated ginger root and ground dried pineapple to rub. Use 1 pound cubed ham, 2 cups pineapple chunks, and green pepper.

Prepare Pork

- Pork tenderloin is one of the more expensive cuts of pork, but there is absolutely no waste and very little fat.

- Be sure the cubes of pork are approximately all the same size and that they match the size of the mango cubes and green pepper pieces.

- The tenderloin is a long, narrow strip of meat with thin ends.

- Cut off the thin ends, cut into squares, then thread 2 pieces together to make a cube.

Add the Dry Rub

- A dry rub provides lots of concentrated flavor without tenderizing. Only use dry rubs on very tender, quick-cooking meats.

- Marinate the mixture in the refrigerator, covered, for 2–3 hours. Any longer, and the mango will get too soft.

- You can vary the rub recipe as you'd like. Use plain sugar, grind other types of seeds, or add your favorite spices.

- You could marinate just the pork in the rub for up to 24 hours, then assemble the kabobs.

MIXED GRILL

Yes, it's possible to cook 2 or 3 meats on 1 skewer; size and timing are the keys

When you want to cook 2 or more meats on a skewer, getting everything cooked to the proper temperature and doneness is the challenge. You can do it, by paying some attention to size and cooking time.

Place the foods on the skewers according to how long they take to cook. For example, shrimp can be placed at the end of the skewer; then that end can be cooked over indirect heat, while the rest of the kabob is right over the coals.

You can also use foil, either placed on the grate under the skewers, or wrapped around the food, to shield it from the hottest heat. With a little practice, everything will cook perfectly. *Yield: 6 kabobs*

Ingredients

3 cloves garlic, minced

1 shallot, minced

2 tablespoons olive oil

1/3 cup honey mustard salad dressing

2 tablespoons lemon juice

1 tablespoon chopped fresh thyme
    leaves

1 teaspoon salt

1/4 teaspoon pepper

3/4 pound rib eye steak

3/4 pound salmon steak

16 large raw shelled shrimp, deveined

8 ounces cremini mushrooms

1 yellow summer squash, cubed

Surf 'n' Turf Kabobs

- Cook garlic and shallot in oil until tender. Remove from heat; add dressing, juice, thyme, salt, and pepper.

- Cut steak into 1¼-inch cubes; cut ½-inch slit in center of each cube. Cut salmon into 1-inch cubes. Combine with shrimp in large bowl; pour marinade over mixture.

- Refrigerate for 1–2 hours. Drain, reserving marinade. Thread all ingredients onto metal skewers, alternating meat with vegetables.

- Grill on direct heat for 9–10 minutes, brushing with marinade, until shrimp and salmon are done.

Tex-Mex Mixed Grill Kabobs

Add ¼ cup minced onion, ½ cup salsa, and 2 minced jalapeño peppers to marinade. Omit shallot, salad dressing, thyme, steak, salmon, and squash. Add 1½ pounds pork tenderloin cut into 1¼-inch cubes, corn on cob cut to 2-inch pieces, and red bell pepper slices.

Lamb and Salmon Kabobs

Omit all ingredients except salmon. Add 1 pound boneless leg of lamb, cut into 1-inch cubes. Combine 2 tablespoons lemon juice, 2 tablespoons orange juice, ¼ cup fresh chopped mint, 1 teaspoon salt, and ¼ teaspoon pepper for marinade. Add green and red bell peppers, cut into strips, and whole mushrooms. Grill for 9–11 minutes. *Yield: 8 kabobs*

Prepare Ingredients

- Use a ruler to be sure that you are cubing the meat to the proper size.

- The salmon has to cook to more doneness than the steak does, so it's cut to a smaller size.

- Cut around any visible fat in the steak; don't include it in the cube because it won't completely melt during the cooking time.

- You can use other vegetables with the same texture. Zucchini, green onions, or bell pepper squares would work well.

Assemble Kabobs

- These types of kabobs need heavier skewers, preferably metal skewers, for best results.

- There's a lot of food on each kabob, and these skewers, especially flat skewers, are best at preventing kabob spinning.

- You could also use sugar-cane sticks to accent the sweet flavors. Alternate foods for best appearance.

- Use foil to shield parts of the kabobs that are cooking faster than others. Move foil around with your tongs.

SHRIMP AND SCALLOPS

Delicate shrimp and scallops make elegant kabobs perfect for entertaining

Shrimp and scallops are perfect kabob partners. They cook in about the same amount of time. This seafood can only be marinated for a few hours or it will become too tough.

Shell and devein the shrimp before you thread it on the skewer. The flavors will penetrate the meat and the shrimp will be easier to eat.

Partially cooked bacon, threaded around the seafood, adds great flavor, and helps add fat to these low-fat foods.

This type of seafood cooks in about 4–5 minutes, so bamboo skewers are appropriate. Keep the seafood on 1 half of the skewers, and the vegetables on the other half, so you can shield food if necessary. *Yield: 4 kabobs*

Ingredients

¼ cup minced red onion

3 cloves garlic, minced

1 tablespoon olive oil

1 tablespoon lemon juice

¼ cup seafood cocktail sauce

¼ cup tomato sauce

16 slices bacon

½ pound large raw peeled shrimp

½ pound sea scallops

1 red and 1 yellow bell pepper

8 ounces button mushrooms

Shrimp and Scallop Kabobs

- Cook onion and garlic in oil. Add lemon juice, cocktail and tomato sauces; simmer 4 minutes. Let cool.

- Partially cook bacon until translucent but still pliable.

- Using double skewers, skewer 1 end of bacon, add shrimp, and wrap the bacon around. Add scallop and wrap bacon around. Continue until seafood is used, using 2 strips bacon per skewer.

- Add bell peppers and mushrooms to the other half of the skewers. Grill on direct heat for 5–7 minutes, brushing with sauce, until done.

~ VARIATIONS ~

Tex-Mex Scallop Kabobs
For sauce, combine 2 tablespoons olive oil, ¼ cup orange juice, ½ teaspoon salt, ⅛ teaspoon pepper, and ½ teaspoon dried thyme leaves. Omit shrimp, cocktail sauce, tomato sauce, and mushrooms. Use 1 pound sea scallops, sliced zucchini, and red bell pepper.

Spicy Shrimp Kabobs
Omit scallops, cocktail sauce, and tomato sauce. For sauce, combine 2 tablespoons olive oil with 3 tablespoons lemon juice, 2 teaspoons chili powder, ¼ teaspoon pepper, and ½ teaspoon salt. Wrap partially cooked bacon around each piece of shrimp.

Skewer Shrimp and Bacon

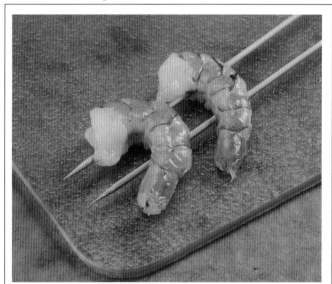

- Shrimp and scallops are some of the most notorious "spinners" on skewers.

- Even when they're placed on flat skewers, they will still turn around as the skewers are turned.

- Use 2 skewers for these types of food. Make sure the skewers are very sharp, and push through the food about ½ inch apart.

- Wind the bacon loosely around the seafood, as it will shrink as it cooks.

Grill Kabobs

- Don't be afraid to move skewers around on the grill. Once the food has seared, the kabobs can be moved to control doneness.

- As you brush the kabobs with sauce, avoid the bacon so it becomes crisp as it cooks.

- Since the bacon is wound loosely around the food, keeping the sauce away isn't too difficult.

- When you're cooking just shrimp on skewers, push them together so they stay moist and tender while on the grill.

MEATBALL LOLLIPOPS

Ground meat, flavored any way you'd like, and shaped onto a skewer, is a fun way to grill

Lollipops are just like meatballs, but they're formed around a skewer and cooked on the grill. You can make just a plain meat lollipop, or add vegetables and fruits to the skewer to add flavor and nutrition.

The meat mixture must be moist but fairly firm to hold its shape on the grill. If you choose to make these from ground chicken or turkey, cook them on perforated foil for best results.

The meat isn't shaped into a ball, but an oval so the inside will cook by the time the outside is crisp and caramelized.

The meat must be cooked to 165 degrees F, so choose sturdy vegetables like parboiled potatoes or ears of corn to accompany the lollipops. *Yield: 8 kabobs*

Ingredients

2 tablespoons ketchup

1 tablespoon mustard

½ teaspoon grill seasoning

⅛ teaspoon pepper

⅓ cup soft breadcrumbs

1 tablespoon yogurt

2 tablespoons chopped parsley

1½ pounds lean ground beef

16 small potatoes, parboiled

3 ears of corn

2 tablespoons butter, melted

American Meatball Lollipops

- In large bowl, combine ketchup, mustard, seasoning, pepper, breadcrumbs, yogurt, and parsley.

- Add meat and mix gently. Form ⅓ cup around the end of a metal skewer. Press firmly but gently to keep the meat together, but don't compress too much.

- Alternately add potatoes and corn to the skewers, leaving about 2 inches at the end.

- Grill lollipops on direct heat for 6–8 minutes until the meat is thoroughly cooked, turning frequently, brushing vegetables with butter.

~ VARIATIONS ~

Hawaiian Pork Lollipops

Omit ketchup, mustard, grill seasoning, buttermilk, beef, potatoes, and corn. Combine 3 tablespoons pineapple juice, 1 tablespoon lemon juice, and 1 minced jalapeño pepper with breadcrumbs and 1¼ pounds ground pork. Thread pineapple chunks and green bell peppers on skewers. Grill for 10–12 minutes, brushing with more pineapple juice, until pork registers 160 degrees F on meat thermometer.

Medium Rare Lollipops

To serve these lollipops medium rare, follow the instructions for Medium-Rare Burgers on page 42 to prepare the beef. The meat must be cooked immediately after it has been ground and mixed with the remaining ingredients.

Form Lollipops

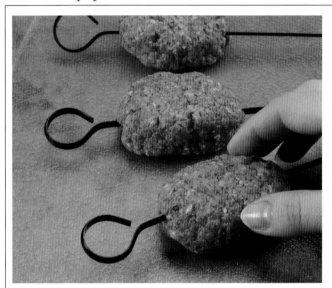

- Just like burgers, lollipops take some special handling to cook well on the grill.

- Work the meat mixture gently but thoroughly. You can make this mixture up to 3 hours ahead of time; chill it in the fridge.

- Shape the meat into an oval on the skewers. The meat should be no more than 1 inch thick so it cooks completely.

- You can brush the kabobs with barbecue sauce as they cook to add extra flavor and moisture.

Add Remaining Ingredients

- Potatoes and corn on the cob can be difficult to thread even onto metal skewers.

- You may want to use another skewer or other sharp object to push a hole through hard ingredients before adding them to the skewers.

- To parboil the potatoes, add them to boiling water and cook for 3–5 minutes until they are almost tender.

- You can use frozen corn on the cob that is already cut into pieces.

ETHNIC KABOBS

Flavors from around the world spice up kabobs to make dinnertime fun

Kabobs have been around since man discovered fire and how to cook over it. Different ethnic groups and cuisines have taken advantage of this easy cooking method and add delicious seasoning techniques to many meats.

Flavored wooden kabobs are one of the newest toys on the market, and they add great taste to your grilled food, espe-

cially more exotic meats and flavors. Also think about using cinnamon sticks, lemongrass stalks, and herb stalks.

Serve any kabob with a rice or couscous pilaf to soak up the juices and to act as a neutral contrast to the highly flavored meats and vegetables. Cook the rice or couscous in chicken broth for more richness. *Yield: 8 kabobs; serves 4*

Ingredients

8 (7-inch) fresh rosemary sprigs

¼ cup minced onion

4 cloves garlic, minced

1 tablespoon olive oil

3 tablespoons lemon juice

¼ cup plain yogurt

2 tablespoons chopped fresh mint

⅛ teaspoon mint extract

½ teaspoon salt

¼ teaspoon pepper

1¼ pound lamb tenderloin

8 ounces button mushrooms

2 green bell peppers, sliced

Indian Lamb Kabobs

- Be sure the rosemary stems are sturdy and not bent. Soak in water for 1 hour.

- Cook onion and garlic in olive oil until tender. Stir in remaining ingredients except lamb, mushrooms, and peppers.

- Trim visible fat from lamb.

- Cut lamb into 1½ inch cubes and add to marinade; stir well. Cover and refrigerate for 1 hour.

- Thread lamb and vegetables on rosemary stems. Grill over direct heat for 7–9 minutes until lamb is at medium doneness, brushing with all remaining marinade.

Lamb tastes so rich because its fat has a low melting point. That's why it coats your mouth, and why lamb is served with rosemary, mint, garlic, and lemon. Those types of foods with a sharp taste cut through the fat and counteract its richness. These foods combined in one recipe flavor and balance the lamb.

• • • • RECIPE VARIATION • • • •

Mediterranean Swordfish Kabobs: Omit rosemary, yogurt, mint, and mint extract. Add ¼ cup buttermilk to marinade. Use 1¼ pounds swordfish steaks, cut into 2-inch cubes. Marinate swordfish for 3–4 hours. Thread the swordfish onto metal skewers alternating with fresh whole bay leaves and onion wedges. Grill on direct heat 9–10 minutes. Do not eat bay leaves.

Blend the yogurt marinade

Thread Food on Rosemary

- Yogurt has a natural acidity and mild flavor, which makes it the perfect base for marinades.

- If you can find it, Greek yogurt is much thicker, with a more pronounced flavor, than the plain yogurt Americans are used to.

- Don't marinate meats or vegetables in yogurt for more than 2–3 hours or the meat will become mushy.

- Use your favorite herbs and spices to flavor yogurt for a variety of marinades.

- Rosemary sprigs are sturdy enough to hold the meat, but they aren't strong enough to start a hole in the meat.

- Use a metal skewer to make a hole in each piece of the meat and vegetables before threading them on the sprigs.

- Rosemary leaves grow pointing in one direction on the stem. Thread the meat onto the stems with the leaves.

- Because rosemary sprigs only grow to 6 or 7 inches, each person gets 2 skewers in this recipe.

FRUIT KABOBS

You can make a salad or dessert from grilled fruit, easily made with these kabobs

Fruit and the grill are natural partners. The heat of the grill caramelizes the sugar in the fruits, and it also softens fruits that aren't quite ripe, so they become smooth and rich.

Fruits have a relatively high water content. The heat of the grill evaporates the water as they cook, concentrating the flavor.

Marinating fruits can add a lot of flavor. Cinnamon sticks,

allspice, star anise, or peppercorns add a depth of flavor to fruit marinades.

Use grilled fruit as a dessert, as a topping for your breakfast oatmeal or pancakes, or as part of a salad.

The only fruits that do not grill well are those with high water content, like watermelon or delicate berries. *Yield: 6 kabobs*

Ingredients

¼ cup lemon juice, divided

½ cup sparkling wine or water

1 tablespoon sugar

1 tablespoon Canola oil

Pinch of salt

2 Granny Smith apples

2 pears

¼ cup sugar

2 tablespoons butter, melted

3 cups ice cream

⅓ cup caramel ice cream topping

Apple Pear Kabobs

- In bowl, combine 2 table-spoons lemon juice, wine, sugar, and salt. Cut fruit in half and core.

- Cut fruit into quarters, then in half crosswise, sprinkling with remaining 2 table-spoons lemon juice. Add to marinade; refrigerate for 1 hour, then thread fruit on

- skewers. Sprinkle with sugar.

- Use a wire brush to clean the grill, then oil it.

- Brush on butter and grill over direct heat for 2–3 minutes, turning once, until grill marks appear and fruit is soft. Serve over ice cream with caramel sauce.

Stone Fruit Kabobs

Cut 3 nectarines and 3 plums in half; remove pit. Brush with 3 tablespoons lemon juice and sprinkle with ⅓ cup sugar. Omit sparkling wine. Thread fruit on metal kabobs so the fruit will lay flat, cut side down on the grill. Grill over direct medium-low heat for 3–5 minutes, turning once, until fragrant.

Pineapple on Sugar Cane

Prepare a pineapple and cut into 2-inch x 2-inch pieces. Omit lemon juice and wine. Pierce a hole in the pineapple pieces with a metal skewer, then thread onto sugarcane. Sprinkle with ⅓ cup brown sugar and grill, turning frequently, for 4–6 minutes until brown and caramelized.

Prepare the Fruit

Grill until Golden

- The flesh of fruit like bananas, pears, peaches, and apples turns brown when exposed to air.

- Enzymes in the fruit's cells react with oxygen when the cells are cut. This is called enzymatic browning.

- Acids and heat inactivate the enzymes, keeping the flesh bright. Lemon, orange, and pineapple juice are usually used.

- Choose fruit that is firm, and cut the pieces all to the same size. Leave some skin on each piece to help hold the fruit together.

- The grill grate must be impeccably clean before the fruit is cooked.

- Fruit doesn't take long to cook on the grill, so watch it carefully as it cooks. Don't even walk away; it can burn in that short time.

- Fruits are high in sugar, which caramelizes and burns quickly in the high heat.

- For a crisp crust, sprinkle the fruit with granulated or brown sugar just before putting it on the grill.

REGIONAL KABOBS

American regional foods and flavors spice up these kabob recipes

American regional flavors are very distinct and complicated, built around native and easily accessible foods.

The Northeast is famous for its clam and lobster bakes, and the Southeast is built around fresh seafood and Low Country cuisine. Tex-Mex holds sway in the south, and California cuisine is an entity unto itself.

Midwestern cuisine includes dairy products, fresh vegetables, cheese, and fish from abundant lakes. And the North-west is all about salmon, comfort foods, and fresh produce.

Wisconsin is a state with lots of native foods, from cheese from its many dairy farms to fresh cherries and vegetables from Door County. These Wisconsin Grilled Cherry Cheese Kabobs are excellent appetizers for any cookout menu.
Yield: 12 kabobs

Ingredients

8 ounces Muenster cheese

8 ounces provolone cheese

2 eggs, beaten

1 tablespoon water

½ teaspoon dried thyme leaves

2 cups panko breadcrumbs

3 cups pitted large bing cherries

1 tablespoon canola oil

Wisconsin Grilled Cherry Cheese Kabobs

- Cut cheeses into 1½ inch cubes and refrigerate. Beat eggs, water, and thyme together and place in shallow bowl.

- Place breadcrumbs in another bowl. Dip cheese cubes into egg mixture, then into breadcrumbs to coat. Repeat.

- Place on plate and place in freezer for 30 minutes. Remove and thread on bamboo skewers with cherries.

- Clean grate and lightly oil with canola oil. Grill kabobs on direct heat for 1–2 minutes, turning once, until crumbs are toasted. Serve immediately.

California Veggie Cheese Kabobs
Omit cherries. Add 14-ounce can artichoke hearts, well drained, and 1 (9-ounce) jar pearl onions, drained. Be sure the artichokes and onions are not marinated, but plain. Use aged goat cheese and halloumi cheese instead of Muenster and provolone, then skewer and grill without freezing.

Maine Lobster Bake Kabobs
Use 2 frozen lobster tails, meat removed and cut into 2-inch chunks, 3 ears corn, cut into 2-inch pieces, and 12 baby red potatoes, boiled for 3–4 minutes until almost tender. Brush kabobs with ½ cup honey mustard dressing. Grill for 7–9 minutes until corn and potatoes are done; sprinkle with grated Romano cheese.

Coat Cheese Cubes

- Work carefully and make sure that the cheese is well coated in the egg wash and breadcrumbs.

- Do not skimp and coat the cheese just once. Two layers of egg wash and crumbs are necessary for the recipe to work.

- If some of the cheese is exposed, it will break through the coating and melt off the skewers.

- Panko are Japanese breadcrumbs that are very crunchy. If you can't find them, plain dried breadcrumbs will work.

Freeze the Cheese

- Don't freeze the cheese longer than 30 minutes, or the insides will be cold when the outsides are done.

- You could use other fruits on these kabobs, such as whole strawberries or nectarine slices.

- The grill has to be very clean before you add the kabobs. You don't want other flavors to transfer, and residue on the grates may cause the cheese to stick.

- Tell your guests to be careful when biting into these kabobs; the coating on the cheese will be hot.

POTATO AND ROOT VEGGIE KABOBS

Hard vegetables take special preparation time, but are so good when grilled on a skewer

Potatoes and other hard vegetables like squash and parsnips take on another dimension when grilled. The heat caramelizes the sugars in these vegetables, forming a delicious crisp crust, and the grill adds a wonderful smoky flavor.

Because these types of vegetables take so long to cook, they must be precooked before grilling. You can precook them in boiling water, in the oven, or in the microwave.

These veggies can be served as a side dish, or think about using them in a potato salad. Potato salad was the inspiration for sprinkling the hot precooked veggies with an herbed vinegar mixture before grilling. The vegetables will absorb the vinegar flavor. *Yield: 8 kabobs*

Ingredients

12 3-inch red potatoes

½ butternut squash

3 tablespoons tarragon vinegar

1 teaspoon dried tarragon leaves

1 tablespoon olive oil

2 tablespoons melted butter

1 teaspoon salt

⅛ teaspoon pepper

Mixed Potato and Squash Kabobs

- Cut potatoes in half; place in pot full of cold water.

- Peel squash, remove seeds, and cut into 1½-inch cubes. Add to pot with potatoes and bring to a boil. Simmer for 6–7 minutes or until vegetables are crisp-tender.

- Remove from heat, drain, and place in large bowl. Sprinkle with vinegar and tarragon, tossing to coat. Let stand for 15 minutes.

- Thread on skewers. Brush with olive oil and grill over direct heat for 5–7 minutes, brushing with melted butter. Sprinkle with salt and pepper and serve.

~ VARIATION ~

Steakhouse Potato Kabobs
Use 24 small red potatoes, each cut in half. Simmer as directed. Omit squash, tarragon vinegar, and tarragon. Sprinkle the potatoes with 5 tablespoons Italian salad dressing, ½ teaspoon salt, and ⅛ teaspoon pepper when still hot from the water. Skewer and grill on direct medium heat until crisp, 7–9 minutes.

Caramelized Squash and Carrot Kabobs
Use ½ of a butternut squash and baby carrots; cube the squash. Precook both in boiling water for 5 minutes, then thread onto kabobs. Brush with ¼ cup melted butter and sprinkle with salt, pepper, and dried basil leaves. Grill on direct heat until browned, about 6–7 minutes.

Prepare Squash

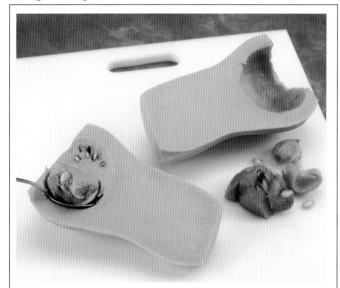

- Squash isn't difficult to prepare, but it does take a bit of time and a bit of muscle.

- Begin by peeling off the skin, using a small paring knife. Cut the squash in half lengthwise, using a large chef's knife.

- Use a spoon to scrape out the seeds and membranes in the hollow. Then cut the squash into cubes.

- You could also use acorn or other types of hard winter squash in this recipe.

Precook Vegetables

- The key to the best grilled potato and root vegetable kabobs is to precook the vegetables properly.

- They must be almost cooked, but still firm enough to resist slightly when threaded onto skewers.

- Coat the vegetables with olive oil or melted butter before they cook so they don't stick to the grill.

- Any fresh herb can be chopped and sprinkled over the hot vegetables; or add some to the fire for smoky flavor.

TENDER VEGGIE KABOBS

Tender vegetables like peppers and tomatoes get smoky in seconds on the grill

Tender vegetables contain more water and have thin skins. They are ideal for very quick grilling. When these vegetables are grilled they become soft and slightly sweet. You can use them as a side dish as is, or add to a green or pasta salad.

Marinades add great flavor to these quick-cooking kabobs. Don't marinate the vegetables in the dressing longer than 8 hours; that will just make them watery. Brush with the marinade as they grill.

Flavored, or compound, butters are a great choice for these types of kabobs. Your guests just slip the veggies off the skewers, and then top with a disc of butter. Everything melts together with wonderful aromas. *Yield: 6 kabobs*

Ingredients

¼ cup butter, softened

1 tablespoon chopped fresh oregano leaves

½ teaspoon lemon zest

1 tablespoon Dijon mustard

⅛ teaspoon pepper

18 cremini mushrooms

18 large cherry tomatoes

1 red onion, cut into eighths

2 tablespoons olive oil

1 tablespoon red wine vinegar

½ teaspoon dried oregano leaves

Greek Mushroom and Tomato Kabobs

- In small bowl, beat together butter, oregano, zest, mustard, and pepper. Form into small log, wrap in plastic wrap, and refrigerate up to 2 days.

- Trim off ends of mushroom stems. Thread onto skewers with tomatoes and onions.

- In small bowl, combine olive oil, vinegar, and dried oregano. Brush over kabobs.

- Grill in kabob basket on direct heat for 4–6 minutes, brushing with marinade, until grill marks appear. Slice the butter into ½-inch rounds and place on hot vegetables.

Skewer Vegetables

- Choose large, firm cherry tomatoes for kabobs. Grape tomatoes cook too quickly.

- You really can't grill tomato wedges or slices; they are too watery and will fall apart in the intense heat.

- Wipe mushrooms with a damp cloth before using.

- Trim off the tough end of the stem and discard.

- Peel onions and cut in half, then cut each half into 4 pieces. Push the skewer through the onion from the outside in to hold the layers together.

Prepare Favored Butter

- Let butter stand at room temperature for about an hour to soften. The microwave will make the butter too soft and can easily melt it in spots.

- Rinse fresh herbs well, then shake off water and blot between paper towels to dry before chopping.

- The herbs must be dry when added to the butter for best results.

- Other good additions to compound butter include pesto, sun-dried tomatoes, and chopped toasted nuts.

DESSERT KABOBS
Nothing caramelizes fruit or cake better than a hot grill

Dessert on a stick is a novel and fun idea popularized by the food at state fairs. And of course everyone knows about s'mores, with toasted marshmallows melting chocolate between crisp graham crackers.

Dessert kabobs can be more sophisticated than that. Cubes of pound cake or angel food cake turn brown on the grill, with a crisp crust and tender interior. And more unusual fruits that you wouldn't think of grilling, like strawberries, add a

wonderful change of pace.

Think about the texture of the fruit you want to grill. Peaches, pineapple, nectarines, pears, and apples are all naturals. But cantaloupe, strawberries, kiwi, or blueberries would also work.

Small fruits should be grilled on perforated foil instead of on a kabob. *Yield: 6 kabobs*

KNACK GRILLING BASICS

Ingredients

2 tablespoons butter

1 tablespoon curry powder

¼ cup brown sugar

1 tablespoon honey

½ cup plus 2 tablespoons apricot preserves

2 nectarines

2 cups large strawberries

¼ angel food cake

1 cup sour cream

¼ cup sugar

Curried Fruit Kabobs with Angel Food Cubes

- Melt butter with curry powder. Add brown sugar; cook and stir until mixture blends, about 2–3 minutes.

- Remove from heat; add honey and 2 tablespoons apricot preserves. Set aside to cool.

- Quarter nectarines, then cut in half. Wash strawberries. Cut angel food cake into 1½-inch cubes. Combine sour cream, sugar, and ½ cup apricot preserves.

- Thread fruit and cake onto bamboo skewers. Brush with butter mixture; grill for 2–4 minutes. Serve with sour cream dip.

• • • • RECIPE VARIATION • • •

Grilled Bananas Foster: Make brown sugar syrup with 2 tablespoons honey, omitting curry powder and preserves. Choose 3 ripe but firm bananas. Cut into 2-inch pieces; brush with 2 tablespoons lemon juice. Skewer bananas; brush with half of syrup. Grill for 1–2 minutes until warm. Drizzle with remaining syrup; serve over ice cream. Omit sour cream dip.

ZOOM

One of the culinary breakthroughs of the 1990s was pairing fruit desserts with fresh herbs. Chop herbs and sprinkle them over the grilled fruit kabobs, or use the herb stems as the skewers. If the stems aren't strong enough to hold the fruit, push a stem or two through the fruit when it's threaded onto the skewers.

Cut Cake into Cubes

Assemble Kabobs

- Because angel food cake is so light and springy, it's difficult to cut. A serrated knife works best to cut the cake into cubes.

- You could substitute pound cake if you'd like; cut that into 1-inch cubes.

- Regular cakes made from a mix, or shortening cakes, are too tender to skewer; they'll fall apart.

- Don't make these kabobs ahead of time; the cake will absorb liquid from the fruit and will fall apart on the grill.

- Yes, you can grill strawberries. Choose large, barely ripe fruit so it holds together on the grill.

- The hard fruits you typically find in the grocery store taste better grilled, with more flavor and a soft texture.

- Think about grilling fruit and using it to make a fruit salad. Any grilled fruit would be delicious with a raspberry or balsamic vinaigrette.

- Grilled fruits are also delicious mixed with some citrus juices and jalapeño peppers for a fresh salsa.

PRECOOKED SAUSAGES

These sausages just heat on the grill, bringing out their juicy flavors

Sausages are one of the easiest foods to grill. With precooked sausages, you don't have to worry about doneness or undercooking. You purchase them fully cooked, so the grill just reheats them.

But that doesn't mean these sausages aren't flavorful! Brush them with glazes and mops as they grill, top them with everything from salsa to raita, and grill them over herb or wood smoke.

Because these sausages can dry out on the grill, keep a pan of beer or stock on the grill. As the sausages finish cooking, add them to the hot liquid and they'll stay hot for an hour for the most flavorful sausages ever. Give them another couple of seconds on the grill to crisp before serving. *Yield: 6 sausages*

Ingredients

1 cup beer

½ cup water

2 onions, chopped

3 cloves garlic, minced

6 fully cooked Polish sausages

6 sausage buns

½ cup grainy mustard

Polish Sausage with Grainy Mustard

- Simmer beer, water, onion, and garlic. Simmer until vegetables are soft. Prick sausages and simmer in beer mixture for 2 minutes.

- Grill sausages over indirect heat, turning frequently and brushing with the beer mixture, until hot.

- Serve immediately, or return to beer mixture for holding. Grill buns; spread with mustard.

- Cut sausages in half lengthwise, place in buns. With slotted spoon, scoop onions and garlic out of beer mixture and place in split sausages.

~ VARIATIONS ~

Polish Kraut Sandwiches

Add 6 slices bacon; partially cook bacon until fat is cooked out but bacon is still pliable. Prick and simmer sausages in beer mixture, then wrap with bacon. Grill over medium direct heat until bacon is crisp, turning frequently. Place on grilled buns with grainy mustard, then top with drained fresh sauerkraut.

Smoked Knockwurst and Potato Salad

Combine 1 cup mayonnaise, ¼ cup whipped salad dressing, ¼ cup mustard, and 3 tablespoons milk. Add 6 cooked chopped potatoes, 3 chopped green onions, and 2 chopped radishes; chill. Grill fully cooked knockwurst over indirect medium heat until crisp and juicy. Slice and serve on potato salad.

Simmer Sausages

- You've been told to never pierce sausages with a fork. Well, piercing won't let out all the fat and juice; it just prevents splitting on the grill.

- Pierce only about ¼-inch deep with a sharp fork, in 2–3 places.

- The sausages are simmered in the beer and onion mixture just to start the cooking process and make a crisp crust.

- Don't partially warm the sausages and hold them; place them on the grill immediately.

Grill Sausages

- Because the sausages are so full of fat, they tend to flare up on the grill.

- Cooking them over indirect heat is the best way to heat them through without burning or overcooking.

- Turn the sausages frequently as they cook, so they heat evenly and the skin becomes crisp. They can be basted with some of the beer mixture if you'd like.

- You can add herbs, smoked wood chips, or beer and barbecue sauces to the drip pan for even more smoky flavor.

FRESH SAUSAGES

Fresh sausages need some preparation before being grilled to smoky perfection

Fresh sausages, including knockwurst and Italian sausages, are not cooked when you buy them. Because they take some time to cook through, it's a good idea to precook them, in a saucepan or in the microwave or slow cooker. Then they finish on the grill, getting a crisp smoky crust bursting with grill flavor.

You can also precook the sausages, then grill them, then put them back into the sauce to finish. Never partially cook any meat and refrigerate or freeze for later cooking. As soon as meat is partially cooked, it has to be finished.

Once these sausages are grilled, they can be served in buns with toppings, or sliced and placed on pizza or in grilled sandwiches. *Yield: 6 sausage sandwiches*

Ingredients

½ cup beer

¼ cup barbecue sauce

⅓ cup water

½ teaspoon salt

⅛ teaspoon pepper

10 dashes hot sauce

6 sweet or hot Italian sausages

2 green bell peppers, sliced

1 cup sliced mushrooms

6 6-inch x 2-inch slices provolone cheese

6 sausage buns

½ cup barbecue sauce

Grilled Italian Sausage Sandwiches

- In large saucepan, combine beer, barbecue sauce, water, salt, pepper, and hot sauce. Bring to a simmer over medium heat. Place on grill.

- Add sausages and bring to a simmer. Cover pan; simmer for 8–9 minutes or until sausages are almost done.

- Place sausages on direct heat; grill until fully cooked and nicely marked. Combine peppers and mushrooms in grill basket; grill for 3–4 minutes.

- When sausages are done, top with cheese. Grill buns. Assemble sandwiches.

Fresh sausages can be frozen when you get them home from the store. Wrap in freezer wrap or place in freezer bags. Label and freeze up to 6 months. To thaw, let stand in the refrigerator overnight; never thaw at room temperature. Cook the thawed sausages just as you would fresh ones.

• • • • RECIPE VARIATION • • • •

Philly Cheese Sausage Sandwich: Add 1 cup sliced mushrooms to beer mixture. Omit barbecue sauce, bell pepper, and provolone cheese. Grill 1 chopped onion with mushrooms. Grill split, buttered steak sandwich buns, spread with processed cheese spread, then top with grilled sausages and onion mixture, then more Cheez Whiz.

Precook Sausages

Grill Sausages and Veggies

- Precooking the sausages by simmering them in beer holds in their juices and adds flavor.

- They can also be precooked by simply simmering them in about an inch of water, or use apple juice or cider for the kids.

- The sausages can also be precooked in the microwave oven.

- Prick the sausages, place in a microwave safe dish, and add ½ cup water. Microwave on high for 3–4 minutes, turning once, until almost cooked.

- Place the vegetables in a grill basket so it's easy to turn them on the grill.

- You can baste the vegetables with the beer and onion mixture too; it adds great flavor.

- Any tender vegetable is a good addition to this sandwich. Sliced zucchini or onions are delicious.

- Start grilling the vegetables when the sausages are about halfway cooked. Then grill the buns, cut side down, for 1–2 minutes just as everything is finishing.

PORK AND BEEF HOT DOGS

Classic hot dogs can be dressed up in many ways, with relishes and sauces

Everyone has had a dry, burnt hot dog served at a backyard barbecue. Never again! With some glazes and marinades, even plain old pork hot dogs can become a feast.

Here's where the toppings really shine. Every region in America has a different favorite hot dog, based on condiments and extras added after the juicy dog is nestled in the bun.

You can grill hot dogs over direct heat and they will be crisp and juicy in just a few minutes. Or you can use a hot dog roller, a great gadget that makes the dogs taste like ballpark franks.

It's also fun to play with hot dogs. When cut in certain ways, they turn into rings or even an octopus, perfect for temping little appetites. *Yield: 8 hot dogs*

Ingredients

2 onions, sliced

2 tomatoes, chopped

½ cup sweet pickle relish

⅓ cup chopped celery

¼ cup ketchup

2 tablespoons olive oil

½ teaspoon salt

⅛ teaspoon pepper

½ teaspoon grill seasoning

8 beef hot dogs

8 poppyseed hot dog buns, sliced

3 tablespoons butter

¼ cup mustard

Chicago Hot Dogs

- Thread onions on wooden skewer pushed through the rings. Grill for 6–8 minutes until tender.

- Remove onions from skewers and chop. Combine with tomatoes, relish, celery, ketchup, salt, and pepper in medium bowl. Combine oil and seasoning in small bowl.

- Thread hot dogs onto metal skewers or heat a hot dog roller over direct heat.

- Grill dogs, brushing with oil mixture. Spread buns with butter and toast for 2 minutes on grill. Spread buns with mustard, top with hot dogs, then spoon on tomato mixture.

A hot dog roller is a great toy for the grill if you cook a lot of hot dogs. It is made of round stainless steel tubes placed about ½ inch apart. You preheat the roller, and then add the hot dogs, rolling them as they heat.

Hot Dog Octopus: Place hot dogs on work surface. Starting 2 inches from end, cut hot dog in half. Cut each one of those pieces in half, then in half again, to make the 8 "legs" of the octopus. Cook on perforated foil or a grill mat over direct heat until hot dogs are hot and the "legs" curl.

Skewer Hot Dogs

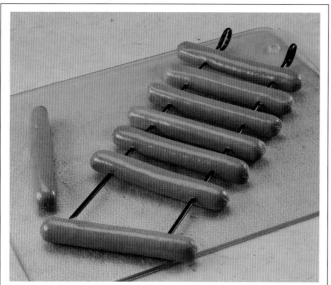

- Use large metal skewers and thread the hot dogs onto 2 of them, placed about 3 inches apart.

- If you don't own a hot dog roller, this is the most efficient way to cook a large number of hot dogs.

- Use tongs and your hand in a mitt to pick up one of the skewers on each side and turn the hot dogs.

- When you cook hot dogs with this method, they stay juicier because the large mass reduces moisture loss.

Grill Hot Dogs

- Don't worry about the hot dogs being pierced; they will lose some juice, but not enough to make a difference.

- The only way to ruin a hot dog is to overcook it. Keep an eye on the grill, since these foods do cook quickly.

- A toasted bun is a nice touch, as is a bun with poppy seeds or sesame seeds.

- Spread the cut sides with butter and grill, cut side down, for about 2 minutes until brown and crisp.

CHICKEN HOT DOGS

Delicate chicken hot dogs are a special treat, served in soft buns

Chicken hot dogs are naturally tender and have less fat than beef or pork dogs. Read the label carefully to see if they are precooked or not. If not precooked, they should be cooked over indirect heat until internal temp is 170 degrees F.

These hot dogs are also available in cured and uncured versions. That just affects the flavor and look, not the cooking process.

Their mild flavor takes naturally to lots of different seasonings and toppings, so don't just rely on mustard and ketchup. Salsa, caramelized onions, and fresh vegetable and fruit chutneys all work well.

Cook your chicken hot dogs over indirect heat, or precook them in water or beer before placing on the grill. *Yield: 6 hot dogs*

Ingredients

1 onion, sliced

1 green bell pepper, quartered

1 tablespoon butter

1 tablespoon olive oil

3 cloves garlic, minced

2 stalks celery, chopped

¼ cup chopped celery leaves

½ cup chunky salsa

½ teaspoon salt

⅛ teaspoon cayenne pepper

2 teaspoons chili powder

6 chicken hot dogs

6 sesame hot dog buns

¼ cup grainy mustard

Chicken Dogs with Jambalaya Topping

- Grill onion and green bell pepper over medium heat until tender. Remove and chop. In saucepan, heat butter and olive oil.

- Add onion, green pepper, garlic, celery, leaves, salsa, salt, pepper, and chili powder. Simmer for 5–6 minutes until hot. Remove from heat.

- Brush chicken dogs with olive oil. Grill over indirect heat for 10–12 minutes, turning frequently, until chicken reaches 170°F.

- Toast buns, spread with mustard, and add chicken dogs. Spoon on jambalaya topping and serve.

You can also find turkey hot dogs in the supermarket and online. These dogs taste more like beef or pork hot dogs. Cook them according to package directions. Chicken hot dogs sometimes taste more like chicken sausage than hot dogs, and they are usually less spicy than beef or pork hot dogs. But you can find them in spicy versions with peppers and Tex-Mex seasonings.

Tex-Mex Turkey Dogs: Spread 6 flour tortillas with refried beans. Grill turkey dogs over medium heat until thoroughly cooked, crisp, and hot. Place tortillas on grill, bean side up, and grill for 1–2 minutes until tortillas are softened. Top with salsa and shredded cheddar and provolone cheeses, then add the turkey dogs and roll up.

Grill Chicken Hot Dogs

Make Jambalaya Topping

- If you'd like, you can simmer the chicken dogs in about 1 inch of water or beer over medium-high heat for 5–6 minutes or until partially cooked.

- Drain, brush with olive oil, then grill, turning frequently, until the hot dogs are crisp with good grill marks.

- You have to use a meat thermometer to make sure these hot dogs are thoroughly cooked.

- Like other sausages, you can hold these chicken hot dogs in simmering beer or water in a pan on the grill.

- Grilling the vegetables for the jambalaya topping adds more smoky flavor to the recipe.

- You can place the vegetables in a grill basket and grill, turning frequently.

- However, you don't have to grill the vegetables. Instead, cook the onion and garlic in butter and olive oil, then add remaining jambalaya ingredients and simmer.

- The jambalaya topping can be served hot or cold on the hot chicken dogs. The spice level will be more intense when cold.

STUFFED HOT DOGS

You can stuff a hot dog with just about anything, but cheese and bacon are favorites

Hot dogs are the kids' favorite, of course, and there are so many ways to cook them on the grill. Stuffed Hot Dogs take a bit more work, but they are easy enough for children to assemble, and they add so much flavor and interest to a plain dog.

Partially cooked bacon is wrapped around cheese-stuffed dogs, then grilled to crisp perfection in this easy recipe. The kids can stuff the cheese into the dogs, but an adult should handle the bacon and the grilling.

Mixing several kinds of shredded cheese makes a more interesting stuffed dog than just inserting a slice of cheese. Use your favorite cheeses to make the recipe your own. *Yield: 6 hot dogs*

Ingredients

1 cup shredded cheddar cheese

½ cup shredded provolone cheese

¼ cup grated Parmesan cheese

⅓ cup minced green onion

6 large hot dogs

6 slices bacon

6 hot dog buns

¼ cup mayonnaise

¼ cup Dijon mustard

Bacon Wrapped Cheese Dogs

- In small bowl, combine cheeses with green onion; mix well. Divide into 6 portions. Press each portion into a ½-inch x 4-inch cylinder.

- Cut a slit in the side of each dog, going about ¾ of the way through. Stuff cheese mixture into hot dogs; refrigerate.

- Cook bacon in large skillet until partially cooked but still pliable. Loosely wrap bacon around the slit area of the hot dog.

- Grill the hot dogs, turning frequently, until bacon is crisp and cheese is melted. Serve on buns with mayo and mustard.

German Stuffed Hot Dogs

Melt 2 tablespoons butter in skillet; add 1 chopped onion and 3 cloves chopped garlic; cook until tender. Add 1 cup drained sauerkraut, 2 tablespoons mustard, 2 tablespoons horseradish, and 1 cup shredded Gouda cheese. Stuff 8–10 hot dogs. Partially cook 8–10 strips of bacon and wrap around hot dogs. Grill over indirect heat for 10–12 minutes. Spread mustard and mayonnaise on Kaiser rolls; add hot dogs.

Tex-Mex Stuffed Hot Dogs

Use 2 (6-ounce) cans whole green chiles. Stuff each chile with some shredded Pepper Jack cheese. Stuff 8–10 hot dogs with the chiles. Grill until hot dogs are crisp and juicy. Spread softened corn tortillas with guacamole and sour cream and add hot dogs; roll up.

Put Cheese in Hot Dog

- Choose larger, thicker hot dogs for this recipe, so they can hold the cheese without ripping.

- You can use cheese slices cut to ½-inch x 4-inch, about the same size as the shredded cheese mixture.

- Be careful not to tear the hot dog as you add the cheese. If necessary, trim the cheese so it fits easily.

- Think about mixing the shredded cheese with other ingredients, like chopped sun-dried tomatoes, chopped pickles, or grilled chopped onions.

Grill Bacon-Wrapped Dogs

- Concentrate on keeping the bacon around the cheese to help protect it from the heat.

- Don't tightly wrap the bacon around the hot dog. As it cooks, the hot dog will expand, and will tear the bacon if it's wrapped too tightly.

- Turn the hot dogs frequently to make sure that the bacon cooks evenly and becomes crisp.

- You may want to drain the hot dogs on some paper towel before serving them to remove bacon fat.

SAUSAGE PIZZAS

Sausage is the perfect topping for pizza cooked on the grill

Pizza on the grill burst onto the scene in America in 1980, although grilled pizzas had previously been made in Italy. If you think of the grill as a big outdoor oven, you'll see that pizzas are a natural fit.

Pizzas cooked on the grill have a wonderful crisp and chewy crust and a delicious smoky flavor. Once you learn how to handle the dough, you can make pizzas with just about any topping. Sausages, however, are the classic pizza topping.

You can make your own pizza dough, which is easy and fun, or use frozen pizza dough, some you've purchased from your local pizza place, or refrigerated dough. You can also use a prebaked pizza crust; just top and grill until the cheese melts and the pizza is hot. Pick your sauce and toppings and let's grill! *Yield: 2 pizzas*

Ingredients

4 Italian sausages

2 tablespoons olive oil

2 green bell peppers, sliced

2 onions, sliced

2 (12-inch) pizza dough rounds

1½ cups pizza sauce

1½ cups grated part-skim mozzarella cheese

1 cup grated sharp cheddar cheese

¼ cup shredded Parmesan cheese

Grilled Sausage Pizza

- Cook sausages in saucepan with ½ cup water over medium heat for 8 minutes, then drain.

- Brush with oil; grill. Grill vegetables in grill basket. Slice sausages ½ inch thick.

- Roll out dough to ¼-inch thickness. Brush with olive oil; flip onto pizza peel; brush with olive oil again.

- Flip onto grill; grill for 2–3 minutes until bottom is crisp; rotate when dough firms. Remove with peel, and flip onto cookie sheet. Add sauce and toppings. Return to grill, cover; grill 2–5 minutes until done.

Pizza Crust

For crust, thaw frozen bread dough according to the package directions. For homemade dough, combine 2½ cups flour, 1 cup cornmeal, 1 package yeast, 1 cup warm water, ¼ cup olive oil, and ½ teaspoon salt, and knead. Let rise for 1 hour, then punch down and roll out. Any type of crust needs to be rotated as it grills; build a two-level fire and move the pizza around as needed.

Pizza Sauce

Cook 1 chopped onion and 3 cloves garlic in 2 tablespoons olive oil. Add 1 cup tomato sauce, ¼ cup tomato paste, 1 chopped tomato, 1 teaspoon dried basil, ½ teaspoon dried Italian seasoning, 2 tablespoons mustard, and ⅓ cup stock or red wine. Simmer for 20–30 minutes.

Grill the Crust

Top the Pizza

- On a charcoal grill, make sure that the crust is 2 inches smaller than the coal surface area, all the way around. This will ensure that the crust cooks evenly.

- If you use a pizza stone, be sure to heat it according to the manufacturer's instructions.

- Oil the crust on both sides before placing it on the grill.

- When the crust is cooked on the first side, the dough will be fairly firm, even on the second side.

- Flip crust onto a pizza peel, then place on your work surface and add sauce and toppings.

- Open grill and place peel on the grate or stone. Give it a slight jerk and slide pizza onto cooking surface.

- Check bottom of the crust frequently. Rotate the pizza as it cooks, over direct and indirect heat, so it browns evenly.

- If the crust finishes before the cheese melts, pull pizza off and cover with tented foil until the cheese melts.

CLASSIC STEAK

The ultimate grilled meal: a good cut of steak, perfectly and simply grilled

A steak is considered one of the best meals, and a grilled steak the best of the best. Only the high, concentrated heat of the grill can make a crisp, caramelized crust on a juicy, tender steak.

Even with a recipe this simple, there are some steps you need to take for the perfect result.

Pick a quality steak. You usually can't find prime grade in the supermarket, because that grade is sold mostly to restaurants. Choice is the next best grade. Buy the best quality steak you can afford. And grill it within 1–2 days of purchase.

A hot grill, some simple seasonings, and knowledge will help make your steaks the talk of the neighborhood. *Yield: 4 steaks*

Ingredients

4 tight-grained steaks (rib eye, T-bone, porterhouse, New York strip, or sirloin)

2 tablespoons olive oil

1 tablespoon red wine vinegar

½ teaspoon salt

⅛ teaspoon pepper

2 teaspoons grill seasoning

Grilled Rib Eye Steak

- If you want to marinate the steak, combine olive oil, vinegar, salt, and pepper. Coat steaks with marinade; refrigerate for 2–3 hours.

- Either way, dry the surface. Steak should char and sear, not boil or steam, so the drier the surface, the better.

- Pat steaks dry with paper towels and let stand at room temperature for 30 minutes.

- Brush on a light coating of oil, then a sprinkle of salt, pepper, and grill seasoning. Place on a hot grill over direct heat; grill as desired.

A meat thermometer is useful, but learning how meat tightens as the steak cooks is a faster way to judge doneness. Touch your thumb to your first finger; the base of your thumb feels like a rare steak. Touch the middle finger and the pad will feel medium. And touching your pinkie, the pad feels like a well done steak.

Steaks deserve a rest after all that work! When you pull the steaks from the grill, they must sit undisturbed for 5–6 minutes so the juices can redistribute. Cover them with foil and let stand while you finish other dishes. Then go ahead and slice into that juicy, flavorful steak.

Turn the Steaks

- As with all meat, when it releases easily from the grill, it's time to turn.

- But there are other signs that a steak is ready for the first turn. The sounds of sizzling will decrease as the steak caramelizes.

- And the heat from the grill will push the liquid inside of the steak to the surface.

- When you see liquid start to accumulate on the surface of the steak that's not against the grill, turn it.

Surface Caramelization

- Deep brown grill marks and a crisp texture are what you're looking for.

- Caramelization, that deep brown color, is what gives grilled steaks their fabulous flavor.

- The sugars and proteins in the meat react with each other on the high heat, breaking down and forming hundreds of compounds.

- Be careful not to burn the steaks. The caramelization process will continue until you remove the steaks from the heat; eventually that turns to charcoal.

MARINATED STEAKS
Cheaper cuts of beef can be just as tender as a filet when marinated

Think of a marinade as a small science project. A marinade consists of an acid, oil, and flavoring ingredients. The acid breaks down the tougher fibers of the meat so it becomes tender. The oil seals in moisture, while the flavoring ingredients, well, add flavor!

The steaks that need a marinade are the more inexpensive cuts, like round, skirt, blade, and hanger steaks. These steaks have a looser grain than the expensive tender cuts with tight grains. This allows the marinade to penetrate the fibers.

These steaks are also much tastier when carved against the grain. The grain looks like lines running through the steak. Cut perpendicular to these lines to cut the fibers, for a more tender bite. *Yield: 4 steaks*

Ingredients

2 tablespoons olive oil

1 tablespoon butter

1 onion, chopped

1 teaspoon sugar

1 teaspoon salt

⅛ teaspoon pepper

¼ cup red wine vinegar

¼ cup steak sauce

1½ pound hanger steak

Caramelized Onion Hanger Steak

- Cook onion in olive oil and butter until tender. Add sugar, salt, and pepper; cook over low heat, stirring frequently, until onions brown, about 30–40 minutes.

- Remove from heat; puree in food processor. Add vinegar and steak sauce; let cool.

- Add steak, cover, and marinate for 8–12 hours in refrigerator.

- Drain steak, reserving marinade. Pat steak dry; let stand for 30 minutes. Grill over direct heat for 10–12 minutes, turning twice, brushing with marinade, until desired doneness. Discard marinade.

The size of the steak matters! A steak that is 1 inch thick will cook over direct heat in 8–10 minutes to medium doneness. A thicker steak should be cooked using direct and indirect heat. Sear the steak on both sides, then move over a drip pan to finish cooking. A 1½-inch thick steak will take 12–15 minutes to cook.

Oil and Wine Marinade: Combine ⅓ cup red wine, ¼ cup olive oil, ½ teaspoon salt, 1 teaspoon dried Italian seasoning, and ⅛ teaspoon pepper. Marinate steak in refrigerator for 5–8 hours. Hearty Steak Marinade: Mix ½ cup each beer and ketchup, 2 tablespoons each soy sauce, vegetable oil, mustard, lemon juice, 1 teaspoon grill seasoning. Marinate in refrigerator for 8–12 hours.

Prepare the Marinade

Dry Steaks before Grilling

- Most marinade recipes use too much oil. A classic marinade should be about 1:1 oil to vinegar or another acid like lemon juice.

- It's possible to marinate steaks too long. Any more than 12 hours and the acid in the marinade will start to break down the fibers of the meat, making it mushy.

- A marinade only has to have oil and an acid. Any other ingredients are optional, so use your imagination and have fun.

- Just as with steaks that don't need marinating, marinated steaks must be dry when they hit the grill.

- You won't be losing flavor; the first ¼ inch of the steak has already absorbed the seasoning.

- Brush the steaks with marinade while they grill. But be sure to cook off the marinade: When you add it to the steak, cook that side before serving.

- Discard any leftover marinade; or you can boil it for 2 minutes and serve it with the steaks.

FILET MIGNON AND TENDERLOIN

The most expensive cut of beef can be improved only one way: by grilling

A filet mignon, which is a slice of beef tenderloin, is one of the most expensive and tender cuts of beef, with less fat. The fat is intramuscular, marbled inside the meat, so it melts evenly for great texture.

Filet mignon isn't the most flavorful steak, because the muscle isn't attached to the bone, which adds flavor.

A simple sauce can add a lot to the flavor and presentation of these steaks. The mild flavor of the meat pairs well with many different seasonings.

As with all steaks, let them rest, covered, for 5 minutes before you serve them. The steaks are delicious plain, or served with a sauce or just melted butter poured on top. *Yield: 4 steaks*

Ingredients

2 tablespoons butter

3 cloves garlic, minced

2 tablespoons brown sugar

1 tablespoon honey

⅓ cup balsamic vinegar

⅓ cup beef stock

1 teaspoon salt, divided

¼ teaspoon pepper, divided

4 (6-ounce) filet mignon steaks

2 tablespoons olive oil

Filet Mignon with Caramel Glaze

- Cook and stir garlic in butter for 3 minutes. Add brown sugar and honey; cook and stir until mixture combines.

- Add vinegar, stock, half of the salt, and pepper and bring to a simmer. Reduce heat to low and simmer for 10–15 minutes or until syrupy. Remove from heat.

- Let steaks stand at room temperature for 30 minutes, then pat dry. Sprinkle with remaining salt and pepper and brush with olive oil.

- Grill over direct heat for 8–11 minutes, turning twice, until desired doneness. Plate and top with sauce.

Creating Quadrillage

Finishing the Steaks

- *Quadrillage* is the French term that means "to quarter" or to divide into squares.

- It refers to the squares created by the grill grates when meats and other foods are cooked, then rotated in a certain pattern on the grill.

- Think of the steaks as being the straight hands of a clock set at 6 o'clock.

- Place the steaks on the grill so they look like clock hands pointed at 10 minutes to 4. Grill for 2½ minutes.

- Then carefully move the steaks, lifting completely off the grate with tongs, and place the steaks at 20 minutes to 2.

- Let them grill for another 2½ minutes, then turn the steaks over.

- Repeat this process on second side. If you need to turn the steaks again, be sure to carefully align the marks with the grill so they are clear.

- For more flavor, you can wrap bacon around the edges of the filet and still create the grill marks.

STEAK

FLANK AND FLAT IRON STEAKS

Flank and flat iron steaks are special cuts of marinated steak that can be used in many recipes

Flank steaks and skirt steaks didn't become popular until recently. In the 19th century, these cuts were considered throwaway meat and were usually given to ranch hands and cowboys in lieu of payment.

Flank steak is the cut used in fajitas. The cut has lots of beefy flavor, and when marinated and cut against the grain, it be-

comes quite tender.

The flat iron steak is a new cut of meat. University researchers looked at so-called "undervalued" meat cuts and discovered that if the gristle on the blade roast was removed, they could create the flat iron steak. This cut is almost as tender as the tenderloin, with more flavor. *Yield: 4 servings*

Ingredients

1½ pounds flat iron steak

¼ cup brown sugar

1 tablespoon grated ginger root

½ teaspoon dry mustard

2 cloves garlic, minced

1 teaspoon seasoned salt

¼ teaspoon pepper

2 tablespoons dark rum

2 tablespoons butter, softened

Brown Sugar Marinated Flat Iron Steak

- Cut steak into serving size pieces. In small bowl, combine all ingredients except rum, butter, and steak. Brush rum on steaks; rub with mixture.

- Place steak in large plastic bag and seal bag, place in large bowl. Refrigerate for 2–3 hours.

- Remove steak from bag and place on direct heat over medium-hot coals. Grill for 5–7 minutes per side, turning frequently, until desired doneness.

- Top steak with a tablespoon of butter, cover, and let stand for 5–6 minutes, then serve immediately.

The flat iron steak, like the Flatiron Building in New York City, may have been named because it looks like an old-fashioned cast iron "flat iron" when viewed from the top. The steak, however, which is cut from the blade roast, has to be cut away from hard gristle, which may be the true source of the name.

Tex-Mex Flank Steak: For marinade, combine ¼ cup oil, 3 tablespoons red wine vinegar, 2 minced jalapeño peppers, ¼ cup minced onion, 3 cloves minced garlic, and 2 tablespoons adobo sauce. Rub this mixture into both sides of a 1½ pound flank steak, cover, and marinate for 12–18 hours. Grill as desired; slice against the grain and serve.

Score or Pierce the Meat

Add Dry Rub

- The meat grain is determined by the type of muscle the steak is cut from.

- The rule of cutting tougher cuts of meat against the grain also applies to meats like brisket or skirt steak.

- For cuts like flank and skirt steak, you can pierce the meat with a fork to let the marinade penetrate.

- Alternatively, you can lightly score the surface of the steak, no deeper than ⅛ inch, to get the flavors further into the meat.

- A dry rub will add more flavor and helps tenderize the steak a bit.

- Brush the steak with rum, wine, or vinegar before sprinkling on the rub so it will stick. This also helps the rub melt into the meat.

- To slice against the grain, place the steak on a cutting board and use a fork to hold it in place.

- Hold the knife at a 45-degree angle to the steak and slice against the grain, for larger thin pieces.

STUFFED STEAKS

You can stuff a thin steak with everything from bacon to cheese to mushroom duxelles

A steak is such a hearty meal, it's hard to think of a way to improve upon it. Here's an idea: stuff it!

Steaks can be stuffed with everything from bread or rice stuffing to meat and cheese, or seasoned fruit and cheese.

Whatever stuffing you choose, there's one key to a successful stuffed steak: Don't overstuff it. This is not the time when "more is better." Too much stuffing will just leak out of the steak into your grill and may make a rolled stuffed steak explode or break apart.

Handle the steaks carefully and follow the recipe and you can serve elegant pinwheels and swirls to your guests. *Yield: 8 pinwheels*

Ingredients

3 tablespoons apple cider vinegar

¼ cup olive oil

I tablespoon lemon juice

I teaspoon dried basil

½ teaspoon dried oregano

¼ teaspoon onion powder

I tablespoon soy sauce

I teaspoon salt

¼ teaspoon garlic pepper

1½ pounds flank steak

6 slices crisply cooked bacon, crumbled

I ounce cream cheese, softened

I cup grated cheddar cheese

⅓ cup crumbled feta cheese

½ cup diced roasted red bell peppers

Bacon Stuffed Flank Steak Swirls

- Combine vinegar, oil, lemon juice, basil, oregano, onion powder, soy sauce, salt, and garlic pepper.

- Pound steak to ¼-inch thickness. Place in large bag with marinade. Refrigerate for 12–18 hours.

- Drain, discarding marinade.

- Combine bacon, cheeses, and bell pepper and spread on steak, roll up, and secure with 8 skewers. Cut between skewers to form swirls.

- Grill steak, turning once, over medium direct heat for 4–5 minutes per side until steak is medium rare.

Flatten the Steak and Fill

Roll and Skewer the Steak

- Start at the center of meat and pound toward the edges. Be careful to not tear or rip the meat; work slowly.

- Marinate the meat, then remove from marinade. Discard the marinade and pat the steak dry.

- Place steak on work surface with the grain running from right to left. This way you'll slice the meat against the grain.

- Spread filling evenly over steak, leaving a border of about ½ inch all the way around.

- Roll the steak up, pressing gently as you work. You may want to tie the steak until the first skewers are inserted.

- Place the skewers about 2 inches apart, starting 1 inch from each end. Be sure the skewers go straight through the meat.

- Cut evenly in between each skewer with a sharp serrated knife, making sure to leave the same amount of beef on each side of each skewer.

- When grilling, you may need to slide a spatula under each swirl to loosen before turning.

MORE STUFFED STEAKS

Butterflying steak makes lots of surface area to fill with stuffing

Stuffed and rolled steaks can be cooked whole. For this recipe, they are butterflied, or cut in half to make them thinner, then filled, rolled, tied with string, and grilled. After they rest for a few minutes, they are cut into pinwheels.

When you butterfly a steak, you have to use a very sharp knife. Use a steel to sharpen the knife just before you use it. You may be able to ask your butcher to butterfly the steak for you. If not, work slowly and stop to check that you are cutting

the meat in half evenly.

Again, make sure that you don't overfill the steak. It should be easy to roll up and handle. Be sure you cut the string off before you slice and present this gorgeous steak. Think about creating new types of stuffing, and enjoy! *Yield: 6 steaks*

Ingredients

1½ pounds flank steak

¼ cup red wine vinegar

¼ cup olive oil

1 teaspoon grill seasoning

⅛ teaspoon pepper

3 slices bacon

2 tablespoons butter

3 cups chopped mushrooms

½ cup chopped onion

3 cloves garlic, minced

½ teaspoon salt

1 teaspoon dried marjoram leaves

½ cup grated Parmesan cheese

1½ cups fresh spinach leaves

Mushroom Spinach Stuffed Flank Steak

- Butterfly steak; place in large plastic bag. Add vinegar, ¼ cup olive oil, seasoning, and pepper. Seal bag, and chill for 12–18 hours.

- Cook bacon until crisp; crumble. Add butter, mushrooms, onion, and garlic to pan; cook until mushrooms turn dark and water evaporates. Cool for 20 minutes.

- Stir in salt, marjoram, and cheese. Open up steak and top with spinach, then mushroom mixture. Roll up; tie with twine.

- Sear over direct heat, then cook over indirect heat until done, 20–30 minutes.

106

~ VARIATIONS ~

Vegetable Stuffed Flank Steak

Prepare steak as directed and marinate. Cook 1 onion, 2 diced carrots, 2 cups mushrooms, and 4 cloves garlic until tender. Stir in 1 cup soft breadcrumbs and 1 cup shredded Grùyere cheese. Use this mixture to stuff the steak; roll and grill as directed.

Herb Stuffed Flank Steak

Combine ½ cup minced parsley, ¼ cup minced fresh basil leaves, and ¼ cup minced fresh cilantro with 1 cup grated provolone cheese, ⅓ cup grated Parmesan cheese, and 3 chopped green onions. Prepare steak as directed, marinate, then stuff, roll, and grill.

Butterfly the Steak

- To butterfly the steak, place it with the short end facing you. Working slowly and evenly, cut the steak in half, leaving ½ inch uncut at the end.

- When you spread the steak to add the filling, be sure that the meat grain runs from left to right.

- Roll up so the grain runs along the roll, not around it.

- As with all flank steaks, this means you'll cut it against the grain when the roll is finished, for tender results.

Stuff and Roll

- Only use 100 percent cotton kitchen string to tie meats and other foods cooked on the grill.

- Twine and other types of string may melt in the heat of the grill. That will ruin your recipe.

- Your meat thermometer is your friend in this recipe. Be sure that it doesn't extend into the stuffing though, or you'll get an incorrect reading.

- The final temperature should be 140°F. Let the meat stand, covered, for 5 minutes before slicing into rounds.

ETHNIC STEAKS

Flavors from around the world add zing and interest to grilled steaks

There are a few countries in the world where beef is revered. The United States is one, but in Argentina and Japan, you'll find the best steaks in the world. In Japan, the cattle that become Kobe beef are massaged by hand.

In Argentina, beef cattle are free-range and graze on natural grasses. If you've ever had grass-fed beef, you understand the difference. The meat is rich and tender, with a full beefy flavor that's almost impossible to describe.

But you can approximate this steak by buying local grass-fed and organic beef from farms near you and adding a few extras. The flavors from the cuisines of other countries add a special touch to traditional steak cuts. Steak can be seasoned with the spices and herbs from any cuisine in the world. *Yield: 4 steaks*

Ingredients

6 tablespoons butter, divided

1 onion, finely chopped

3 cloves garlic, minced

¼ cup chopped oil-packed sun-dried tomatoes

2 teaspoons fresh oregano leaves

¼ cup sliced Greek black olives

¼ cup sliced kalamata olives

1 tablespoon lemon juice

4 8-ounce rib eye steaks

1 tablespoon olive oil

½ teaspoon salt

⅛ teaspoon pepper

½ cup crumbled feta cheese

Grilled Greek and Olive Steak

- In small saucepan, melt 2 tablespoons butter. Cook onion and garlic until tender, about 6 minutes.

- Remove from heat and stir in tomatoes, oregano, olives, and lemon juice; set aside to cool.

- Pat steaks dry. Brush all sides with olive oil and sprinkle with salt and pepper.

- Grill steaks over direct heat for 4–6 minutes on each side until medium rare. Remove from grill, top each with 1 tablespoon butter and feta, and let rest for 5 minutes. Serve with olive sauce.

Argentine Skirt Steak
Choose the best flat iron steaks you can find. Pat dry, brush with olive oil, and sprinkle with salt and pepper. Grill as desired, and top each steak with 2 tablespoons butter. Remove from grill, cover, and let stand for 5 minutes. Serve with Chimichurri Sauce.

Chimichurri Sauce
In blender, combine 1 cup parsley, ⅓ cup chopped cilantro, 3 cloves minced garlic, ½ cup extra virgin olive oil, 3 tablespoons white balsamic vinegar, 1 tablespoon fresh oregano, ½ teaspoon salt, and ¼ teaspoon crushed red pepper flakes. Blend until combined, then refrigerate until steak is ready.

Trim Fat from Steak

- There has to be some fat on your steak because it carries the meat flavor. But if there is more than ¼ inch on the steak, trim off the excess.

- Use a sharp knife for trimming and be careful not to cut into the meat itself.

- Meat that has lots of thin veins of white fat running through it is the best choice for the grill.

- This intramuscular fat melts when heated, keeping the steak moist and adding lots of flavor.

Make the Olive Sauce

- Onion and garlic should be cooked until translucent. This reduces the harsh sulfur compounds in the vegetables and brings out the sweetness.

- Sun-dried tomatoes packed in oil have more flavor than dried tomatoes. Drain them, then chop into small pieces.

- There are many types of olives available. Kalamata olives are from Greece. These dark brown olives have lots of flavor.

- Don't use inexpensive olives in this recipe. Look for olives from Greece or Spain, often found in international aisles at food stores.

HAM STEAKS

Ham steaks are quickly grilled and can be combined with different ingredients

Grilling a ham steak is a great way to get ham flavor without the hassle of heating a whole or half ham.

Ham steaks can be purchased boneless or bone-in. They are literally slices of ham, cut about 1 inch thick. Try to find a ham steak that is more than 1 inch thick. Thinner steaks will dry out quickly on the grill.

The ham is fully cooked, so only needs to be heated on the grill. Because the ham is so simple, you can have fun with glazes, sauces, and accompaniments.

This mild, salty meat really takes well to sweet sauces, barbecue sauce, and spicy glazes. *Yield: 6 servings*

Ingredients

1 (18-ounce) can apricot halves, drained, juice reserved

2 tablespoons vegetable oil

¼ cup apricot preserves

1 tablespoon lemon juice

½ teaspoon salt

⅛ teaspoon pepper

2 tablespoons Dijon mustard

1 (2-pound) ham steak, 1½ inches thick

Ham Steak with Grilled Apricots

- Drain apricots, reserving juice. In large casserole dish, combine oil, preserves, lemon juice, ⅓ cup reserved juice, salt, pepper, and mustard and mix well.

- Add steak; turn to coat, then cover and marinate for 1–2 hours.

- Remove steak from marinade. Slash edges of the fat. Place over direct heat and grill, brushing with marinade, for 7–10 minutes per side.

- Add apricots to grill for the last 5 minutes, turning, until warmed through. Serve with steak.

Tangy BBQ Ham Steak

In small bowl, combine ¼ cup barbecue sauce, ¼ cup ketchup, 2 tablespoons yellow mustard, 1 tablespoon honey, and ⅛ teaspoon pepper. Brush over both sides of ham steak, and refrigerate for 1–2 hours. Grill the ham steak for 8–9 minutes on each side, basting occasionally with marinade, until hot.

Pineapple Ham Steak

In large casserole dish, combine ½ cup pineapple juice with ¼ cup honey, 2 tablespoons chili sauce, ¼ cup finely minced onion, 2 tablespoons Dijon mustard, and ⅛ teaspoon pepper. Marinate ham steak for 30 minutes at room temperature, and grill as desired.

Marinate Ham Steak

Grill Ham and Fruit

- So the steak won't curl on the heat of the grill, make vertical slashes on the fat on the outer edges of the meat.

- Even smoked hams will improve in flavor and juiciness when marinated.

- Don't marinate them longer than 1–2 hours, because the meat is already cured.

- Because the meat is fully cooked, you don't need to worry about leftover marinade; just serve it on the side.

- Canned apricots are much easier to use than fresh, and they cook in about the same amount of time.

- This tender and delicate fruit is really just warmed on the grill. Nice grill marks add a caramelized flavor and look pretty, too.

- You might want to place the fruit in a grill basket, or use a grill mat so it doesn't stick to the grill and burn.

- Brush the fruit with any remaining marinade as it grills, too, for great flavor.

111

MORE STEAKS AND ROASTS

PORK ROAST

Tender and juicy pork roasts, cooked using indirect heat, are a wonderful entree

Grill roasting is just like grilling over indirect heat, but for a longer period of time. This is an easy way to make a flavorful roast without heating up your indoor kitchen.

With a gas grill, just keep an eye on the roast. But with a charcoal grill, you have to add more briquettes or lump charcoal after an hour. Get them up to grilling temperature in a chimney starter, then add about 10–15 briquettes every hour. It's important to keep the lid closed as much as possible when you're grill roasting.

A center cut pork loin roast is the best choice for grill roasting. This cut has a thin layer of fat and is very tender and juicy. Enjoy the tender, smoky results of your grill roast! *Yield: 8 servings*

Ingredients

2 cups wood chips

1 cup water

3-pound boneless pork loin roast

5 cloves garlic, slivered

3 sprigs fresh rosemary, cut into
    1-inch pieces

⅓ cup Dijon mustard

⅓ cup honey

¼ cup apple cider vinegar

2 tablespoons olive oil

1 teaspoon salt

⅛ teaspoon pepper

Tuscan Pork Roast

- Soak wood chips in water. Meanwhile, make ½-inch-deep holes about 1½ inches apart over top of roast.

- Insert garlic slivers and rosemary sprigs into the holes in the meat.

- Combine remaining ingredients. Rub over roast.

- Cover meat and leftover marinade and refrigerate for 12–18 hours.

- Brown roast over direct heat, about 5 minutes; place over drip pan filled with drained wood chips and cover. Roast for 25–30 minutes per pound, brushing with leftover marinade.

Mediterranean Pork Roast

Insert thyme leaves instead of rosemary, and garlic slivers into roast. Combine ¼ cup olive oil, ⅓ cup lemon juice, 1 teaspoon salt, 2 tablespoons honey, 1 teaspoon dried thyme leaves, and ⅛ teaspoon pepper in small bowl. Rub over roast, refrigerate for 12–18 hours, and grill roast.

Herbed Pork Roast

Mash 4 cloves of garlic with 1 teaspoon salt until a paste forms. Stir in 2 tablespoons olive oil, ⅓ cup fresh chopped parsley, 1 tablespoon fresh oregano, and ⅛ teaspoon pepper. Rub this mixture over roast; refrigerate for 12–18 hours. Grill roast as directed.

Prepare Roast

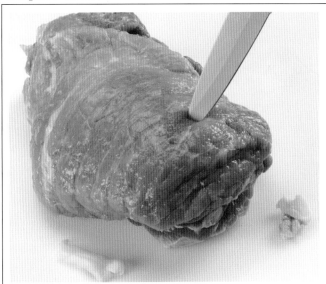

- Use a sharp knife to poke the holes for the herbs and garlic, and make an even pattern.

- It's easiest if you prepare the herbs and garlic first, then slide them in right by the knife as you make the hole.

- Be sure that you cut the garlic into very thin slivers so it melts into the meat as it grills.

- Tell your guests not to eat the rosemary; it's just there for the aroma and flavor.

Insert Herbs and Garlic

- Remember, today's pork only has to be cooked to 155°F, which is slightly pink in the middle.

- First brown the roast over direct heat, then move it right over the drip pan. You can put cider, wine, or beer in the drip pan, or more herbs.

- Cover the grill and cook. Check for doneness at the shortest cooking time.

- Let the roast stand for 10 minutes, covered, after it comes off the grill, then slice and serve.

POT ROAST

Yes, you can cook a pot roast on the grill, with some patience and a few tricks

There's nothing as comforting and savory as a long-cooked pot roast. The meat literally falls apart and the flavor and texture evoke memories of Grandmother.

But did you know that you can grill a pot roast? This method is fun and easy as long as you follow a few rules.

The meat can be cooked on the grill in a Dutch oven, in a rib rack, or directly on the grill. It does need moisture for ideal tenderness, so add liquid to the drip pan. Beer, wine, or water are all delicious.

Take advantage of the grill and cook vegetables with your roast, just like you do in the oven. Tender grilled carrots, onions, and potatoes are delicious too. *Yield: 8 servings*

Ingredients

1 teaspoon salt

1 teaspoon grill seasoning

1 teaspoon cracked black peppercorns

1 teaspoon cracked green peppercorns

1 teaspoon cracked white peppercorns

3 tablespoons olive oil

2 pound beef tri-tip roast

2 cups beer

Grilled Pepper Roast

- For rub, combine all ingredients except oil, meat, and beer in small bowl.

- Brush meat with oil and sprinkle with rub; gently rub into the meat. Let stand for 15 minutes.

- Prepare grill for indirect low heat, placing 2 cups beer in the drip pan. Sear roast on all sides over direct heat, then place over drip pan.

- Insert a heat-resistant meat thermometer and cover grill. Grill for 50–60 minutes or until meat reaches 155°F. Let meat stand, covered, for 10 minutes before slicing to serve.

The type and size of roast will determine how long it cooks. Tenderloin, tri-tip, and standing rib are classic roasts for grilling and can be done directly on the grill, cooked for about 20 minutes per pound. Rump roast and round roasts do better if cooked in a Dutch oven over indirect heat; they cook for 45–55 minutes per pound.

• • • • RECIPE VARIATION • • • •

Grandma's Grilled Pot Roast: Marinate 4-pound rump roast in red wine vinaigrette overnight. Dry meat and sprinkle with salt and pepper. Sear on grill, and place in Dutch oven with 2 cups red wine. Add carrots, onions, and potatoes. Place oven over indirect medium heat, cover, and grill for 2–3 hours until roast is tender. Turning every hour and add more charcoal.

Sear Roast

- A tri-tip roast got its name because it is cut in a triangular shape. It's also called triangular steak.

- It's a piece cut from the bottom sirloin and is fairly new in supermarkets because there are only two per cow.

- This cut is tender enough that it doesn't have to be marinated before grilling. You can marinate it if you'd like.

- Dry rubs can be made of any spice combination. Make them fairly heavy on salt and pepper.

Grill-roast the Meat

- The beer or other liquid in the drip pan will simmer and start to evaporate as the roast cooks.

- Insert a heat-resistant thermometer into the meat before grilling. Cook the roast to 155°F.

- Add vegetables to your roast by placing baby carrots, chopped onions, and cubed potatoes on heavy duty foil.

- Sprinkle vegetables with olive oil, salt, and pepper and wrap. Grill for 40–50 minutes until done, turning packets twice.

LEG OF LAMB

A boneless leg of lamb takes on extraordinary flavor when grilled

Leg of lamb isn't just for Easter anymore. When marinated and grilled, it is flavorful, tender, and juicy. When prepared with everything from garlic to mint to mustard, it is a great choice for grilling.

A boneless leg of lamb is easiest to grill. You can usually find them prepared at the supermarket. The leg should be butterflied so you can add a paste or rub over the largest area. You can grill the lamb as is, or roll and tie it for longer cooking.

Ask the butcher to butterfly the lamb for you if it isn't already done. When not rolled, the lamb will cook 10–12 minutes per side. If it's rolled and tied, it will cook for about 20 minutes per pound. *Yield: 6 servings*

Ingredients

½ cup yogurt

½ cup Dijon mustard

2 tablespoons horseradish

¼ cup olive oil

2 teaspoons mustard seed

3 tablespoons honey

2 tablespoons minced fresh rosemary

1 teaspoon salt

¼ teaspoon pepper

1 (3-pound) butterflied boneless leg of lamb

Grilled Rosemary-Mustard Leg of Lamb

- In small bowl, combine yogurt, mustard, horseradish, oil, mustard seed, honey, rosemary, salt, and pepper; mix well.

- Place lamb in glass baking dish; spread yogurt mixture on both sides. Cover and refrigerate for 8–12 hours.

- When ready to cook, prepare grill. Remove lamb from marinade; discard marinade.

- Cook lamb on direct medium-high heat for 13–18 minutes per side, turning once. Grill until meat thermometer registers 145°F for medium rare, 155°F for medium.

Asian Rolled Leg of Lamb

Blend ¼ cup low-sodium soy sauce, ¼ cup hoisin sauce, 3 tablespoons white wine vinegar, 1 teaspoon toasted sesame oil, 2 tablespoons brown sugar, ¼ cup minced onion, 4 cloves minced garlic, ⅛ teaspoon pepper, and ½ cup chopped parsley in blender. Spread all over butter-flied leg of lamb; cover and refrigerate for 12–18 hours. Roll lamb skin side out and tie with 100 percent cotton kitchen string. Place 5 star anise pods and 1 cup soaked wood chips in drip pan. Sear lamb over direct heat, and grill over indirect medium heat for 65–75 minutes until meat thermometer registers 155°F.

Marinate Lamb

- Any well-seasoned marinade will work beautifully with this cut of meat.

- You can marinate the lamb for 30 minutes at room temperature or up to 12 hours in the refrigerator.

- Remember that ingredients like mint, garlic, citrus juices, and mustard help accent and complement the flavor of the lamb.

- One side of the lamb will have a layer of fat and perhaps skin. Start grilling with this side against the cooking surface.

Grill Marinated Lamb

- The butterflied leg of lamb is a fairly large piece of meat and can be difficult to handle.

- Be sure that the charcoal area is larger than the lamb by 2 inches all the way around.

- Flare-ups are going to be an issue with this cut. Keep an area clear of coals so you can move the lamb as needed to control them.

- Use tongs or two–three skewers inserted into the center to make handling the lamb easier.

MORE STEAKS AND ROASTS

SEAFOOD STEAKS

From salmon to halibut to swordfish, seafood steaks are delicious

Seafood steaks are a great choice for dinner, and they are easy to grill. Did you know that you are supposed to eat at least 2 servings of fatty fish each week for good health? Tuna, swordfish, and salmon steaks cooked on the grill are delicious ways to fulfill this requirement.

Salmon steaks don't need much help on the grill. Tuna steaks work well with more assertive flavors, and swordfish and halibut steaks have the meatiest taste. Mahi mahi steaks

are tender and delicate.

The most important thing to remember with seafood steaks is that they are very tender. Think about grilling these meats on a bed of onions, herbs, or other vegetables to add a protective layer between the meat and the heat. *Yield: 4 steaks*

Ingredients

3 tablespoons olive oil

¼ cup orange juice

2 tablespoons honey

1 teaspoon fresh tarragon leaves, minced

1 teaspoon salt

⅛ teaspoon pepper

4 tuna steaks

2 leeks

6 whole tarragon sprigs

Leek Scented Tuna Steaks

- In small bowl, combine olive oil, orange juice, honey, tarragon, salt, and pepper.

- Place tuna in large resealable plastic bag and pour marinade over. Seal bag and chill for 1–2 hours.

- Slice leeks lengthwise and rinse well to remove grit.

- Place on grill over direct medium heat. Turn leeks after 5 minutes, and top with tarragon sprigs. Remove tuna from marinade and pat dry.

- Place tuna on leeks, cover grill, and cook for 11–14 minutes or until tuna flakes with fork.

• • • • RECIPE VARIATION • • • •

Honey Mustard Salmon Steaks: Combine ¼ cup Dijon mustard, 2 tablespoons honey, 2 tablespoons lemon juice, ½ teaspoon salt, 1 teaspoon mustard seeds, and ⅛ teaspoon pepper in small bowl. Brush on both sides of salmon steaks and let stand for 20 minutes. Grill over direct medium heat for 5–8 minutes per side.

Marinate Tuna

- As with most seafood, tuna should not be marinated for a long time.

- The maximum is 3 hours in the refrigerator, or the acid in the marinade will make the fish mushy.

- You can reserve the marinade and spoon it over the steaks as they begin cooking, but make sure the steaks cook for at least 7 minutes after brushing with marinade.

- If you top the tuna with marinade, turn it once while it's grilling so the marinade cooks off and is safe.

Place Tuna Steak on Vegetables

- Leeks, onions, and even onion husks all make great beds to grill tender meats like seafood.

- The bed of leeks and tarragon will start to char and smoke, and that's what gives the seafood such great flavor.

- You can serve tuna or salmon when it's slightly rare in the center. But be sure to cook the fish to 145°F.

- The leeks will be tough and dry after grilling this way, so don't try to eat them. Also discard remaining marinade.

STEAK SALAD
Thin slices of juicy steak are combined with flavorful ingredients in these main dish salads

Whether you use a freshly grilled steak or want to make use of leftovers, a steak is the perfect addition to a main dish salad. Hot steak right off the grill is a marvelous contrast to cold salad ingredients, while a cold steak blends with the lettuce and vegetables.

The leftover steak should be sliced against the grain for the most tender texture. You can reheat it before slicing for a minute or two on each side over direct medium heat if you'd like.

You can make your own salad dressings or use your favorite bottled variety. It's also fun to dress up purchased dressings with more herbs and spices, minced onion and garlic, or cheese. *Yield: 6 servings*

Ingredients

3 tomatoes, chopped

2 orange bell peppers, chopped

3 cups red leaf lettuce, torn

3 cups romaine lettuce, torn

2 potatoes

3 tablespoons olive oil, divided

Salt and pepper to taste

2 rib eye steaks

Dressing:

⅓ cup olive oil

3 tablespoons Dijon mustard

¼ cup red wine vinegar

2 tablespoons lemon juice

¼ cup minced red onion

Salt and pepper to taste

Steak and Vegetable Salad

- In large bowl, combine dressing ingredients. Mix. Add tomatoes, peppers, and lettuce.

- Cut potatoes into ½-inch-thick slices; toss with 1 tablespoon olive oil; sprinkle with salt and pepper.

- Place potatoes on grill on medium-high direct heat for 8 minutes. Rub steak with 2 tablespoons olive oil and sprinkle with salt, pepper.

- Place steak on grill; turn potatoes. Grill steak until desired doneness. Remove food from grill. Chop potatoes, let stand for 5 minutes, slice, and add to salad; toss.

~ VARIATIONS ~

Steak House Salad

In large bowl, combine ¼ cup each steak sauce, olive oil, lemon juice, and mayonnaise, adding 1 teaspoon dried thyme leaves, 1 teaspoon sugar, and salt and pepper to taste. Add 2 cups sliced leftover steak with 4 cups romaine lettuce, 1 cup sliced mushrooms, ½ cup crumbled blue cheese, and ½ cup toasted walnut pieces; toss.

Tex-Mex Steak Salad

In large bowl, combine ½ cup each salsa, mayonnaise, yogurt, and ¼ cup Cotija cheese. Add 3 cups sliced leftover steak, 1 can drained baby corn, 2 chopped red bell peppers, 1 minced jalapeño pepper, 2 cups corn, and 2 cups baby spinach. Garnish with crushed blue corn tortilla chips.

Grill Steak and Potatoes

- The potatoes take a longer time to grill than the steak does, so add them to the grill first.

- For more flavor, you could brush the potatoes with some of the salad dressing before grilling.

- Cook the steaks for 7–9 minutes for medium rare to medium doneness, turning once. Cover and let stand to let the juices redistribute.

- For faster preparation, grill canned potatoes until brown, and use leftover grilled steak. Prepare the dressing and vegetables ahead of time.

Toss Salad

- Keep the vegetables and dressing in the refrigerator while you're grilling the potatoes and steak.

- The temperature contrast between hot steak and potatoes and cold vegetables and dressing is delicious; serve this salad as soon as you can.

- Substitute other vegetables for the tomatoes and bell peppers. Good choices include mushrooms, sliced zucchini, or cherry tomatoes.

- If using leftover steak, just grill the potatoes and add to the salad, or you can use canned potatoes, drained and sliced.

FAJITAS AND QUESADILLAS

Freshly grilled or leftover steak is delicious in these quick and easy Tex-Mex recipes

If you have some cooked leftover steak, some vegetables, cheese, and tortillas, you have a meal! Slice the steak thinly against the grain for best texture and flavor.

Fajitas and quesadillas are Tex-Mex creations that combine meats, vegetables, and cheese with tortillas. Quesadillas are grilled or pan-fried until the tortillas are crisp, while for fajitas

you just fold the food into a softened tortilla.

These sandwiches can be served as a meal or as appetizers. Look for small tortillas to make mini fajitas, or, cut the crisp quesadillas into wedges or quarters for finger food.

Serve these easy sandwiches with salsa, guacamole, sour cream. *Yield: 6 servings*

Ingredients

2 tomatoes, chopped

1 red onion, chopped

2 cloves garlic, minced

1 jalapeño pepper, minced

¼ cup minced cilantro

2 tablespoons lemon juice

1 avocado, peeled and cubed

Salt and pepper to taste

8 (10-inch) flour tortillas

3 cups sliced Caramelized Onion
    Hanger Steak (see page 98)

1 cup shredded cheddar cheese

2 avocados, peeled and sliced

1 cup shredded Pepper Jack cheese

⅔ cup sour cream

Avocado Steak Quesadillas

- Combine tomatoes, onion, garlic, jalapeño, cilantro, lemon juice, cubed avocado, salt, and pepper.

- Wrap tortillas in foil and grill, turning once, for 3–4 minutes to soften.

- Place 1 tortilla on work surface. Add some of the

steak, cheddar cheese, sliced avocado, and Pepper Jack cheese. Top with second tortilla and press down gently.

- Repeat with remaining food. Grill over medium direct heat, turning once, until tortillas are crisp and cheese is melted. Serve with sour cream and tomato mixture.

~ VARIATIONS ~

Chili Beef Fajitas

Combine ¼ cup olive oil, ¼ cup soy sauce, 3 tablespoons lemon juice, 2 tablespoons vinegar, 2 teaspoons Worcestershire sauce, 1 tablespoon chili powder, 2 cloves garlic, and 2 tablespoons Dijon mustard. Marinate 1 pound flank steak and chopped red and green bell peppers. Discard marinade, then grill steak and vegetables, and wrap in softened tortillas with sour cream, avocados, shredded cheddar cheese, and salsa.

Beef and Bean Quesadillas

Slice 1 pound cooked steak and combine with 1 (15-ounce) can refried beans, 1 chopped red onion, 2 cloves garlic, 1 cup cooked black beans, and 1 chopped red bell pepper. Spread on 6 flour tortillas, and top with 2 cups shredded cheddar cheese and 6 tortillas. Grill until tortillas are crisp and cheese melts.

Prepare Salsa

Assemble Quesadillas

- Salsas are easy to make. Just combine chopped vegetables, including tomatoes, hot peppers, bell peppers, onion, and garlic.

- An acidic ingredient like lemon or lime juice, and seasonings like salt, pepper, chili powder, and Tabasco add flavor.

- Chop the vegetables so they are all about the same size so it's easy to scoop up the salsa.

- You can substitute purchased salsa for homemade to save some time. Dress it up by adding some chopped green onions or cilantro.

- Arrange the food evenly on the tortilla, leaving a space of about ½ inch on the edges so the food doesn't fall out on the grill.

- Use a large spatula to flip the quesadillas for best control.

- When the quesadillas have nice grill marks and the tortillas are crisp, they are done. Remove to a wire rack to let cool for a few minutes.

- Then place the quesadillas on a flat surface and cut into quarters or wedges to serve.

STEAK SANDWICHES
Everything from cheese to spinach to sun-dried tomatoes

Everyone loves a juicy steak sandwich, topped with flavorful ingredients and encased in nice sturdy bread. Grill the ingredients and serve in anything from a pita to tortillas, or pile ingredients in a bun or roll and grill until the bread is crispy.

Any steak sandwich should be made with thinly sliced steak, sliced against the grain. Think about complementary flavors and cuisines to create your sandwich.

An Italian sandwich would use peppers, onions, garlic, oil, tomatoes, and mozzarella cheese, while a Tex-Mex sandwich could be made with hot peppers, corn, black beans, and steak in salsa all wrapped up in a corn tortilla. And a California sandwich would include sun-dried tomatoes, fresh spinach, and avocado. *Yield: 4 sandwiches*

Ingredients

¼ cup honey mustard

1 tablespoon horseradish

⅓ cup sour cream

½ teaspoon dried oregano leaves

½ teaspoon dried basil leaves

⅛ teaspoon pepper

4 hoagie buns, sliced

¼ cup butter, softened

2 leftover grilled rib eye steaks

1 (7-ounce) jar roasted red peppers

2 cups shredded provolone cheese

2 cups baby spinach or arugula leaves

Italian Steak Sandwiches

- Combine mustard, horseradish, sour cream, oregano, basil, and pepper.

- Spread cut sides of hoagie buns with butter; grill until golden brown. Place on work surface.

- Slice the steak against the grain. Drain peppers on paper towel; cut into thin strips. Spread buns with mustard mixture; layer on steak, cheese, peppers, spinach.

- Top with hoagie bun tops. Wrap in foil. Grill sandwiches over medium direct heat, turning several times and pressing with spatula, for 9–12 minutes.

~ VARIATIONS ~

Philly Cheese Steak Sandwich

Slice 2 Grilled Rib Eye Steaks (see page 96) very thinly. Toss with 1 tablespoon olive oil and red wine vinegar; add ½ teaspoon each dried thyme, basil, onion powder, salt, and pepper. Grill 2 sliced green bell peppers and 1 onion. Butter 4 split hoagie rolls and top with steak, vegetables, and 2 cups Swiss. Grill open-faced until cheese melts, then put together.

Saucy Steak Sandwiches

Thinly slice 2 Grilled Rib Eye Steaks. Cook 1 chopped onion and 4 cloves minced garlic in 2 tablespoons olive oil. Add 2 cups pasta sauce; simmer. Split 1 baguette; remove some bread; brush with ¼ cup olive oil. Grill, cut sides down; add steak to sauce and simmer. Top baguette with steak, sauce, and 2 cups shredded mozzarella cheese. Grill until cheese melts; cut into serving pieces.

Layer Sandwich Ingredients

- Watch the buns carefully when you're toasting them on the grill before adding the sandwich ingredients. They can burn quickly.

- You may want to remove some of the bread from the insides of the buns to make more room for the filling.

- Don't overfill the sandwiches. They will be pressed down, but too much filling will make the sandwiches fall apart.

- These sandwiches can be grilled, one at a time, on a dual contact indoor grill with a floating hinge.

Wrap and Grill Sandwiches

- Use heavy duty foil, or 2 layers of regular foil to wrap the sandwiches.

- Wrap tightly to hold the sandwiches together on the grill. Secure the edges with a double fold so the juices don't leak.

- Pressing with a spatula is a good idea. This compresses the bun and forces juices into the bread.

- You can also place a clean brick, wrapped in foil, on top of each of the sandwiches; turn the sandwich once during grilling.

STEAK AND SALAD

A hot, juicy steak topped with cold, crunchy salad is a marvelous combination of flavors and textures

No, this isn't steak salad; it's steak topped with a salad. The contrast between a hot juicy steak and cold crisp salad, whether sweet or savory, is really delicious.

It's best to have the salad made ahead of time. Keep it in the refrigerator until it's time to eat so the ingredients are as cold as possible. While the steak is resting after being grilled, bring out the salad and get everyone ready to eat.

You can use your favorite salad and just plop it on top of a nice grilled steak, or use the fruits or vegetables that look best in the market. The salads don't have to be savory; fresh berries with baby spinach would be delicious. *Yield: 4 servings*

Ingredients

¼ cup extra virgin olive oil

3 tablespoons lemon juice

2 tablespoons Dijon mustard

½ teaspoon dried thyme leaves

½ teaspoon salt

⅛ teaspoon pepper

¼ teaspoon sugar

I cup sliced mushrooms

I cup grape tomatoes

I cup red leaf lettuce, torn

I cup green leaf lettuce, torn

4 skirt steaks

2 tablespoons olive oil

I teaspoon grill seasoning

Steak and Veggie Salad

- In medium bowl, combine oil, lemon juice, mustard, thyme, salt, pepper, and sugar and whisk until blended.

- Toss mushrooms, tomatoes, and lettuces with the dressing mixture and refrigerate.

- Rub steaks with oil and sprinkle with grill seasoning. Grill over direct medium-high heat, turning twice, until desired doneness, about 10 minutes for medium rare.

- Let steak stand for 5 minutes, covered, then place on serving plates. Top with salad mixture and serve immediately.

~ VARIATIONS ~

Steak with Pepper Salad

Slice 1 red bell pepper, 1 orange bell pepper, and 1 yellow bell pepper and finely chop 1 red onion; toss with zesty Italian salad dressing; refrigerate. Grill rib eye or T-bone steaks; let stand for 5 minutes, then top with the bell pepper salad. The bell peppers could be grilled and chilled first if desired.

Steak with Berry Salad

Combine ½ cup blueberries, ½ cup raspberries, and ½ cup chopped strawberries with 1 cup baby spinach leaves and ⅓ cup raspberry vinaigrette; chill in refrigerator. Top hot grilled filet mignon with this mixture and serve immediately. This mixture can top grilled salmon steaks.

Prepare Salad Ingredients

- Use your favorite salad dressing in this easy recipe instead of making one, or use a different herb.

- You could vary the salad by using all tomatoes or all mushrooms, or try different varieties of salad greens.

- Salad greens should be torn to bite size so they are easier to eat and sit nicely on top of the steak.

- Don't make a salad with fresh mushrooms more than ½ hour ahead of time; the mushrooms will darken as they stand.

Assemble Salad

- Use the tongs to grasp a portion of the salad, then place on top of the steak.

- Twist the tongs slightly as you release to help the salad stay in place on the steak.

- You can serve the salad on the whole steak, or thinly slice the steak against the grain and fan it on the plates, then top with salad.

- You could drizzle the salad dressing in the bottom of the bowl or over the steak and salad.

127

STEAK GRILL-FRY

Yes, you can stir-fry on the grill! These quick and easy recipes are one-dish meals

Stir-frying on the grill is just as fast as stir-frying on your stovetop. You must have everything ready to cook before you start, and keep the food moving.

There's something different about grill-frying, though. You have two choices; you can grill on a closed wok, or on a wok that is pierced with holes.

The closed wok will give you the same results as indoor cooking, while using the pierced wok means the finished dish won't have a sauce, but will have smoky grill flavor.

Be sure to use a heat-resistant spatula when you're stir-frying the food on the grill. And don't be afraid to move the food around so it cooks evenly. *Yield: 4 servings*

Ingredients

¼ cup soy sauce

2 tablespoons hoisin sauce

1 clove garlic, minced

1 tablespoon grated fresh ginger root

2 tablespoons rice wine vinegar

2 tablespoons oil

⅛ teaspoon pepper

1 pound boneless sirloin steak

1 green bell pepper, sliced

2 cups snow peas

1 onion, sliced

Asian Steak Grill-Fry

- Combine soy sauce, hoisin sauce, garlic, ginger root, vinegar, oil, and pepper.

- Cut steak into ½-inch-thick and 4-inch-long strips. Add to marinade and chill for 8–12 hours. Add remaining ingredients to steak and marinade. Let stand for 20 minutes.

- Drain steak mixture, discarding marinade. Spray pierced grill wok with nonstick grilling spray; place over direct high heat for 5 minutes.

- Add steak and vegetables; grill, stirring constantly, until steak is done and vegetables are crisp-tender. Serve immediately.

~ VARIATIONS ~

Spicy Steak Stir-Fry

Combine 2 tablespoons cornstarch, ¼ cup soy sauce, ½ cup beef broth, 2 minced jalapeño peppers, 1 finely minced onion, ⅓ cup chili sauce, 1 tablespoon lime juice, and ¼ teaspoon cayenne pepper. Marinate 1 pound sirloin steak for 12–18 hours in fridge. Heat a non-pierced grill wok over medium-high heat. Drain steak, reserving marinade. Heat 2 tablespoons peanut oil in wok; grill-fry steak; remove and grill-fry 2 sliced bell peppers, 2 cups mushrooms, and 2 sliced poblano peppers. Return steak and marinade to wok; grill-fry until mixture thickens.

Preheat Wok

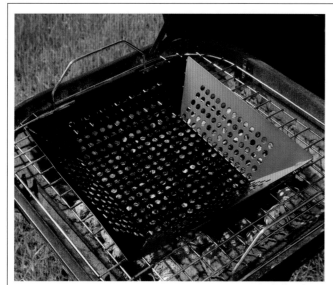

- Nonstick cooking spray is the best choice for a pierced grill wok. There are cooking sprays made just for the grill that you could use.

- Preheat the wok according to the manufacturer's directions.

- Test by dropping a bit of water on the grill; if it sizzles the wok is ready. It must be very hot before you add the food.

- A lot of steam will rise as the food hits the grill; be sure to protect your arms and face.

Grill-fry Steak and Veggies

- Slice the steak against the grain for the most tender results. Don't marinate the steak longer than 18 hours.

- Because you're working on a pierced grill wok with no sauce, the food needs to be very well seasoned.

- You can boil the marinade in a small pot for 2 minutes, and then pour it over the grill-fried food just before serving.

- Serve this recipe over rice that has been cooked in beef broth and seasoned with soy sauce and pepper.

ETHNIC STEAK RECIPES

Flavors from Greece to Hawaii flavor these delicious and easy steaks

A tender, juicy, well-grilled steak is perfect on its own, but it's fun to add flavors and foods from other cultures.

Tex-Mex recipes use chiles, limes, garlic, onion, and tomatoes, while Asian steak recipes feature soy sauce, hoisin sauce, lemongrass, and sesame oil.

Take foods and flavors from your favorite ethnic cuisines and use them to make marinades for steak, or slice up some leftover steak and toss it with a pasta mixture flavored with those ingredients.

This pasta dish is a variation of pastitsio, a classic Greek baked casserole typically made of ground beef, onion, garlic, and pasta in a rich cheesy cream sauce. It is delicious and hearty, a nice twist on the classic casserole. *Yield: 6 servings*

Ingredients

1 (2-pound) flat iron steak

3 tablespoons red wine vinegar

1 teaspoon grill seasoning

½ teaspoon dried oregano

1 onion, sliced ½ inch thick

3 eggs, beaten

½ cup heavy cream

½ teaspoon salt

⅛ teaspoon nutmeg

½ cup grated pecorino cheese

¼ cup crumbled feta cheese

2 tomatoes, halved

1 pound dry penne pasta

¼ cup chopped fresh parsley

Greek Steak with Pasta

- Rub steak with vinegar; sprinkle with grill seasoning and oregano; let stand for 20 minutes. Skewer onion.

- Bring pot of salted water to a boil on grill. In small bowl, combine eggs, cream, salt, nutmeg, cheeses; mix well.

- Grill steak for 8–9 minutes, onions for 5 minutes, tomatoes for 2–3. Remove from heat; let stand.

- Cook pasta until al dente. Slice steak, chop onions and tomatoes. Drain pasta; return to pot. Add egg mixture and stir over heat for 2 minutes. Add remaining ingredients and toss.

~ VARIATION ~

Tex-Mex Grilled Steak

In casserole dish, combine ⅓ cup tequila, ¼ cup chili sauce, 2 tablespoons lime juice, 1 teaspoon salt, ⅛ teaspoon cayenne pepper, ¼ teaspoon red pepper flakes, 2 cloves garlic, and 2 minced jalapeño peppers. Marinate steak in refrigerator. Grill steak as desired and serve with salsa.

Hawaiian Steaks with Fruit

In casserole dish, combine ½ cup pineapple juice, ¼ cup soy sauce, 2 tablespoons brown sugar, 1 finely chopped onion, and ⅛ teaspoon pepper. Marinate steak for 3 hours in refrigerator. Grill as desired. Grill 1 sliced pineapple and 2 sliced oranges. Slice steak and serve with fruit; sprinkle with toasted coconut.

Grill Food on Skewers

- Threading sliced onions on skewers is a great way to keep the rings together on the grill so they cook evenly.

- Watch the food carefully as it grills. The tomatoes will be done first, but the onions may take as long as the steak.

- You want to see nice grill marks on the onions and they should be tender when pierced with a fork.

- While the steak rests, chop the vegetables and attend to the pasta.

Toss Pasta and Eggs Mixture in Pot

- The eggs will cook on contact with the hot pasta, and together with the cream, form a sauce that will coat the pasta.

- Gently toss all the ingredients, using 2 large spoons, until they are all hot and everything is evenly distributed.

- Other strong flavored cheeses could be used, including Romano, Cotija, blue cheese, or goat cheese.

- This recipe is similar to Spaghetti Carbonara, and should be served immediately.

BONELESS CHICKEN BREASTS
Chicken breasts cook in minutes to juicy perfection and can be flavored in myriad ways

Boneless, skinless chicken breasts are probably the most versatile meat available. They can be flavored many ways, combine with almost any ingredient, and are very easy to overcook on the grill.

So watch your time carefully when grilling this simple meat. The chicken has to be cooked to an internal temperature of

165 degrees F, but the temperature will rise about 5 degrees after it's pulled from the grill. So cook the chicken to 160 degrees F, then let it stand, covered, for 5 minutes.

You can flavor boneless, skinless chicken breasts so many ways; just use your imagination. Soon you'll have a huge repertoire of your own excellent recipes. *Yield: 6 servings*

Ingredients

3 cups water

1 cup apricot nectar

⅓ cup salt

⅓ cup sugar

1 cup apple cider vinegar

6–8 boneless, skinless chicken breasts

½ cup apricot preserves

1 tablespoon lemon juice

1 tablespoon honey

1 teaspoon vanilla

1 teaspoon ground ginger

3 tablespoons Dijon mustard

Apricot Glazed Chicken Breasts

- Combine water, nectar, salt, sugar, and vinegar; mix well. Pound chicken until ½ inch thick; add to brine; cover; refrigerate for 3–4 hours.

- Combine remaining ingredients and refrigerate.

- Preheat grill. Drain chicken. Place over direct medium-high heat. Brush with half of the preserves mixture.

- After 3 minutes, turn chicken and brush with remaining glaze. Grill for 3–4 minutes or until chicken is almost cooked. Turn once more, cook for 30–45 seconds until temp reaches 160°F. Let stand; serve.

RECIPE VARIATION

Honey Glazed Chicken: Combine 3 tablespoons olive oil, ¼ cup honey, 2 tablespoons each lemon juice and low-sodium soy sauce in a plastic bag. Add 6 boneless, skinless chicken breasts, seal, and place in a casserole; refrigerate for 12–24 hours. Drain chicken, reserving marinade. Grill over direct heat until done, brushing occasionally with reserved marinade.

GREEN●LIGHT

Foods that cook best over direct heat are those that cook quickly, like thin steaks and pork chops, boneless chicken breasts, kabobs, and tender vegetables. Indirect heat and two-layer cooking is for bone-in chicken, burgers, and thicker steaks and chops. These foods cook with an initial sear, then a finish over cooler coals so they cook thoroughly and evenly.

Marinate Chicken

- You can flavor brines any way you'd like. As a variation, you could use pineapple juice and pineapple preserves along with tarragon.

- Be sure that you marinate chicken according to the recipe directions.

- If chicken is brined for longer than 24 hours, it will start to "cook" in the acid and become tougher when cooked.

- To keep chicken submerged in the brine, cover it with a plate a bit smaller than the diameter of the bowl.

Grill Chicken and Brush with Sauce

- Since the chicken has been pounded almost to a paillard, it will cook more quickly than a plain chicken breast.

- An unpounded chicken breast will cook for 5–6 minutes on each side.

- For a sauce to accompany the chicken, just double the glaze. Boil it for 2 minutes before serving with the chicken.

- Serve this chicken with a simple hot rice or couscous mixture, cooked with apricot nectar and some grated ginger root.

CHICKEN PACKETS

Combine chicken with tender fruits or vegetables in a one-dish meal cooked on the grill

Packets, filled with delicious food are a great way to serve a crowd. This is basically one-dish cooking on the grill.

Fish and chicken cook very well using this method. Burgers and steaks, which require direct high heat to caramelize, don't work quite as well.

Again, almost any combination of flavors willbe delicious.

Use only about ¼ cup of sauce for each packet; any more and the packets will leak.

Seal the packets by folding over the ends twice, first the long way, then the short way. But be sure to leave room for expansion in the heat of the grill; don't fold the foil tight against the food. *Yield: 4 servings*

Ingredients

4 boneless, skinless chicken breasts

½ teaspoon salt

¼ teaspoon lemon pepper

1 lemon, thinly sliced

1½ cups blueberries

4 green onions, sliced

⅓ cup lemon juice

¼ cup olive oil

2 tablespoons honey

1 teaspoon fresh thyme leaves

Lemon Blueberry Chicken Packets

- Sprinkle chicken with salt and lemon pepper. Tear off 4 18-inch x 12-inch pieces of heavy duty foil and place on work surface.

- Place 1 chicken breast on each piece of foil. Top with lemon slices, blueberries, and green onions.

- Combine lemon juice, olive oil, honey, and thyme; mix well. Drizzle over packets.

- Fold with a double fold, leaving some room for heat expansion. Grill over direct medium-high heat for 18–22 minutes, moving packets around, until chicken is done.

Mexican Chicken Packets

Combine 3 tablespoons lemon juice, 2 tablespoons olive oil, 1 minced jalapeño pepper, 1 tablespoon chili powder, ½ teaspoon cumin, ½ teaspoon salt, and ⅛ teaspoon pepper. Prepare foil, then top chicken breasts with 1 pint cherry tomatoes, 2 cups frozen corn, and ½ cup salsa. Drizzle with lemon juice mixture, fold, and grill.

Pepper Orange Chicken Packets

Combine ⅓ cup frozen orange juice concentrate, thawed, ¼ cup orange marmalade, 1 tablespoon chopped fresh basil, 2 tablespoons olive oil, ½ teaspoon salt, and ⅛ teaspoon pepper. Top chicken with sliced red, yellow, orange, and green bell peppers and 1 chopped red onion. Drizzle with orange sauce, fold packets, and grill.

CHICKEN I

Assemble Packets

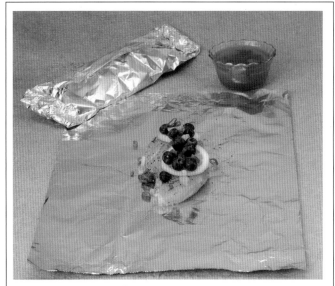

Grill Packets

- Don't skimp on the foil for these packets; use a full 18-inch x 12-inch piece and use heavy duty foil, or doubled plain foil.

- Spray the area where you'll place the food with non-stick cooking spray. Then stack the food.

- Drizzle with the sauce, then bring the 18-inch sides to the middle; fold once, then twice.

- One at a time, fold the 12-inch sides together, once, then twice. There should be air space around the food.

- It's best to have a two-level fire when cooking these packets for more control over the temperature.

- Move the packets around on the grill. Start over direct heat, then move them to indirect.

- You can check doneness by sticking a meat thermometer probe through the foil into the chicken, or carefully unwrap 1 packet to check.

- The packets may finish cooking at different times; pull them off as they are finished and cover to keep warm.

STUFFED CHICKEN BREAST

Boneless, skinless chicken can be stuffed with everything from cheese to chutney

There are two ways to stuff boneless, skinless chicken breasts: by cutting a pocket in the flesh, or by pounding the meat thin, stuffing, then rolling to enclose the filling.

Both techniques work well; it just depends on the look you want. You can get a bit more filling into breasts that are pounded and rolled around the filling.

Be careful to keep the meat whole while you're pounding it; don't tear holes with the mallet or rolling pin.

You can fasten the breast after it's stuffed by using toothpicks to hold the opening closed or by tying the breast with 100 percent cotton kitchen twine. Remove the toothpicks or twine when the chicken is done. *Yield: 6 servings*

Ingredients

2 cups water

2 tablespoons salt

2 tablespoons sugar

6 boneless, skinless chicken breasts

3 slices bacon

2 tablespoons butter

⅓ cup finely minced onion

3 cloves garlic, minced

1 red bell pepper, chopped

3 tablespoons ricotta cheese

¼ cup shredded extra-sharp cheddar cheese

Bacon Cheese Stuffed Chicken

- In bowl, combine water, salt, and sugar; stir until dissolved. Add chicken; cover and refrigerate while preparing filling.

- Cook bacon in large skillet until crisp; drain and crumble. Drain skillet; do not wipe; add butter.

- Add onion, garlic, pepper to skillet; cook and stir until tender. Remove to small bowl; let cool. Add bacon and cheeses to filling.

- Remove chicken from brine; cut pocket or flatten; stuff with bacon mixture. Grill over direct medium heat 9–12 minutes.

MAKE IT EASY

Your ear is an important tool when grilling. Listen to your food cooking on the grill. When the coals and the rack are at the correct temperature, there should be a sharp snap of sizzling when the food is first added to the hot grill. As the food cooks, the sound will decrease.

• • • • RECIPE VARIATION • • • •

Brine chicken as directed. For filling, combine 1 cup crumbled feta cheese, ⅓ cup minced kalamata olives, ¼ cup chopped green onion, and 1 teaspoon dried oregano leaves. Flatten chicken and spread filling over; roll up and secure with twine. Brush with olive oil and sprinkle with salt, pepper, and paprika. Grill until chicken is thoroughly cooked.

Cut Pocket or Flatten Chicken

- When cutting the pocket, use a sharp knife and place your palm on the chicken.

- Sweep the knife back and forth inside the chicken; don't pierce the sides. Make the pocket larger than the entrance hole.

- When pounding the chicken, place between sheets of waxed paper or plastic wrap. Start at the middle and pound out toward the sides.

- Move the chicken around occasionally to be sure you're not pounding holes in the chicken or making one area too thin.

Stuff Chicken and Secure

- Don't overstuff the chicken, or as filling expands in the heat of the grill, it may break through the meat.

- Handle the chicken carefully on the grill and use tongs and a spatula to turn it.

- When you check on the internal temperature, be sure that the probe doesn't extend into the stuffing; you'll get an inaccurate reading.

- Since the chicken is so thin, you can rely on clear juices or careful timing to make sure it's thoroughly cooked.

137

MORE STUFFED CHICKEN BREASTS
Stuffing can also be placed under the skin on bone-in breasts

There is an easier way to stuff chicken breasts: just loosen the skin from the flesh and add the stuffing. This method uses bone-in, skin-on chicken breasts, which take a longer time to cook on the grill.

For a really crisp skin, when marinating the chicken, air dry in the fridge. This just means you marinate the chicken with the skin exposed, uncovered. This lets the skin dry a bit and concentrates the sugars, so it will brown and crisp on the grill.

With this type of stuffing, it's important to secure the skin to the flesh so it doesn't shrink when cooking. Toothpicks are the best tools for this. Be sure you remove the toothpicks before you serve the chicken. Enjoy these delicious recipes.
Yield: 6 servings

Ingredients

½ cup plain yogurt

2 tablespoons curry powder

2 tablespoons grated fresh ginger root

6 bone-in, skin-on chicken breasts

4 tablespoons olive oil, divided

1 onion, chopped

4 cloves garlic, minced

1½ cups chopped cremini mushrooms

1 jalapeño pepper, minced

¼ cup minced sun-dried tomatoes

2 tablespoons lemon juice

¼ cup chopped cilantro

1 teaspoon salt

¼ teaspoon pepper

Tandoori Indian Stuffed Chicken

- Combine yogurt, curry powder, and ginger root. Loosen skin from chicken; spread mixture under skin. Cover; refrigerate for 8–24 hours.

- Cook onion, garlic, mushrooms, jalapeño in olive oil until tender; stir in tomatoes, lemon juice, cilantro.

- Stuff mixture under skin; secure with toothpicks. Brush chicken with rest of olive oil; sprinkle with salt and pepper.

- Place chicken, skin side up, on indirect medium heat. Cover; grill for 45–55 minutes or until chicken is thoroughly cooked.

Loosen Chicken Skin from Flesh

Add Stuffing

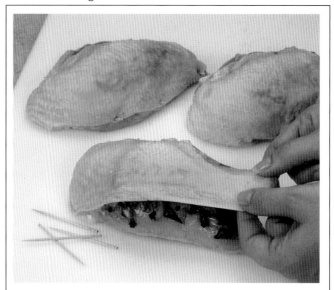

- When you loosen the skin from the breast, be sure to leave it attached at 1 side to hold the filling.

- Yogurt is an excellent marinade for chicken. The acidic nature of this dairy product is perfectly balanced to make the chicken tender.

- Don't marinate the chicken longer than 24 hours, or it may start to become tough.

- You don't need to remove the yogurt mixture from the chicken after it has finished marinating; it adds flavor to the chicken.

- Don't overstuff the chicken, or the skin may split as it cooks. Use the amount specified in the recipe.

- Spoon the stuffing onto the chicken lightly; don't compact the filling; it will expand in the heat of the grill.

- Bone-in, skin-on chicken cooks for a much longer time than boneless, skinless breasts because the bone protects the flesh from the heat.

- Let the chicken stand, covered, for 5–6 minutes after grilling to let the juices redistribute.

CHICKEN DRUMSTICKS

Kids love drumsticks! And there are a thousand different ways to flavor and glaze them

Chicken drumsticks are perfect foods for kids. They come with a handle attached, and the tender meat is delicious.

You can flavor drumsticks in many different ways, from a simple herb and lemon glaze to more complicated recipes.

Stuffing herbs under the skin of chicken drumsticks—or thighs or breasts, for that matter—is a nice way to add flavor to the meat and also to make a beautiful presentation.

Pull the meat back from the flesh and arrange whole leaves of sage or tarragon on the flesh, then carefully smooth the skin back over the drumsticks. Chopped herbs make a delicious pattern, too, and you can combine several for flavorful blends.
Yield: 8 drumsticks

Ingredients

8 chicken drumsticks

2 tablespoons lemon juice

1 tablespoon melted butter

2 tablespoons chopped parsley

2 tablespoons chopped fresh thyme

2 tablespoons chopped fresh tarragon

1 teaspoon salt, divided

¼ teaspoon pepper, divided

2 tablespoons olive oil

Herbed Chicken Drumsticks

- Pat chicken dry and gently remove skin, keeping it attached at the bone.

- In small bowl, combine lemon juice, butter, herbs, and half of the salt and pepper; mix well. Spread over chicken flesh, then smooth skin back over chicken.

- Cover and refrigerate chicken for 2–3 hours. Prepare grill.

- Brush chicken with olive oil and sprinkle with remaining salt and pepper. Grill over indirect heat, turning occasionally, for 45–55 minutes until chicken is thoroughly cooked.

Tex-Mex Drumsticks

Combine ¼ cup ketchup with 2 tablespoons lime juice and 1 tablespoon chili powder. Pull back skin from drumsticks and rub this mixture on flesh; pull skin back over, fasten with toothpicks, and rub with ketchup mixture. Marinate for 4–5 hours in the fridge, then grill as directed. Serve with dip made by combining equal amounts of sour cream, salsa, and chopped avocado.

Creamy Cheese Dips

Serve these dips with any of these drumsticks. Kids love anything they can hold by hand and dip into something delicious. Combine 1 cup sour cream, ½ cup mayonnaise, ½ cup grated Parmesan cheese, and ⅓ cup chopped parsley. Or combine an 8-ounce package of softened cream cheese with ½ cup milk, 8 ounces processed cheese spread, and cooked crumbled bacon.

Pull Back Skin

- Chicken drumsticks usually come about 4 to the pound.

- Pull the skin back, starting at the meaty end and pulling back down toward the bone.

- They can be grilled with the skin off, but leaving the skin on lets you create patterns with herbs and marinades.

- The skin also protects the meat as it cooks, keeping it moist. If you don't eat the skin, the calorie count between skinless and skin-on is about the same.

Place Herbs under Skin

- You can substitute dried herbs, but change the amounts. Use ⅓ the amount of dried herbs when substituting for fresh.

- Grill the drumsticks until a meat thermometer registers 175°F. Be sure the thermometer doesn't touch the bone.

- Let the chicken stand, covered, for 10 minutes after grilling so the temperature increases to 180°F. This will also let the juices redistribute.

- Be sure to serve these drumsticks with dipping sauces and lots of napkins and wet wipes.

CHICKEN WINGS

Wings not only make great appetizers, they can also be a satisfying and inexpensive meal

Everyone has had chicken wings for an appetizer. But did you know that you can make a meal with them? All you need to do is serve enough wings. Make several different kinds and offer an assortment, with dipping sauces and condiments.

Each person should be served about a pound of chicken wings for a meal, and just 3–4 wings for an appetizer. Give everyone a dish for the bones.

Because the wings are so small, they do best when cooked over indirect medium-low heat. Turn them frequently and brush with sauce as they cook. They cook in about 15 minutes, so you can start brushing with sauce as soon as they hit the grill.
Yield: 8 appetizer servings

Ingredients

1 cup sour cream

⅓ cup crumbled blue cheese

2 celery stalks, chopped

3 pounds meaty chicken wings

½ cup hot sauce

½ cup butter, melted

1 cup beer

4 cloves garlic, minced

⅓ cup flour

2 teaspoons paprika

1 teaspoon salt

¼ teaspoon pepper

1 tablespoon canola oil

Grilled Buffalo Chicken Wings

- Combine sour cream, blue cheese and celery; chill.

- Cut wings into 3 pieces; discard tips. Combine with hot sauce, butter, beer, garlic in large saucepan; refrigerate for 3 hours.

- Remove wings from sauce. Combine flour, paprika, salt, pepper. Coat wings in this mixture, place on rack, and refrigerate for 1 hour.

- Brush grill with oil. Place sauce in saucepan on grill and simmer. Grill wings on indirect medium-low heat for 15–20 minutes until done, toss in sauce. Serve with sour cream mixture.

Honey Mustard Wings

In large bowl, combine ½ cup mustard, ¼ cup honey, 1 teaspoon seasoned salt, 2 cloves garlic, minced, 1 teaspoon onion powder, 1 teaspoon dried basil leaves, and ¼ teaspoon pepper. Prepare wings as directed and marinate in mixture. Grill as directed. Discard marinade when wings are done. Serve with sauce made of sour cream and honey mustard.

Asian Wings

In large bowl, combine ⅓ cup low-sodium soy sauce, ¼ cup hoisin sauce, ¼ cup brown sugar, 2 tablespoons grated ginger root, ⅓ cup rice wine vinegar, 1 teaspoon garlic powder, ⅓ cup water, and ⅛ teaspoon pepper. Add wings, marinate, then grill as directed, brushing with marinade Discard marinade after wings are done.

Prepare Chicken Wings

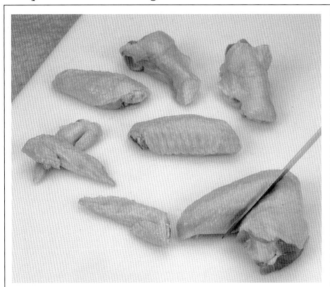

- Look for chicken wings with a lot of meat on the bone. They should be plump, with smooth skin.

- Grilling is a great way to cook wings because they do contain a fair amount of fat, which this method removes.

- To cut the wings into pieces, use a sharp knife and cut gently into the joint between the sections.

- The wing tips don't have much meat, but they do have flavor to add to stocks. Freeze them for later use.

Grill and Glaze Wings

- Chicken wings should be grilled to 170°F for food safety reasons.

- It's kind of tricky to get an accurate temperature reading on wings, so depend on timing and a touch test.

- When they're done, they'll look done, will give gently when pressed, and the juices will run clear.

- Simmer the sauce the entire time that the wings are cooking, then toss them in the sauce as they finish to add more flavor and keep them moist.

ROAST WHOLE CHICKEN

Using indirect heat, it's easy to cook a whole chicken on the grill, with almost no work

Cooking a whole chicken on the grill is very easy, once you've set up the grill for indirect heat and the chicken has been brined. Brining is really necessary for the best result.

Brining the chicken guarantees a moist, well-flavored bird with nicely browned skin. The chicken doesn't sit in the brine for a long period of time—just about 4 hours in the fridge.

The most important thing when cooking chicken is that it be cooked to the correct internal temperature.

It's important to let the chicken stand, covered, after grilling so the juices redistribute. To carve the chicken, start by removing each breast and slicing it, then remove the drumsticks and slice the rest of the dark meat. *Yield: 4 servings*

Ingredients

I gallon cold water

⅔ cup plus I teaspoon salt

⅔ cup brown sugar

2 tablespoons plus I teaspoon dried basil leaves

3 lemons

I (3–4-pound) whole chicken

I lemon, sliced

I bunch fresh basil

¼ cup minced onion

½ teaspoon pepper

3 tablespoons butter

3 tablespoons olive oil

Brined Lemon Basil Chicken

- In large bowl, mix water, ⅔ cup salt, brown sugar, 2 tablespoons dried basil. Squeeze 2 lemons; add with rind to bowl.

- Slice lemon; add. Discard neck, giblets. Place in brine; chill 4–5 hours.

- Remove chicken; pat dry.

Place sliced lemon and whole fresh basil leaves in cavity. Truss chicken.

- Mix onion with remaining salt and pepper until paste forms. Add remaining dried basil, butter, olive oil. Rub into meat. Grill over indirect heat, breast side up, for 75–90 minutes until 180°F.

Weather does play a part in cooking on a charcoal grill. Read your manufacturer's instructions to see if there are any special instructions for cooking in very cold, stormy, or windy weather. Charcoal grills cook faster on calm, warm days and slower on cold, windy days, so adjust recipes accordingly. To grill in winter or rainy weather you'll need more charcoal to sustain a consistent fire.

Spicy Grilled Chicken: Use regular sugar in brine instead of brown sugar; omit lemons. Stuff chicken with 2 sliced jalapeño peppers and 2 sliced onions. Omit basil from paste; add 1 tablespoon chili powder, 1 teaspoon cumin, and 2 tablespoons adobo sauce. Cook chicken as directed in recipe.

Brine Chicken

- Brining adds moisture and flavor to the chicken. Salt wants to move from highly concentrated to less concentrated solutions.

- To be sure the chicken is completely immersed in the brine, place a plate on the chicken and top with a can.

- After the chicken is removed from the brine and drained, don't rinse it. Pat it dry and rub in the onion mixture.

- You can rub the onion mixture under the chicken skin as well as on the outside.

Grill-roast Chicken

- This chicken can also be cooked on a rotisserie. Follow manufacturer's directions for using the rotisserie.

- Baste the chicken with chicken broth if you'd like. This will add more flavor and help the chicken brown.

- If you don't have a V-rack, you can use an aluminum roasting pan, with slits cut in the bottom to let smoke in.

- Or line the grill with a grill mat, then cover with onion or lemon slices. Top with the chicken and grill.

ANY CAN CHICKEN
Whatever type of canned liquid you use, this chicken is unbelievably moist and tender

Everyone has heard of the famous Beer Can Chicken, in which a plump chicken sits on a can of beer on the grill. The beer bastes the chicken from the inside out.

You don't have to use beer in this recipe. Anything will do! A can of chicken broth makes the chicken even more flavorful, while pineapple can be used with sweet and sour seasonings.

Just be sure to use a can without a paper covering, and completely remove the top of the can. Even if you remove the paper, the glue will remain, and it's probably not food safe.

There are special racks made to hold the can and the chicken securely so you don't have to balance them. *Yield: 1 chicken; 4–6 servings*

Ingredients

2 cloves garlic

1 teaspoon salt

½ teaspoon pepper

2 teaspoons paprika

2 teaspoons grill seasoning

2 tablespoons butter

1 (3–4-pound) whole chicken

1 (11-ounce) can chicken broth

¼ cup barbecue sauce

½ small apple

Rich and Spicy Can Chicken

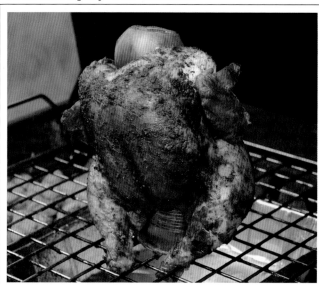

- Mash garlic and salt with knife until a paste forms. Stir in pepper, paprika, grill seasoning, butter.

- Loosen skin from chicken and rub half garlic mixture under skin. Smooth skin over chicken and rub rest on skin.

- Pour half of the chicken broth into a small bowl add barbecue sauce to can and stir. Set chicken on can. Refrigerate broth in bowl.

- Using legs and can, balance chicken over indirect heat. Put apple in neck. Cover and grill, basting chicken occasionally with reserved chilled broth, for 75–90 minutes

Cola Chicken

Rub chicken with mixture of 3 tablespoons each brown sugar and chili powder, 1 teaspoon each salt, pepper, and paprika; refrigerate chicken for 12–24 hours. Open a cola can by completely removing the top. Pour out half the cola; add 1 tablespoon chili powder and 1 tablespoon brown sugar to cola in can. Place chicken on can; proceed with recipe.

Beer Can Chicken

Use the same rub as in Rich and Spicy Can Chicken, but add ½ teaspoon dried mustard. Use a 12-ounce can of beer with the top completely removed. Pour off half the beer and add ¼ cup mustard. Put a small onion in neck of chicken instead of apple.

Balance Chicken on Can

- You may have to work a bit to get the chicken balanced on its legs and the can.

- There are special racks available that will hold the chicken and the can securely upright on the grill.

- Be sure the can you use doesn't have a paper cover or glue. It should be a plain metal can.

- Be sure that the can is half empty, because the liquid inside will expand and boil in the heat of the grill.

Grill Chicken

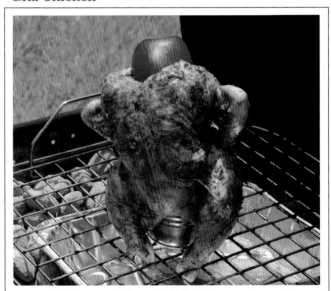

- The grill is being used like an oven in this recipe, so refrain from opening the lid.

- Baste only 2–3 times during grilling. Work quickly so the heat is restored rapidly.

- Be careful removing the chicken from the grill. The can will be very hot, so use large heavy oven mitts.

- Recruit a helper to get the can out of the chicken; one person should hold the can, the other the chicken. Lift off, and carve.

CHICKEN AND TURKEY

CHICKEN PIECES

A cut-up chicken on the grill lets everyone have their favorite

Chicken pieces on the grill give you lots of flexibility. You can flavor them many different ways, and everyone gets the type of chicken they like best.

Dark meat—drumsticks, wings, and thighs—will take longer to cook than white meat, or the chicken breasts. You can often find the drumstick with the thigh attached; that cut takes the longest of all on the grill.

For best results, brown the chicken over direct heat, then move the breasts to the edge of the grill on indirect heat. Place the dark meat closer to the center of the grill.

There is a lot of fat in chicken, which will burn off as it cooks. Keep an eye on flare-ups, and be ready to move the chicken around. *Yield: 6 servings*

Ingredients

1 tablespoon minced ginger root

4 cloves garlic, minced

1 teaspoon salt

1 tablespoon five-spice powder

1 teaspoon sesame oil

2 tablespoons honey

¼ cup orange juice

3 tablespoons canola oil

2 tablespoons hoisin sauce

¼ cup chili sauce

3 pounds chicken parts

Five-Spice Grilled Chicken

- In small bowl, combine all ingredients except chicken and mix well.

- Place chicken in large plastic bag with marinade. Seal bag and knead. Chill for 12–18 hours. Remove chicken from marinade; reserve marinade.

- Pat chicken dry, then brown over direct medium heat for 8–9 minutes. Then move chicken to indirect heat.

- Grill over indirect medium heat, basting occasionally with reserved marinade, until breast pieces register 165°F (25–35 minutes) and thigh pieces 175°F (35–45 minutes).

Grill charms are the latest accessory. You can use the charms to label the pieces of chicken that your guests prefer, or to mark chicken that is seasoned or sauced differently. The charms come in different collections, including the "rare, medium, well done" collection and "charmed life" charms, which represent activities of a charmed life, like sailing.

• • • • RECIPE VARIATION • • • •

Grill Roasted Chicken: Soak chicken in 3 cups buttermilk, 1 teaspoon salt, 2 teaspoons paprika, and 3 cloves minced garlic. On plate, mix ¼ cup each flour, dry seasoned breadcrumbs, and crushed cornflake cereal. Coat drained chicken in dry mixture. Place in large aluminum pan on low heat. Cover and grill for 1–1¼ hours, turning chicken once, until done.

Marinate Chicken

Grill Chicken, Brush with Marinade

- Don't marinate the chicken longer than the specified time or it may become tough.

- You may want to knead and turn the bag several times during the marinating process so all the pieces are exposed to the marinade.

- For really crisp skin, after the chicken marinates, remove it from the marinade and place on jelly roll pan.

- Let the chicken stand, uncovered, in the refrigerator for 3–4 hours so the skin dries.

- As the chicken starts to cook, brush with the reserved marinade. Be sure to discard any unused marinade.

- Grill the chicken breasts for 35–45 minutes, and grill the thighs and drumsticks for 25–35 minutes.

- The chicken breasts should register 165°F, and the thighs and drumsticks 175°F.

- As chicken finishes cooking, remove to a warm clean plate. Cover with foil and let rest for 10 minutes before serving.

SPATCHCOCKED CHICKEN

By cutting out the back, cook a flattened chicken to juicy perfection on the grill

Spatchcock sounds like such a fancy English term. It actually originated in Ireland. All it means is a chicken with its backbone removed so it will lay flat on the grill; it's a butterflied chicken.

This is an easy way to evenly cook chicken on the grill. It's also very simple to brush the chicken with glaze. The chicken will cook very evenly.

All you need is a sharp set of kitchen shears or a sharp knife, patience, and a whole chicken. You could always ask the butcher to do it! Then brine or marinate it, and grill.

When the chicken is done, let it stand so the juices redistribute, then cut the breast, thighs, wings, and drumsticks apart. *Yield: 4–6 servings*

Ingredients

6 cloves garlic, minced

2 teaspoons salt

½ teaspoon pepper

½ teaspoon garlic powder

2 teaspoons paprika

¼ cup olive oil

2 tablespoons butter

1 (3–4-pound) whole chicken

Spatchcocked Chicken with Garlic Marinade

- Mix garlic with salt, pepper, garlic powder, and paprika, oil and butter.

- With kitchen shears or sharp knife, cut the backbone out of the chicken. Place chicken, bone side down, on work surface. Press down on the chicken breast to flatten chicken.

- Loosen skin and rub on half of the garlic mixture. Smooth skin over flesh and rub in remaining mixture.

- Refrigerate for 8–12 hours. Grill chicken, skin side down, on direct medium heat for 15 minutes. Turn; grill for 20–25 minutes longer until 170°F.

Tex-Mex Spatchcocked Chicken

For marinade, combine 1 (4-ounce) can chopped green chiles, drained, ¼ cup olive oil, ¼ cup lemon juice, 2 tablespoons chili powder, and 1 teaspoon cumin. Spatchcock chicken and marinate for 12–18 hours in the refrigerator. Drain chicken, reserving marinade. Grill chicken until done, turning twice and brushing with marinade.

Greek Spatchcocked Chicken

For marinade, combine ⅓ cup olive oil, ⅓ cup lemon juice, ⅓ cup chicken broth, ¼ cup minced olives, 3 cloves garlic minced, and 1 minced onion. Spatchcock chicken and marinate for 12–18 hours in the fridge. Drain chicken, reserving marinade. Strain marinade. Grill chicken until done, turning and brushing with marinade as it cooks.

Cut Out Backbone

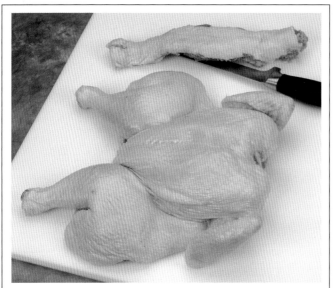

Cut Up Grilled Chicken

- Work carefully and slowly as you cut through the chicken. There's no need to rush.

- Save the backbone to make chicken stock; it's full of flavor. Just freeze it until you've accumulated enough chicken bones.

- After you've finished cutting, turn the bird over and press down on the center of the breast to flatten it.

- The chicken is now ready for marinating. Turn the chicken over several times while it is marinating.

- An easy way to tell if the chicken is done is to see if the juices run clear and if the leg moves freely in the joint.

- After the chicken is done, cover it with foil and let it stand for 10 minutes.

- When you look at the chicken, you'll be able to see the breasts, thighs, drumsticks, and wings.

- Using those (washed) kitchen shears, or a sharp knife, cut the chicken up along the joints. You could also use a sharp chef's knife.

WHOLE TURKEY

For Thanksgiving or anytime, cook a whole turkey on the grill for a fabulous taste

A whole turkey, cooked on the grill, is a bird for a celebration. The bird will be beautifully browned, with a crisp skin and moist meat that has a light smoky flavor. The turkey should weigh less than 16 pounds.

For food safety reasons, don't stuff a turkey cooked on the grill. This makes cooking the turkey easier too. Brine the tur-key or marinate it for best results. Use traditional flavors like onion, garlic, and sage, or try something new: an Asian grilled turkey or a turkey with a Tex-Mex flair.

For a charcoal grill, you'll have to add 10–15 briquettes per hour to keep the heat consistent. Start the coals in your chimney starter for best results. *Yield: 8–10 servings*

Ingredients

1 (11–12-pound) whole turkey

3 tablespoons lemon juice

1 tablespoon lemon zest

⅓ cup butter, softened

2 teaspoons dried thyme leaves

2 teaspoons salt

½ teaspoon pepper

4 cloves garlic, minced

2 lemons, cut in half

3 sprigs thyme

3 onions, sliced

3 carrots, sliced lengthwise

3 cups chicken stock

Lemon Roasted Turkey

- Remove giblets, neck from turkey; cover parts with water and simmer for gravy.

- Mix lemon juice, zest, butter, thyme, salt, pepper, and garlic. Rub the cavity under the skin, and on skin. Place lemon halves and thyme sprigs in cavity.

- Sear turkey on each side over direct medium heat for 10 minutes. Place onions and carrots in heavy duty roasting pan; place on indirect medium heat. Add turkey and chicken stock.

- Cover; grill for 2 ½–3 hours, or until meat thermometer in thigh registers 180°F.

Charcoal briquettes must extend at least 2 inches beyond the foods you are cooking for best results. When you add more coals to the grill, move them around and mix them together so the newly lit and dying coals are combined, or start them in a chimney. A grill with a hinged rack makes this easier. Never squirt lighter fluid on hot coals.

• • • • RECIPE VARIATION • • • •

Classic Roast Turkey: Brine turkey in mixture of 3 quarts water, ½ cup salt, and ½ cup brown sugar for 8 hours in refrigerator. Drain, rinse turkey, and pat dry. Combine ¼ cup mustard, 3 cloves minced garlic, 2 teaspoons onion powder, 2 teaspoons salt, and ½ teaspoon pepper; rub under skin and on skin. Prepare turkey as directed.

Stuff and Truss Turkey

- For more lemon flavor, prick the lemons with a fork before you place them inside the cavity.

- You can truss the turkey before cooking it using 100 percent cotton twine. Tie the legs to the bird and fasten the wings down.

- When you're searing the bird, you're adding color and flavor. Watch the timing carefully and turn the bird twice.

- For gravy, place a drip pan filled with chicken stock under the turkey. Use this mixture in your favorite recipe.

Grill Turkey

- The turkey can be cooked in a heavy duty roasting pan or on a grill rack. Either way, close the grill so the turkey roasts.

- Use a heat-proof thermometer inserted into the thigh for most accurate results. Be sure the probe doesn't touch the bone.

- Let the turkey stand, covered, for 15 minutes after cooking to let the juices redistribute.

- Place the turkey on a large platter decorated with lemon slices and sprigs of thyme.

TURKEY BREAST

A turkey breast is easy to cook on the grill when paired with these marinade and rub suggestions

KNACK GRILLING BASICS

If you prefer white meat, a turkey breast is a great solution for entertaining or the holidays. A turkey breast is easier to handle, can be safely stuffed, and cooks in less time.

If you're grilling a whole turkey for a holiday meal, think about grilling an extra breast or two to have more white meat. Even if you don't use them, the meat is invaluable for leftovers.

You can brine or marinate a turkey breast just as you do a whole turkey or chicken.

If you use a boneless breast, you can cut it in half lengthwise and treat the halves like large chicken breasts. Think about using them in your favorite chicken breast recipes, just increasing the grilling time. *Yield: 8 servings*

Ingredients

2 tablespoons apple butter

3 tablespoons butter

3 tablespoons Dijon mustard

3 cloves garlic, minced

1 teaspoon salt

¼ teaspoon pepper

1 (3-pound) boneless turkey breast

2 cups soaked apple wood chips

Boneless Apple Mustard Grilled Turkey Breast

- In small bowl, combine apple butter, butter, mustard, garlic, salt, and pepper.

- Loosen skin from turkey and rub half of apple mixture on flesh. Smooth skin back over flesh and secure with toothpicks.

- Rub remaining apple mix-

ture into skin. Place wood chips in drip pan; set up grill for indirect medium heat.

- Brown turkey over direct medium heat on both sides, about 12 minutes. Place over drip pan, cover, and grill for 55–65 minutes, turning once, until meat thermometer registers 165°F.

Simple Grilled Boneless Breast

Combine ½ cup minced onion, 3 cloves minced garlic, 3 tablespoons soy sauce, 2 tablespoons sugar, 3 tablespoons olive oil, and ¼ cup orange juice. Marinate turkey for 4 hours in fridge. Drain, reserving marinade. Grill on direct medium heat for 30–40 minutes until 165°F, brushing with marinade.

Brined Bone-in Turkey Breast

Combine ⅓ cup each salt and brown sugar, 2 quarts water, and 2 sliced lemons in large bowl. Add turkey breast; refrigerate for 12–24 hours. Rinse turkey; pat dry. Mix ¼ cup chopped parsley, 3 minced garlic cloves, 3 tablespoons lemon juice, and 1 teaspoon salt. Spread under and over skin. Grill over indirect heat for 2¼–3 hours until 165°F.

Rub Turkey with Seasonings

- If the turkey is frozen, make sure it's completely thawed before you brine or marinate.

- Never thaw turkey on the counter; in the refrigerator or under cold running water are the only safe ways to thaw.

- The toothpicks will hold the skin in place. After it's been loosened for flavoring, it will shrink, which exposes the meat to high heat.

- Be sure to remove the toothpicks after the turkey is done and has finished standing time.

Grill Turkey Breast

- The turkey can be cooked on direct or indirect heat; the time will be longer for indirect heat.

- Brush the turkey with the reserved marinade as it grills. Use a silicone brush for easiest cleanup.

- The temperature of the turkey will rise to 170°F while the meat is standing after it comes off the grill.

- As with all meats, let the turkey stand, covered, on a clean platter after it has reached the correct temperature.

CHICKEN SALADS

Moist and smoky grilled chicken is the perfect addition to fruit or vegetable salads

Chicken salads have come a long way from the mayonnaise and grape mixture favorite of our grandmothers (although that salad can also be delicious!).

Grilled chicken combined with a flavorful dressing and fruits or vegetables makes a fantastic meal. Grill the chicken especially for the salad or use leftover chicken from the night before.

Cube leftover chicken and drizzle with some of the dressing, or the liquid from the dressing, so it will absorb some flavor and stay moist. Then mix it with the rest of the salad ingredients.

Use your imagination when thinking about these salads. Grill the vegetables or fruit, or add fruit juices or preserves to the salad dressing. *Yield: 6 servings*

Ingredients

¼ cup apricot preserves

1 teaspoon salt

2 teaspoons chili powder

⅛ teaspoon cayenne pepper

⅛ teaspoon pepper

4 boneless, skinless chicken breasts

⅔ cup mayonnaise

⅓ cup orange juice concentrate, thawed

¼ cup light cream

¼ teaspoon salt

⅛ teaspoon white pepper

1 head romaine lettuce, halved

1 tablespoon oil

8 canned apricot halves, drained

4 green onions

½ cup pecan pieces

Grilled Spicy Apricot Chicken Salad

- Combine preserves, salt, chili powder, peppers. Brush onto chicken breasts; let stand for 20 minutes.

- In large bowl, mix mayo, concentrate, cream, ¼ teaspoon salt, white pepper.

- Brush lettuce with oil; grill, cut side down, on direct heat for 2–3 minutes. Remove; chop. Grill apricot halves, turning once, for 2–3 minutes. Chop; add to bowl with lettuce.

- Grill chicken for 7–9 minutes, turning once, until done. Add green onions, pecans to salad. Chop chicken; add to salad; toss and serve.

Southwest Chicken Salad

Combine ½ cup sour cream, ½ cup low-fat mayonnaise, and 1 (12-ounce) jar of salsa in large bowl. Add 3 grilled chicken breasts, cut into strips, 1 cup cubed cheddar cheese, 2 cups thawed lima beans, 2 red bell peppers, chopped, 2 cups frozen corn, thawed, and 1 cup thawed edamame. Mix well and chill.

Fruity Chicken Salad

In large bowl, combine ½ cup sour cream, ⅓ cup plain yogurt, and ⅓ cup milk with ⅓ cup raspberry preserves. Add 3 cubed grilled chicken breasts, 2 cups red grapes, 2 cups sliced strawberries, 1 cup chopped kiwi, and 1 cup chopped celery. Beat 1 cup cream and fold into salad; garnish with raspberries.

Cut up Grilled Chicken

Toss Salad

- Using boneless chicken breasts that are glazed on the grill lets you add more flavor since the glaze is directly on the meat.

- If you use skin-on chicken, for less fat remove the skin, then cube, chop, or shred the chicken after it has been grilled.

- Use other fruits and fruit juices for recipe variations. Or combine fruits, juices, and preserves for a unique recipe.

- Apple juice and grilled apples, or pear juice and grilled pears, are good substitutions.

- Think about different greens to use in this flavorful recipe. Baby spinach, endive, butter lettuce, and green lettuce are all good choices.

- Softer lettuces, like spinach or green lettuce, won't stand up to grilling, so just chop them and add to the salad.

- If you're using leftover chicken, remove and discard the skin, then pull the meat off the bone. Save the skin and bones to make stock.

- With freshly grilled chicken, the temperature contrast in this salad is really marked.

GRILLED CHICKEN RECIPES

CHICKEN SANDWICHES
Grill your sandwich with tender chicken for a delicious treat

Once you have some grilled chicken on hand, think of your refrigerator as a deli. There are infinite variations on chicken sandwich recipes. You can make a sandwich out of next to noting! A perfectly grilled chicken breast, sliced, is delicious layered on some good bread with mustard, mayonnaise, and a sliced tomato.

Fancier sandwiches are just as easy. Transform your favorite hot chicken dishes, like casseroles and soups, into sandwiches by using the same ingredients and flavors.

Make several chicken sandwich spreads and leave them in the fridge for quick lunches and snacks. Along with a good selection of dinner rolls, whole grain breads, and tortillas, you never need serve the same chicken sandwich twice! *Yield: 6 sandwiches*

Ingredients

4 slices bacon

2 red bell peppers, sliced

1 (3-ounce) package cream cheese

1/3 cup sour cream

1/4 cup Dijon mustard

2 tablespoons chopped fresh tarragon

1/2 teaspoon salt

1/8 teaspoon pepper

2/3 cup cubed Havarti cheese

2 cups sliced grilled chicken

12 slices whole wheat French bread

4 tablespoons butter, softened

Grilled Chicken and Vegetable Tarragon Sandwiches

- On dual contact indoor grill, cook bacon until crisp. Remove and crumble. Add red bell pepper to grill; cover and grill for 2–3 minutes until tender.

- In bowl, beat cream cheese, sour cream, mustard, tarragon, salt, and pepper. Add cheese and chicken and stir.

- Place bread on work surface. Add half of chicken mixture, then bacon and red bell peppers. Top with remaining chicken mixture, then bread.

- Spread sandwiches with butter. Grill on dual contact grill for 5–6 minutes until bread is crisp and cheese is melted.

GREEN ● LIGHT

Dual contact indoor grills are a good choice when the weather is bad or you want to grill a small amount of food. You can also use grill pans that are placed over gas or electric burners on your stovetop. Follow directions for outdoor cooking. The result won't be the same, but can approximate the taste of grilled foods.

•••• RECIPE VARIATION ••••

Curried Chicken Spread: Mix ⅓ cup each mayo, sour cream, orange juice, 1 tablespoon curry powder, 2 chopped grilled chicken, ½ cup each dried cranberries, sliced celery, chopped walnuts. Tex-Mex Chicken Spread: Mix ⅔ cup mayo, ½ cup salsa, 2 teaspoons chili powder, 3 chopped grilled chicken, 2 chopped red bell peppers, 1 minced jalapeño, 2 chopped tomatoes.

Assemble Sandwiches

- If the chicken is a bit dry, chop or slice it, then drizzle with a bit of chicken broth; let stand until broth is absorbed.

- You could chop the chicken to make a sandwich spread. Mix in the bacon and bell peppers.

- Sturdy bread is necessary for the best sandwiches. Whole wheat or whole grain bread is best, and it's better for you, too.

- Low-fat ingredients work in this recipe: use low-fat sour cream, cream cheese, and cheese.

Grill Sandwiches

- When you purchase your dual contact grill, look for one with a floating hinge that will accommodate thick sandwiches.

- Unless you have a large dual contact grill, cook the sandwiches one at a time for best results.

- These sandwiches can also be grilled directly on an outside grill or on a grill pan.

- Wrap the sandwiches in foil, place on the grill, and cover with a foil-wrapped brick to mimic the indoor grill results.

CHICKEN PASTA SALADS

Chicken and pasta are a natural combination, and adding grill flavor makes these salads spectacular

Add pasta to a chicken salad and not only do you stretch the chicken, but you add a delicious ingredient that contributes texture, flavor, and, yes, nutrition.

Pasta has gotten a bad rap because of the low-carb craze. But if you use one of the whole-grain pastas now on the market, you'll add fiber, B vitamins, and healthy carbs to your diet.

Yes, you can cook pasta on the grill. Just use a heavy duty pot to boil the water. The pot won't be damaged by the smoke if you rub a thin layer of liquid dish soap over the exterior before you begin.

Enjoy pasta salads made with grilled chicken and have fun with dressings and ingredient combinations. *Yield: 8 servings*

Ingredients

1 cup small pecans

4 boneless, skinless chicken breasts

1 tablespoon olive oil

½ teaspoon salt

⅛ teaspoon pepper

⅔ cup mayonnaise

½ cup vanilla yogurt

¼ cup pineapple juice

4 cups farfalle pasta

¾ cup dried sweetened cranberries

1 cup chopped celery

1 cup red grapes

Cranberry Pecan Chicken Pasta Salad

- Bring a large pot of water to a boil. Meanwhile, in small saucepan, toast pecans over direct medium-high heat for 2–3 minutes, shaking pan constantly; cool.

- Brush chicken with olive oil and sprinkle with salt and pepper. Grill over medium direct heat for 4–5 minutes per side. Remove, set aside.

- In large bowl, mix mayonnaise, yogurt, and juice. Cube chicken and add.

- Cook pasta until al dente and stir into dressing along with cooled pecans, cranberries, celery, and grapes. Chill for 4–5 hours.

Orange Chicken Pasta Salad

Cut 3 leftover grilled chicken breasts into 1-inch pieces. Place in bowl; drizzle with ¼ cup orange juice; toss. In small bowl, combine ½ cup each mayonnaise, yogurt, and thawed frozen concentrated orange juice; salt and pepper; and 1 tablespoon fresh thyme. Add 15-ounce can drained mandarin oranges, 1 cup celery, ⅓ cup green onions, 1 (12-ounce) package cooked farfalle, and chicken.

Ginger Sesame Chicken Salad

Cut 6 grilled chicken thighs into 1-inch pieces. Drizzle with 1 tablespoon sesame oil; toss. Combine ⅓ cup each low-sodium soy sauce, apple cider vinegar, and oil. Add 2 tablespoons each minced ginger root, chili sauce, and honey. Cook 12 ounces pasta and add along with chicken, ⅓ cup green onion, parsley, 1 cup pea pods, and 1 cup sliced mushrooms.

Cook Pasta on Grill

- Be sure the water is at a hard boil before you add the pasta. Salt the water before adding the pasta.

- When you add the pasta to the water, stir so it doesn't settle to the bottom. Stir the pasta every minute while it's cooking.

- Any pasta that is comparable in shape to farfalle can be used; think about penne, mostaccioli, or medium shells.

- Taste the pasta to test for doneness. It should still have a bit of resistance.

Toss Salad

- Add pasta to these salads while it's still hot so it can absorb the dressing and its flavors.

- If you rinse the pasta with cold water after cooking, it will stop the cooking process but the pasta won't absorb dressing and will taste flat.

- You can serve these salads immediately, or chill them in the fridge for a few hours.

- You will need to stir the salad before serving, as it will solidify as it cools.

GRILLED CHICKEN RECIPES

CHICKEN PIZZA

Grilled pizzas are so fun to make, and chicken adds a light touch to this classic

Once you've learned how to make pizza on a grill, it's hard to go back to pizza cooked in the oven, or even pizza delivery! The grill is like a big brick oven, and the chewy, crisp and smoky crust that it produces is just sublime.

Chicken on pizza isn't traditional, but it is delicious. The chicken must be fully cooked before it's added to the piz-

za, since grilling just cooks the crust and melts the cheese toppings.

It's important to rotate the pizza after the crust has set, so it cooks evenly and doesn't burn on the bottom.

For entertaining, it's easy to have a pizza party on the grill. Use grill charms to mark each pizza. *Yield: 4 servings*

Ingredients

1 (3-ounce) package cream cheese, softened

½ cup ranch dressing

⅛ teaspoon cayenne pepper

1 (4-ounce) can green chiles, drained

2 cups shredded grilled chicken

1 recipe Pizza Crust (see page 95)

2 tablespoons olive oil

1 cup black beans, drained and rinsed

3 plum tomatoes, chopped

½ cup chopped red onion

1 cup shredded Pepper Jack cheese

1 cup shredded sharp cheddar cheese

Southwest Chicken Ranch Pizza

- Beat cream cheese with dressing, pepper, and green chiles. Stir in chicken.

- Roll out dough to ¼-inch thickness. Brush top with olive oil and flip over onto pizza peel; brush with olive oil.

- Flip dough onto grill; grill

for 2–3 minutes until bottom is crisp; rotate over direct and indirect heat when the dough firms. Remove and flip onto cookie sheet.

- Add chicken mixture, black beans, tomatoes, onion, and cheeses. Return to grill, cover, and grill for 5–7 minutes until done, rotating pizza.

Pizza stones are made of the material used to line blast furnaces, so they can tolerate temperatures of 700 degrees F. Place the stone over indirect heat and heat on a closed grill for 1 hour before adding the dough. Once the dough releases from the stone, use your long-handled tongs to rotate the dough so it cooks evenly.

• • • • RECIPE VARIATION • • • •

Buffalo Chicken Pizza: Prepare pizza crust, and slice 3 grilled chicken breasts. For sauce, combine 1 cup ranch salad dressing, ½ cup blue cheese, and 2 table-spoons hot sauce. Sprinkle 1 cup mozzarella and ¼ cup Parmesan cheese on crust and top with sauce, then chicken. Sprinkle with 1 cup chopped celery and 1 cup shredded Swiss cheese. Grill as directed.

Roll out Crust

- Rub the rolling pin with flour for easier handling. For more texture, roll the dough out on a surface sprinkled with cornmeal.

- Roll the pizza evenly. Any thin spots may break on the grill when toppings are added.

- Roll the crust ahead of time and keep it in the fridge so all you have to do is add the toppings and grill.

- You could make the pizza with French bread, pita bread, or focaccia. Adjust grilling times for each base.

Technique Focus 2

- Then add the toppings and return to the grill. Be sure to move the pizza around and rotate it for even grilling.

- For a pizza party, divide each batch of dough into 8 pieces and roll out to 7-inch circles.

- If you use grill charms to mark the pizzas, make sure your guests remove them before they eat.

- If you use a precooked crust, like focaccia or a Boboli™ crust, you don't need to grill it before you add the toppings.

CHICKEN WITH PASTA

The only thing that could make pasta with chicken better is to add the flavor of the grill

Pasta with sauce is one of the fastest and easiest dinner recipes. Add grilled chicken and vegetables to that mix and you have a meal worthy of company.

Red sauces are the most common type of sauce served with pasta, but pesto, cheese, and cream sauces are also delicious. Combine pasta cooked on the grill with grilled chicken and grilled vegetables in a bottled sauce for an easy update on spaghetti and meatballs.

When cooking pasta that you are going to add to a sauce, undercook it slightly. Then add to the sauce with the rest of the ingredients and cook for a few minutes. The pasta will finish cooking and absorb the flavors of the sauce. *Yield: 4 servings*

Ingredients

3 boneless, skinless chicken breasts

1 tablespoon olive oil

1 tablespoon Cajun seasoning

1 red bell pepper, sliced

1 yellow bell pepper, sliced

1 cup cherry tomatoes

½ cup basil pesto

1 jalapeño pepper, minced

2 green onions, minced

⅔ cup heavy cream

3 cups gemelli pasta

⅓ cup grated Cotija cheese

Cajun Chicken with Gemelli

- Brush chicken with olive oil and sprinkle with seasoning. Grill over direct medium heat for 5–7 minutes, turning once, until done.

- Bring a large pot of water to a boil. Meanwhile, place peppers and cherry tomatoes in grill basket; grill for 3–4 minutes until tender.

- In small bowl combine pesto, jalapeño, green onions, and cream; shred chicken and add to sauce.

- Cook pasta until al dente. Drain and return to pot over indirect heat. Add chicken mixture and vegetables; toss gently. Sprinkle with cheese and serve.

Tex-Mex Chicken with Pasta

Grill chicken breasts as directed, using 1 tablespoon chili powder for Cajun seasoning. Cook 12 ounces of penne pasta. Meanwhile, grill 3 ears of corn, 2 poblano peppers, and 2 red bell peppers. For sauce, combine 1 (26-ounce) jar pasta sauce with 1 cup salsa. Remove corn from cob; chop peppers; combine all ingredients. Sprinkle with Cotija cheese.

Chicken and Pasta in Four-Cheese Sauce

Grill chicken breasts as directed, omitting Cajun seasoning, adding salt and pepper. Cook 12 ounces farfalle pasta. Meanwhile, grill 2 cups sliced mushrooms, and 1 sliced onion. Heat 1 (16-ounce) jar Alfredo sauce, and ¼ cup each Parmesan, mozzarella, provolone, and Havarti cheese. Combine all ingredients along with 1 cup frozen baby peas and heat; sprinkle with Parmesan.

Prepare Chicken

- If you time this recipe correctly, it can be done very quickly and efficiently. Start the water boiling first.

- Then grill the chicken and let it stand while you add the pasta to the boiling water and start grilling the veggies.

- When the pasta is done, drain and return to pot and add remaining ingredients.

- You may want to reserve some pasta cooking water to help thin the sauce. Add it if the sauce seems dry.

Combine all Ingredients

- Cook the pasta until it's just shy of al dente. Take a bite and look at the pasta. You'll see a thin line of uncooked pasta in the center.

- The pasta will finish cooking in the sauce and absorb the pesto flavors.

- You can grill the chicken and vegetables ahead of time. Toss the chicken with the sauce and refrigerate.

- Then cook the pasta and combine all the ingredients. Toss over medium heat or medium coals until hot.

GRILLED CHICKEN RECIPES

CHICKEN TACOS

Grilled chicken, whether freshly grilled or leftover, is a delicious addition to spicy tacos

Tacos are a quick and easy meal that can be flavored so many ways. You can use the standard preformed crisp taco shells, or use corn or flour tortillas for soft tacos.

Chicken tacos are a great way to use up leftover grilled chicken. When you're grilling chicken breasts, no matter how they're flavored, cook a few extra and refrigerate or freeze them. Then when you get a craving for Mexican food, chop or shred the chicken and create tacos.

You can make tacos mild or spicy. Make them with vegetables or fruits, with grilled or fresh vegetables, and with a variety of cheeses. This versatile recipe should be in your regular repertoire. *Yield: 6 servings*

Ingredients

1 (15-ounce) can refried beans

3 cups shredded grilled chicken

2 chipotle peppers in adobo, minced

2 tablespoons adobo sauce

6 crisp taco shells

1 cup sour cream

2 avocados, peeled and chopped

¼ cup chopped cilantro

2 cups cherry tomatoes, chopped

1 tablespoon Lemon juice

1½ cups shredded Colby-Jack cheese

2 cups shredded lettuce

1 cup chunky salsa

Hot and Spicy Chicken Tacos

- In heavy pan on grill, heat refried beans until steaming. Add chicken, chipotle peppers, and adobo sauce; cook and stir until hot.

- Meanwhile, heat taco shells as directed on package. You can also grill them over indirect heat, turning frequently, until crisp.

- In small bowl, combine sour cream, avocados, cilantro, tomatoes, and lemon juice.

- Make tacos by adding chicken mixture and cheese to taco shells. Let guests layer on lettuce, salsa, and sour cream mixture. Serve immediately.

Regularly cleaning the grill is a must. Not only do you have to scrape off the grill rack, but you must keep the area under the coals clean. Charcoal grills have deep grill pans that hold the coals. This burns down to ash, which must be removed. Gas grills have grease traps or trays under the burners. Clean them out regularly.

Soft Chicken Tacos: Chop 4 grilled chicken breasts; sprinkle with ¼ cup lime juice and salt and pepper. Let stand for 10 minutes. Add 15-ounce can drained black beans, 1 chopped red onion, and 1 cup corn. Soften 8 flour tortillas by briefly placing on grill. Spread with 1 cup sour cream and add chicken mixture. Top with Monterey Jack cheese and salsa; roll.

Heat bean mixture on grill

Heat taco shells until crisp

- Refried beans are made of cooked pinto beans that are mashed and usually cooked in lard or other fat.

- You can find vegetarian refried beans in the super-market that are cooked in oil, sometimes with season-ings added.

- It's important to heat the chicken thoroughly in the bean mixture so it absorbs flavors and becomes tender.

- Other cheeses that work well in this recipe include Pepper Jack, Monterey Jack, and provolone.

- It won't take long for the taco shells to become crisp on the grill, so have all the other ingredients ready.

- Watch the shells carefully; they should brown and crisp in just a few seconds on each side.

- Set up a taco bar, with fillings of chicken, ground beef, pork, and shrimp. Offer different cheeses and salsas.

- For soft and crisp tacos, spread the outsides of crisp shells with refried beans and wrap in a softened tortilla.

PORK CHOPS

Pork chops, whether boneless or not, are tender and juicy when quickly grilled

Pork chops have a reputation for being rather tough and dry. Solve that by brining the pork and cooking quickly.

Pork no longer needs to be cooked well done. Cook pork to an internal temperature of 155 degrees F. During standing time, the temperature will rise to 160 degrees F. The pork will be slightly pink inside and will be juicy and tender.

The best chop for grilling is a center-cut pork loin chop that is 1 inch thick. Untreated pork chops can be brined before grilling; read labels to know what you're buying.

Chops can be finished with everything from teriyaki sauce to salsa. Add liquid when they come off the grill to ensure juiciness. *Yield: 6 servings*

Ingredients

¼ cup salt

¼ cup sugar

6 cups water

6 1-inch-thick center cut loin pork chops

2 tablespoons olive oil

⅓ cup salsa

2 tablespoons low-sodium soy sauce

¼ cup apple cider vinegar

2 tablespoons chopped fresh thyme leaves

2 tablespoons chopped flat-leaf parsley

1 tablespoon chopped fresh marjoram leaves

⅛ teaspoon white pepper

Herbed Salsa Pork Chops

- ICombine salt, sugar, and water. Add chops; cover; chill for 10–12 hours.

- Remove chops from brine; rinse well and pat dry. Brush with olive oil. In shallow bowl, combine salsa, soy sauce, vinegar, herbs, and pepper and mix well.

- Grill chops over medium direct heat for 10–12 minutes, turning and brushing with salsa mixture, until meat thermometer registers 155°F.

- Pour remaining marinade into small saucepan; boil for 1 minute and pour over chops. Let stand for 1 minute, then serve.

Brines are weaker marinades used to force moisture into food. Make sure that the food you brine is natural, not enhanced. Enhanced meats are already injected with brine. Don't worry about the health effects of salt in brines. The food doesn't absorb much sodium. The salt concentrations between the brine and flesh must equalize, drawing liquid into the meat.

Brine Chops

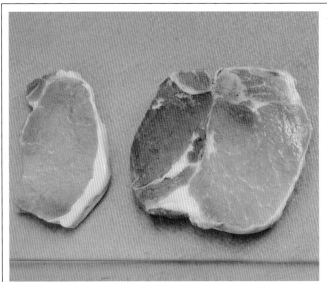

Trim Chops

- Boneless pork chops are the easiest to eat, but bone-in chops can have more flavor.

- There will be a time difference. The bone-in chops will take about 5–8 minutes longer on the grill.

- Any marinade will work well with pork chops. Think about using fruit juices and preserves with some oil, or foods with an Asian twist.

- When brining pork chops, don't go beyond the 12-hour limit in the refrigerator or the chops will become salty and tough.

- If the pork chops have fat around the edge, trim it before cooking to avoid flare-ups.

- Trim the fat to ¼ inch, no less. The remaining fat adds flavor and keeps the meat moist. Discard the trimmed fat.

- If the pork chops in your area aren't 1 inch thick, buy a pork loin and cut 1-inch slices.

- A glaze is always nice, even on marinated chops. Combine fruit preserves with mustard and a bit of oil; brush on in last 5 minutes.

PORK TENDERLOIN

Glazes, rubs, marinades, and sauces change the flavor of this most tender cut of pork

Pork tenderloin, like beef tenderloin, is a more expensive cut of the meat, but there is no bone and no fat, therefore no waste. The meat is tender and flavorful, and it's very easy to grill.

To evenly grill the tenderloin, turn it three times during grilling, moving the tenderloin ¼ turn each time. This will ensure that the meat grills evenly and doesn't overcook.

There are a lot of pre-seasoned marinated tenderloins on the market. Those are very easy to cook; all you have to do is plop them on the grill. Don't add extra flavor to these cuts; it's been injected into the meat.

Use your favorite flavors to create your own special recipes for pork tenderloin. *Yield: 3–4 servings*

Ingredients

2 tablespoons low-sodium soy sauce

2 tablespoons olive oil

2 garlic cloves, minced

2 tablespoons honey

3 tablespoons Dijon mustard

½ teaspoon ground ginger

¼ teaspoon pepper

2 (1-pound) pork tenderloins

Honey Mustard Pork Tenderloin

- Combine soy sauce, oil, garlic, honey, mustard, ginger, and pepper. Add tenderloins; cover and chill for 8–12 hours.

- Drain tenderloins, reserving marinade. Pat tenderloins dry with paper towel.

- Grill tenderloins over direct medium heat for 3 minutes, then turn ¼ turn and cook for 3 minutes longer.

- Move tenderloins over drip pan, turn ¼ turn, and grill, covered, for 7–10 minutes longer, turning and brushing with reserved marinade until temperature registers 150°F.

Even if you're making a direct fire and are grilling only quick-cooking meats and vegetables leave a space in the grill pan where there are no coals. Control flare-ups by moving the food to that area. You can use a water bottle to spritz charcoal to end flare-ups, but never use a water bottle to control flare-ups on a gas grill.

• • • • RECIPE VARIATION • • • •

Asian Pork Tenderloin: In resealable plastic bag, combine ¼ cup each low-sodium soy sauce, red wine vinegar, and chicken broth. Add 1 tablespoon grated ginger root, 3 minced garlic cloves, 1 tablespoon brown sugar, 1 tablespoon oil, and ½ teaspoon five-spice powder. Marinate tenderloin for 8–24 hours. Grill as directed in recipe, brushing with marinade.

Marinate Tenderloin

- Look at the tenderloin carefully before you start cooking. If there's a thin, shiny skin on the meat, remove it.

- That is called silver skin, and it will shrink as it cooks, squeezing juice out of the meat. Pull it off using paper towels.

- Brines or marinades are appropriate for this cut of pork because it's so mild.

- This cut of pork works well in kabobs. Cut into 1½-inch pieces and thread on skewers with pineapple, green pepper, and mushrooms.

Finish the Dish

- When the temperature registers 150°F, remove from the grill, cover, and let rest for 10 minutes.

- For more people, prepare more tenderloins. Each will serve 3 generously.

- Dry rubs work well when the tenderloin has been

brined. If you marinate the pork, boil marinade to serve as a sauce.

- To serve, cut the pork into 1-inch slices. Salsa, red sauce, Alfredo sauce, or a simple mixture of chicken broth and butter finishes off the dish.

STUFFED PORK CHOPS

There are many stuffing recipes that work well in thick cut pork chops

Stuffed pork chops are a delicious choice for any meal. You can stuff chops with everything from Asian flavored rice and vegetables to curried fruit with croutons.

Grilling stuffed pork chops is a bit different from searing and baking them in the oven. Cut a pocket in the chops to hold the filling. If you butterfly the pork, you'll need to tie it together so the filling doesn't fall out when the meat is on the grill.

You can brine the chops before filling and grilling them. Use a basic brine of ¼ cup each salt and sugar to 5 cups water, and refrigerate the chops for 3–4 hours.

Enjoy these stuffed pork chops and have fun creating your own fillings. *Yield: 6 servings*

Ingredients

2 tablespoons butter

1 onion, chopped

2 cloves garlic, minced

1 apple, peeled and chopped

1 cup soft whole-wheat breadcrumbs

⅓ cup raisins

1 teaspoon salt, divided

¼ teaspoon pepper, divided

1 teaspoon dried thyme leaves

2–3 tablespoons chicken broth

6 (1½-inch-thick) loin pork chops

2 tablespoons olive oil

3 tablespoons apple jelly

Apple-Raisin Stuffed Pork Chops

- In small skillet, melt butter. Add onion and garlic; cook over medium heat for 7–8 minutes until soft. Add apple; cook for 3–4 minutes.

- Remove from heat; add breadcrumbs. Stir in raisins, ½ teaspoon salt, ⅛ teaspoon pepper, thyme. Add chicken broth if necessary.

- Cut pocket in pork chops; fill with apple mixture. Brush with olive oil; sprinkle with remaining salt and pepper.

- Grill chops over medium direct heat, brushing with apple jelly and turning once, until meat thermometer registers 155°F.

~ VARIATIONS ~

Pesto Stuffed Pork Chops

For filling, cook 1 chopped onion in 1 tablespoon olive oil. Remove from heat and stir in ½ cup prepared basil pesto, ⅓ cup chopped walnuts, and ¼ cup grated Parmesan cheese. Stuff this mixture into 4 pork chops. Grill over direct medium heat, brushing with chicken broth, until done.

Bacon Cheese Stuffed Pork Chops

For filling, cook 4 slices bacon until crisp; remove and crumble. Drain pan; do not wipe. Add 1 chopped onion, 3 cloves garlic; cook and stir for 5 minutes. Place in bowl with bacon; let cool. Add 1 cup shredded Swiss cheese and ¼ cup grated Parmesan. Stuff 6 pork chops. Brush chops with olive oil and grill until done.

Cut Pocket in Chops

- Work carefully when you're cutting the pocket in the pork chop.

- You want to make as large a pocket as possible, but keep the entry hole smaller.

- It helps to put your hand on top of the chop while you're making the pocket so you can feel where the knife is going.

- Once you've cut 1 side, remove the knife, turn it around, and cut the other side, so the leading edge of the knife is making the cuts.

Stuff Chops

- A small spoon, like an iced-tea spoon or even a baby spoon, works well when stuffing the chops.

- Don't overstuff the chops. The pocket should be full, but not packed. Use a toothpick to hold the entry point closed.

- Use tongs to turn these chops. You may need to place them on indirect heat for a bit.

- Let the chops stand, covered with foil, for 5–6 minutes after cooking so the filling sets up and the juices redistribute.

STUFFED PORK TENDERLOIN

Butterfly pork tenderloin and stuff it with fabulous savory or sweet mixtures for a great recipe

Pork tenderloin is a more tender cut than a pork chop, so when it's stuffed and grilled the filling melts into the meat.

For stuffing, it's best to butterfly the meat and pound it until it's about 1/3–1/2 inch thick. Spread the filling over the meat, then roll up the meat like a jelly roll. Tie the meat closed with 100 percent cotton kitchen twine at 1–2-inch intervals, then grill to perfection.

Because the cooking time is around 1/2 hour, these types of recipes should be grilled over indirect heat. Oil the grill rack, add the meat, cover the grill, and baste the meat occasionally with broth or fruit juices, depending on the stuffing. *Yield: 8 servings*

Ingredients

1/3 cup plus 1 tablespoon lime juice

1/4 cup plus 2 tablespoons olive oil

3 cloves garlic, minced

1 teaspoon salt

1 1/2 teaspoon dried oregano, divided into 1 plus 1/2 teaspoon

1/8 teaspoon white pepper

2 (1-pound) pork tenderloins

1 (3-ounce) package cream cheese

1/4 cup chopped kalamata olives

1/4 cup chopped green olives

1/3 cup crumbled feta cheese

Greek Stuffed Pork Tenderloin

- Combine 1/3 cup lime juice, 1/4 cup olive oil, garlic, salt, 1 teaspoon oregano, and pepper. Add tenderloins; cover; chill for 2–3 hours.

- Drain tenderloins, reserving marinade, and pat dry. Butterfly tenderloins and pound to 1/2 inch thick.

- Mix cream cheese, remaining lime juice, olives, feta, and remaining oregano. Spread over tenderloins.

- Roll up and tie at 2-inch intervals. Brush with leftover olive oil. Grill over medium direct heat; turn and brush with marinade, until temperature registers 155°F.

Herb Mustard Stuffed Pork Tenderloin
For filling, combine ½ cup chopped fresh basil, ½ cup chopped fresh parsley, ¼ cup sliced green onions, ¼ cup ricotta cheese, ¼ cup Dijon mustard, and 2 tablespoons mayonnaise. Butterfly and pound 2 1-pound tenderloins and spread with filling; roll up and tie with 100 percent cotton kitchen twine. Grill on indirect medium heat for 25–35 minutes until 155°F.

Blue Cheese Spinach Stuffed Pork Tenderloin
For filling, combine 1 cup chopped baby spinach, ¾ cup crumbled blue cheese, ¼ cup minced green onion, salt and pepper to taste, and ⅓ cup chopped pecans. Butterfly and pound 2 1-pound pork tenderloins, spread with filling, roll up, and secure. Grill as directed on indirect heat.

Butterfly Pork Tenderloin

Stuff, Roll, and Tie Tenderloin

- To butterfly the tenderloin, use a sharp knife and cut it in half lengthwise to within ½ inch of opposite side.

- Open up the tenderloin like a book. Cover with plastic wrap and pound with a rolling pin until the meat is flat and even.

- Sprinkle with salt and pepper and add the filling. Starting at long end, roll up the meat, enclosing the filling.

- Don't overstuff the tenderloin; the filling should be an even layer about ¼–½ inch thick.

- Roll evenly but firmly. The whole roll should be evenly stuffed and about the same diameter.

- There are several ways to tie the tenderloin. Make individual loops around the meat, tying each off.

- Or use a large single length of 100 percent cotton twine. Tie it at the end, then crisscross down the length of the tenderloin.

- When it's done, let it stand, covered, for 5 minutes. Untie the meat, then slice into 1-inch pieces and place on serving tray.

PORK

GLAZED HAM

Hams take on a wonderfully smoky flavor when grilled

A grilled ham has a wonderful smoky flavor and is a great way to save oven space during the holidays.

The best way to cook a ham on the grill is with a rotisserie. If you don't have one, you'll need to turn the ham regularly as it grills.

Don't use a spiral sliced ham, or one that is already glazed. Glaze the ham yourself so the crust is infused with smoky flavor. A pre-glazed ham will probably burn. If the ham is sliced,

it will dry out.

Grill over low coals so the ham doesn't dry out by the time it is hot. Let the coals die down if you're using a charcoal grill. Set a gas grill to low heat for the juiciest ham ever. *Yield: 8–10 servings*

Ingredients

1 (5–6-pound) half ham

2 cups apple wood chips, soaked

1 cup pineapple juice

2 tablespoons butter

3 tablespoons Dijon mustard

2 tablespoons honey

¼ teaspoon pepper

½ cup brown sugar

Pineapple Glazed Ham Half

- Place ham on grill over indirect low heat. Place soaked wood chips in drip pan. Cover; grill.

- Meanwhile, combine juice, butter, mustard, honey, pepper in small saucepan and bring to a simmer.

- After 10 minutes, turn and brush the ham with juice mixture every 20 minutes. Keep going until the ham registers 150°F in 2 different places, about 1 hour.

- Sprinkle ham with brown sugar. Grill ham; turn frequently and continue sprinkling with sugar, until ham is glazed, 15–20 minutes.

In gas grills, there must be something between the burners and the food; otherwise melting fat and liquid would drip directly on the burners. New grills use ceramic or stainless steel bars. Drippings and food that fall on the bars will usually burn up, but the bars should be cleaned at least once a year with soapy water.

• • • • RECIPE VARIATION • • • •

Honey Glazed Ham: Combine 1 cup honey, 1/3 cup brown sugar, 1/3 cup melted butter, 1/3 cup orange juice, 1/8 teaspoon cardamom, and 1/2 teaspoon pepper in small saucepan; heat until butter melts. Grill ham as directed, using maple chips. During last hour, start brushing with the honey mixture.

Glaze Ham

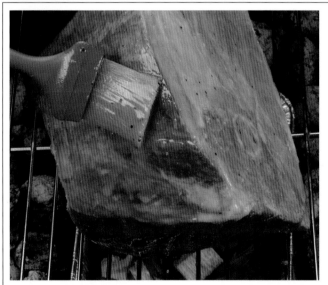

- Make sure that you buy a fully cooked ham that can be served right from the package.

- This time on the grill will not cook a fresh ham to a safe temperature, and fresh ham has a totally different taste.

- Since the ham is already so salty, adding more salt isn't necessary. Add other flavors to complement the ham.

- Flavors of Greece, Tex-Mex, Spain, Asia, Thailand, and France all pair beautifully with ham.

Heat Ham over Indirect Heat

- A whole ham is very large and is more difficult to grill than a half ham.

- Since about 8 ounces of a boneless ham is a good size serving, a 6-pound half ham will feed 10–12 people.

- Think about different flavor combinations for your own glazes. Sweet, hot, tangy, and bitter flavors are good foils for the salty ham.

- Leftover ham is one of the best parts of the holidays. Use your grilled ham in sandwiches, soups, and salads.

ETHNIC PORK

Pork is mild and tender and adapts well to the flavors of any ethnic or regional cuisine

Pork is a mild and naturally tender meat, which takes beautifully to any flavor from any cuisine. Think about recipes and cuisines that you love and use the flavors to create your own recipes.

For Asian pork, combine soy sauce, hoisin sauce, grated ginger root, and a bit of honey for a marinade. Tex-Mex pork chops could be made with brined chops that are glazed with a mix-

ture of taco sauce, olive oil, chili powder, and adobo sauce.

For French pork, combine herbes de Provence with olive oil, chicken broth, and balsamic vinegar. Greek pork would be delicious with a marinade of lemon juice, olive oil, chopped fresh oregano, and salt and pepper. Top the pork with feta cheese as it stands after grilling. *Yield: 6 servings*

Ingredients

2 tablespoons red wine vinegar

2 tablespoons olive oil

3 cloves garlic, minced

1 teaspoon salt

¼ teaspoon white pepper

½ teaspoon dried oregano leaves

6 thin boneless pork chops

3 slices bacon

1 onion, chopped

1 cup chicken stock

1 (8-ounce) can tomato sauce

2 teaspoons chili powder

2 red bell peppers, sliced

1 green bell pepper, sliced

Spanish Style Pork Chops

- Mix vinegar, olive oil, garlic, salt, pepper, and oregano. Add pork chops; cover; chill for 3–4 hours.

- When ready to eat, cook bacon in cast iron skillet on grill until crisp; remove and drain. Add onion; cook until tender, then add chicken stock, tomato sauce, and

chili powder; simmer.

- Place peppers in grill basket. Drain chops, discarding marinade. Grill over direct medium heat until peppers are tender and chops register 150°F.

- Add to skillet on grill; simmer 2–3 minutes to blend flavors.

Greek Pork Chops

Combine ¼ cup salt, ¼ cup sugar, and 6 cups water; add chops; chill for 4 hours in fridge. Combine ⅓ cup lemon juice, 3 tablespoons olive oil, 1 tablespoon fresh oregano, salt, and pepper. Grill chops on direct medium heat for 9–13 minutes, basting with lemon mixture. Boil marinade for 1 minute. Pull chops off grill; pour marinade over, and top with feta cheese.

French Pork Chops

Brine chops as for Greek Pork Chops. Drain, rinse, and pat dry. For mop, combine 1 teaspoon herbes de Provence, ¼ cup balsamic vinegar, ¼ cup olive oil, and salt and pepper. Grill chops, brushing with herb mixture. Boil remaining herb mixture; pour over cooked chops; top with cubed Brie.

Prepare ingredients

- Choose a good quality vinegar and oil for this simple marinade.

- When a recipe uses just a few ingredients, the quality of those ingredients is important. Extra virgin olive oil is necessary.

- You could use other veg-

etables in this easy recipe. Try sliced mushrooms, sliced red onions, zucchini, or summer squash.

- Use more foods from Spain to finish the dish. Sprinkle some chopped Spanish olives and Marcona almonds over the chops just before serving.

Grill chops and veggies

- Finishing the meat and vegetables in a spicy tomato sauce ensures that the meat will be juicy and flavorful.

- The vegetables will take less time on the grill than the chops. So they don't overcook, add them to the sauce with the meat.

- Add any leftover marinade to the tomato sauce as it simmers on the grill for more flavor.

- Serve this one-dish meal over hot cooked rice or couscous. Cook the rice or couscous in chicken broth.

PORK

PORK BABY BACK RIBS

From baby back ribs to spareribs, pork ribs are the classic grilled recipe

Cooking ribs in the slow cooker before finishing on the grill is a great and easy way to get the best result. The sauce caramelizes on the grill to form a rich crust.

There are three kinds of pork ribs: baby back, spareribs, and country style ribs. Baby back ribs are from the loin and have meat covering the bones and in between them.

You can, of course, cook the ribs completely on the grill, but that is a different technique. Precooking the ribs saves time. All you're doing is finishing the ribs on the grill.

Grill the ribs as a whole rack or cut them into individual portions; it's up to you! *Yield: 6 servings*

Ingredients

4 pounds pork baby back ribs

½ cup apple cider

5 cups water

1 onion, sliced

1 tablespoon butter

1 onion, minced

3 cloves garlic, minced

1 cup barbecue sauce

½ cup chili sauce

¼ cup Dijon mustard

¼ cup honey

¼ teaspoon pepper

Baby Back Ribs

- Place ribs in 7-quart slow cooker, cutting if necessary to fit. Add cider, water, and sliced onion.

- Cover and cook on low for 6–7 hours or until meat is tender. Meanwhile, in 1-quart slow cooker, combine remaining ingredients. Cook on low for 6–7 hours until blended.

- Drain ribs and discard liquid. Prepare grill for medium-low heat. Place ribs on grill and brush with sauce.

- Cover grill and cook ribs for 10–12 minutes, brushing frequently with sauce, until browned.

~ VARIATIONS ~

Oven to Grill Ribs

Place ribs in large roasting pan; cover with cider mixture, and bake at 300°F for 2½–3½ hours. Instead of sauce, use a rub on the ribs. Combine 2 tablespoons brown sugar, ½ teaspoon cayenne pepper, 1 teaspoon salt, 1 tablespoon garlic powder, and 1 tablespoon chili powder; rub on ribs. Grill until browned.

Sweet and Sour Ribs

Prepare ribs as in main recipe, cooking in slow cooker. For sauce, combine ½ cup ketchup, ½ cup barbecue sauce, 3 tablespoons lemon juice, 3 tablespoons sugar, and ½ cup chili sauce; simmer for 30–40 minutes until thickened. Use this sauce to glaze the ribs as they finish on the grill.

Slow Cook Ribs

- If the ribs don't fit easily in the slow cooker, think about using 2 of them at the same time.

- For best results, the slow cooker should be filled ⅔–¾ full. Make sure the lid fits securely on the insert.

- If you're at home during the day, turn the ribs around once or twice. If you're away, don't worry about it.

- Stir the sauce a few times. You can make the sauce a day or two ahead of time.

Finish Ribs on Grill

- Slather on the sauce! Not only does it add flavor, but the heat of the grill will caramelize it.

- That deep brown crust has a lot of flavor because the proteins and sugars combine to make new compounds.

- Make sure that you cook off the sauce. After you brush on the sauce, turn that side to the grill.

- Since the ribs are cooked completely before grilling, you can cook ahead of time and refrigerate, then grill until hot; add 5–10 minutes.

BEEF RIBS

Beef ribs are less common, but still very delicious, with tender meat and lots of flavor

These ribs are so tender the beef will fall right off the bone. The beefy flavor is complemented by a rich sauce.

Most beef ribs have a thick membrane that has to be removed before you marinate or grill. And remember that beef ribs have to be cooked slowly, over low indirect heat. Like a roast, low and slow cooking is necessary for the connective tissue to melt.

There are two kinds of beef ribs: back ribs and short ribs. The short ribs are meatier, while back ribs are more tender.

Beef ribs are usually not brined, but flavored with marinades, mops, and pastes. Think about your favorite burger and roast recipes and use those flavors in grilled ribs. *Yield: 6 servings*

Ingredients

4 cloves garlic, minced

1 teaspoon salt

¼ teaspoon pepper

⅓ cup low-sodium soy sauce

½ cup barbecue sauce

2 tablespoons olive oil

¼ cup apple cider vinegar

3 tablespoons adobo sauce

1 tablespoon chili powder

3 pounds individual short ribs, membrane removed

2 cups hickory wood chips

Hot and Spicy Short Ribs

- Mash together garlic and salt until a paste forms; place in large bowl. Add remaining ingredients except ribs and chips.

- Add the ribs and turn to coat with sauce. Cover and chill for 4–5 hours.

- Prepare grill for indirect medium heat. Remove ribs from marinade; reserve marinade. Place ribs on direct heat; brown for 6–7 minutes, turning once.

- Place wood chips in drip pan. Grill ribs, covered, over indirect heat for 90–130 minutes, brushing occasionally with sauce, until very tender.

Coat Ribs with Sauce

- Buy at least 1 pound of ribs per serving to allow for the bone and for shrinkage.

- Adobo sauce is a spicy hot sauce that's usually used to can smoked jalapeño peppers. You could substitute chili sauce.

- Make sure that the ribs are completely covered with the sauce so it flavors every bite.

- You can put some liquid in the drip pan with the wood chips if you'd like; just a bit so they smoke instead of burning.

Grill Ribs

- Watch the ribs when they're browning over direct heat. You want nice color, but don't let them burn.

- Keep the grill closed as much as possible, so the ribs cook evenly and absorb the flavor of the wood smoke.

- Turn the ribs 3–4 times during grilling. Use tongs and a spatula to keep them together as they turn.

- Let the ribs stand, covered, for 5–10 minutes after cooking to let the glaze cool a bit.

RACK OF LAMB
Lamb is a delicate meat, but must be prepared with certain ingredients for best results

Lamb ribs are more commonly known as rack of lamb or lamb rib roast. Eight ribs serve 2–3 people, so for 6 servings buy 16–24 ribs. Have the butcher crack the chine so the ribs are easy to separate after they have been grilled.

Also ask the butcher to French the ribs. This entails removing gristle and fat from the bones. You may need to finish the job and clean the bones with a sharp knife.

This meat is so tender and flavorful it can be grilled with just a coating of olive oil and some salt and pepper. Or use your imagination and incorporate classic lamb ingredients like mustard, mint, and garlic. *Yield: 6 servings*

Ingredients

3½ pounds lamb ribs, Frenched

3 tablespoons olive oil

1 onion, minced

3 cloves garlic, minced

⅓ cup lemon juice

2 tablespoons brown sugar

1 teaspoon salt

¼ teaspoon white pepper

1 teaspoon lemon rind

2 tablespoons finely chopped mint

2 tablespoons chopped flat-leaf parsley

1 tablespoon fresh thyme leaves

Lemon Herbed Lamb Ribs

- Place ribs in large casserole. Combine remaining ingredients in small bowl; pour over lamb.

- Cover lamb; refrigerate for 8–12 hours. Remove from marinade, reserving marinade.

- Prepare grill for indirect heat.

Rub grate with oil, and add lamb ribs, meat side down, over medium indirect heat.

- Grill for 7 minutes, then turn and brush with remaining marinade. Cover; grill for 6 minutes longer. Finish by searing lamb over direct heat for 3 minutes on each side. Let stand 10 minutes.

You can use a roast or rib rack for grill roasting to take the meat away from the heat a bit and make your grill more like an oven. This will also reduce flare-ups, since the fat will drip into the drip pan, and any flame won't reach the meat. You can also use those drippings, if they aren't burned, to make pan gravy after the roast is done.

• • • • RECIPE VARIATION • • • •

Mustard Crumb Lamb Ribs: French 3 racks of lamb, brush with olive oil, and sprinkle with salt and pepper to taste. Brown over medium-high direct heat on first side, about 3 minutes. Turn, then slather with Dijon mustard and press 1 cup soft breadcrumbs mixed with 2 tablespoons chopped fresh rosemary into the ribs. Grill for 6–12 minutes longer, then serve.

Marinate Ribs

- As with most ribs, there may be a membrane covering the meat that must be removed.

- The membrane will prevent flavor and smoke from penetrating the meat. Pull it off with a paper towel.

- Buy a rack of lamb that is firm, with smooth, creamy fat. There shouldn't be too much fat on the ribs, and the meat should be firmly attached to the bone.

- Lamb should be cooked medium rare to medium. The final temperature is 135 to 150°F.

Grill Ribs

- A single rack of lamb is the perfect amount for serving 2 people. For serving more people, buy more racks.

- Because the ribs cook quickly, you can add the sauce or marinade as soon as the first side is browned.

- Think about serving a sauce with these grilled ribs. A purchased mint sauce can be dressed up with fresh mint.

- For plain grilled ribs, combine mustard with honey and garlic and simmer to make a flavorful dipping sauce.

ALL-GRILL BBQ RIBS

Ribs are fabulous slow-cooked on the grill; this is real barbecue

Baby back ribs are smaller and meatier than spareribs, and they usually have less fat. They are easier to handle and eat.

Baby back pork ribs, which are used for this recipe, usually have a membrane covering the meat. For best results, this should be removed before the meat is marinated or grilled. Have the butcher do it, or you can do it yourself. Grab the membrane with a paper towel and pull it off, then discard. Rub or marinate the ribs and you're ready to cook.

Ribs cooked on the bone have a special sweet taste and tender texture. They're definitely finger food. Be sure to offer lots of wet wipes and napkins. *Yield: 6 servings*

Ingredients

3 (2-pound) racks baby back pork ribs

2 teaspoons salt

1 teaspoon pepper

6 cloves garlic, minced

⅓ cup brown sugar

2 teaspoons grated lemon rind

2 tablespoons lemon juice

1½ cups favorite barbecue sauce

All-Grill BBQ Ribs

- Remove membrane from ribs. In small bowl, combine salt, pepper, garlic, sugar, and lemon rind.

- Rub ribs all over with lemon juice, then sprinkle with salt mixture. Rub in well; let stand for 30 minutes.

- Prepare grill for indirect medium-low heat. Place soaked mesquite chips in drip pan. Grill ribs, turning occasionally, until the meat is tender, about 2–3 hours.

- Brush with barbecue sauce during last 30 minutes of grilling. Let stand for 10 minutes, then serve.

~ VARIATIONS ~

Tex-Mex Spareribs

Combine ⅓ cup brown sugar, 1 tablespoon chili powder, 1 teaspoon ground cumin, 1 teaspoon pepper, 1 teaspoon paprika, 2 teaspoons seasoned salt, and ½ teaspoon cayenne pepper; rub into 4 pounds spareribs. Marinate in fridge for 4 hours. Grill over indirect heat, covered, with hickory chips in drip pan for 3–4 hours, brushing with ½ cup jarred salsa during last half hour.

Garlic Onion Spareribs

Cook 1 chopped onion and 3 cloves garlic in 2 tablespoons olive oil. Add ½ cup chili sauce, ½ cup barbecue sauce, and ¼ cup lemon juice. Marinate ribs for 4 hours in fridge. Grill over indirect heat, with apple chips in drip pan, for 3–4 hours, brushing with reserved marinade during last half hour.

Place Ribs on Grill

- For this long cooking time, you'll need to add more lump charcoal or briquettes to a charcoal grill. Keep the temperature constant for a gas grill.

- Every hour, heat 15–20 briquettes in a chimney starter and add to grill. Keep the temperature constant.

- You can jazz up purchased barbecue sauce with a few tablespoons of your favorite ingredients.

- Grilled chopped onion, minced jalapeño pepper, some strong mustard, or roasted garlic are good choices.

Finish Ribs with Sauce

- The final temperature of ribs isn't as critical as with chicken or beef; look for visual cues.

- The ribs will begin to expose on the ends when the meat is done as the meat pulls away from the bone.

- Also, the ribs are done when the meat pulls easily away from the bone.

- The meat will still be pink in the center. A line of dark pink right under the crust is desirable, a mark of perfectly slow-grilled meat.

COUNTRY STYLE RIBS

For an easy dinner after work, cook ribs in your slow cooker or microwave, and finish them on the grill

Country style pork ribs are not really ribs at all, but are pork chops sold in a rack. They are thicker and fattier than spareribs or baby back ribs, and have much more meat. They're cut from the shoulder.

Because there's more meat, you need only about ½ pound per person for a generous serving. These ribs aren't necessar-

ily finger foods, so you may want to offer a knife and fork.

You can also bake the ribs in the oven before finishing on the grill. Bake the ribs, marinated or not, at 325 degrees F for about 2 hours, then finish on the grill with your favorite barbecue sauce or mop. *Yield: 6 servings*

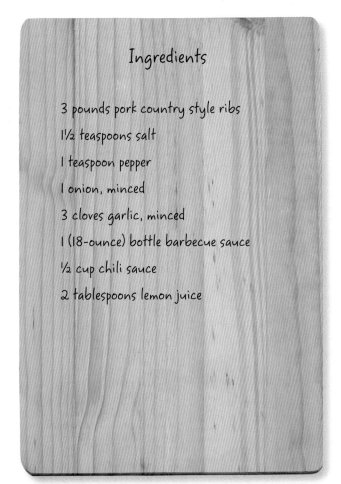

Ingredients

3 pounds pork country style ribs

1½ teaspoons salt

1 teaspoon pepper

1 onion, minced

3 cloves garlic, minced

1 (18-ounce) bottle barbecue sauce

½ cup chili sauce

2 tablespoons lemon juice

Slow Cooker-to-Grill Country Ribs

- Sprinkle ribs with salt and pepper. Place ribs, cut to fit if necessary, in large oval slow cooker.

- Combine onion, garlic, and barbecue sauce in bowl and pour over ribs. Cover and cook on low for 6–7 hours or until ribs are almost tender.

- Drain ribs and place over direct medium heat. For sauce, scoop out ½ cup of the liquid from the slow cooker and add chili sauce and lemon juice.

- Cook ribs, turning frequently and basting with sauce, for 20–30 minutes until glazed, brown, and tender.

MAKE IT EASY

Lots of preparation can be done in advance of cooking time. Mix marinades, rubs, sauces, and pastes and store them in the refrigerator. Cook barbecue and pasta sauces in the slow cooker so they're ready when you are. Prepare desserts and salads ahead of time, so all you have to do is pull them out of the freezer or refrigerator.

• • • • RECIPE VARIATION • • • •

Microwave-to-Grill Ribs: Place ribs on microwave-safe dish at least 2 inches deep. Microwave on medium for 7–9 minutes until edges begin to cook. For glaze, combine ½ cup mustard, ⅓ cup pineapple juice, 3 cloves minced garlic, 2 tablespoons low-sodium soy sauce, and 1 tablespoon grated ginger root. Grill ribs for 20–30 minutes, brushing with sauce, until browned.

Cook Ribs in Crockpot

- If the ribs are fatty, trim off some of the visible fat. You could brown the ribs in a skillet for a few minutes.

- You may need to drain some of the fat ¾ of the way through the cooking time.

- The ribs will be fully cooked after the slow cooker, so you can make them ahead of time and refrigerate.

- Just add 5–10 minutes to their time on the grill to let the refrigerated ribs warm up. Start them over direct heat.

Finish Ribs on Grill

- Use your favorite barbecue sauce or make your own. There are so many varieties on the market.

- Check with a site like Amazon.com, Consumer Reports.org or Epinions .com for reviews on bottled sauces.

- Use your silicone brush to apply the sauce for easiest cleanup. Or you could make a "brush" by tying together some herbs.

- This herb brush can only be used once. But you can finely chop the herbs and add them to the sauce at the end.

ETHNIC RIBS

Ribs can be flavored in so many ways, with ethnic rubs and sauces

Flavoring ribs with foods, spices, and sauces from other cuisines is a great way to expand your grilling repertoire.

There are some classic ethnic rib recipes, including Korean short ribs, German ribs prepared with sauerkraut, and Thai ribs with a peanut sauce.

Both beef ribs and all kinds of pork ribs can be prepared with these seasonings and marinades. You can have a rib party, offering different types of beef and pork ribs cooked with different flavors.

Ethnic cheeses are a great way to add flavor at the end of a recipe. Sprinkle Greek feta or Spanish Manchego cheese, Italian Romano cheese, or even French Brie cheese on ribs after they finish cooking; let the cheeses melt into the meat.
Yield: 6 servings

Ingredients

3 pounds beef short ribs

3 tablespoons lemon juice

1 tablespoon olive oil

4 cloves garlic, minced

2 teaspoons salt

1 teaspoon grated lemon zest

2 teaspoons dried oregano leaves

2 teaspoons dried basil leaves

½ teaspoon garlic pepper

2 cups soaked mesquite chips

⅓ cup crumbled feta cheese

2 tablespoons minced kalamata olives

Greek Short Ribs

- Rub ribs with lemon juice and drizzle with olive oil. Mash garlic with salt until a paste forms; add remaining ingredients except chips, cheese and olives.

- Rub mixture into ribs. Refrigerate for 4–5 hours. Then let stand at room temperature for 30 minutes.

- Place soaked wood chips in drip pan. Brown ribs over direct heat for 6–7 minutes, turning once.

- Grill ribs, covered, over indirect heat for 90–130 minutes, until tender. Remove, sprinkle with cheese and olives, serve.

Korean Short Ribs
In large casserole, combine 1 onion, minced, 4 cloves garlic, ¼ cup low-sodium soy sauce, 2 tablespoons grated ginger root, 2 tablespoons brown sugar, 2 teaspoons sesame oil, and 1 cup beef broth. Add 3 pounds beef short ribs and marinate for 12–24 hours. Sear for 6 minutes, then cook for 100–120 minutes over indirect heat, brushing with reserved marinade.

Thai Pork Spareribs
In bowl, combine 1 minced onion, 1 cup chicken broth, 1 teaspoon ground cumin, 1 teaspoon coriander seed, 2 tablespoons adobo sauce, ¼ cup peanut butter, ⅓ cup ground peanuts, and ¼ teaspoon cayenne pepper. Marinate pork baby back ribs for 24 hours, then grill as in All-Grill BBQ Ribs.

Rub Ribs with Herb Mixture

- You could use fresh herbs rather than dried. Use 3 times the amount of fresh herbs.

- The ribs can be marinated longer than 5 hours, but don't marinate them longer than 12 hours.

- If you wanted to brush these ribs with a sauce when they're on the grill, combine 2 cups beef broth with ¼ cup lemon juice and oregano.

- When the ribs are almost done, boil the sauce for 2 minutes to serve as a dipping sauce.

Sprinkle w/Cheese & Olives

- Wood chips, vines, herbs, and spices added to the drip pan accent these foreign flavors.

- You could also use Spanish Manchego cheese instead of the feta cheese as the rib topping.

- Kalamata olives come from Greece. They have a deep burgundy color and a rich, fruity flavor.

- Serve these ribs with a cooling sauce of Greek yogurt, grated cucumber, and lemon juice.

FISH FILLETS

Delicate fish fillets can be delicious grilled with these easy tips

Fish fillets are boneless and delicate. You can buy everything from salmon fillets to trout or walleye. It's difficult to grill this tender meat directly on the grill. Making a bed of lemons, onions, or herbs not only adds flavor, but prevents sticking. Or you can use cedar planks or cedar paper.

A grill mat or just a layer of heavy duty foil, pierced to allow some smoke through, is a good way to cook the fillets.

Because fish fillets cook so quickly, make them the last item on your menu that you prepare. Have everything else ready and waiting for the fish.

Choose 4–6-ounce fillets; no smaller, or they'll overcook even in the brief grilling time. *Yield: 6 servings*

Ingredients

1 (18-inch x 8-inch) cedar plank

6 (6-ounce) trout fillets

3 tablespoons lemon juice

3 tablespoons orange juice

2 tablespoons olive oil

1 teaspoon grated orange rind

¼ teaspoon white pepper

Planked Citrus Trout

- Be sure you have an untreated cedar plank approved for food contact. Soak it overnight in water.

- Place fish in casserole dish. Combine remaining ingredients and pour over fish; let stand while plank heats.

- Prepare the grill for high direct heat. Place the plank on the grill and cover; heat until plank starts to smoke.

- Drain fish, discarding marinade. Turn plank over and add fish fillets, skin side down. Close grill and cook for 7–9 minutes or until fillets flake when tested with fork.

192

Heat Plank on Grill

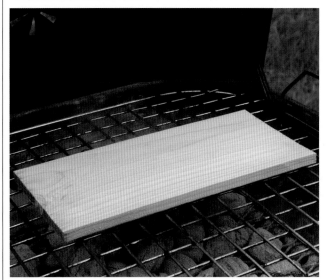

Grill Fish Fillets

- Fish fillets with the skin attached are ideal for cooking on planks, because the skin shields the fish from the burned plank.

- Some recipes using planks call for turning the plank after it has started to smoke so the burned side is against the food.

- Other recipes call for just heating the plank and placing the food on the unburned side.

- The choice is yours; turning the plank will give the food a smokier flavor. If you do turn the plank, place the fish skin side down and don't turn it.

- You can serve the fish right on the plank for a wonderful presentation. There's something primal about this method of serving.

- You can use one large plank, or several small ones for individual servings. Use those grill charms to mark personal preferences.

- After grilling, brush the burned part of the wood away and use sandpaper to get down to the bare wood.

- Then the planks can be reused, after soaking. They must be soaked each time they are used.

WHOLE FISH

Grilled whole fish makes a spectacular presentation, perfect for entertaining

If you have a fisherman in the family, or just want a wow entree, grilling a whole fish can be quite an event.

Unless you're an experienced fisherman or chef, it's best to ask your fishmonger to scale and gut the fish. Once that is done, season the fish the way you like it and grill it to smoky perfection.

To serve the fish, all you need is a spatula. The flesh will come right off the bone, so just slide the spatula between the fish and the ribs and lift it away from the bones.

You can grill a whole fish plain, just rubbed with olive oil, salt, and pepper, or stuff it with lemon, onion slices, or fresh herbs. *Yield: 6 servings*

Ingredients

1 (3-pound) whole walleye or sea bass

¼ cup olive oil

2 teaspoons salt

4 sprigs fresh thyme

1 sprig fresh rosemary

1 fresh lemon

Garlic Herb Grilled Whole Fish

- Rinse the fish and pat dry. Using a sharp knife, slash the fish on both sides about every 3 inches.

- Drizzle the fish with oil, both inside and out. Then sprinkle liberally with salt. Place the herbs inside the fish and tie it closed with kitchen string.

- Clean the grill and rub generously with oil. Place the fish on the grill over direct medium heat.

- Grill for 10 minutes, then carefully flip the fish using a large fish spatula. Grill on second side for 10–12 minutes until flaky. Squeeze lemon over and serve.

Rosemary Orange Trout

Prepare a whole trout. Brush with olive oil and sprinkle with salt and pepper. Slice 1 orange and 1 onion and place in the trout cavity wth fresh rosemary sprigs. Tie with kitchen string. Grill the trout over direct medium heat for 14–20 minutes, turning once, until the fish is done. Serve with orange wedges.

Grilled Orange Roughy

Prepare the fish and sprinkle generously with salt and pepper. Brush the outsides with olive oil. Chop 1 onion and 3 cloves garlic and place inside cavity along with a bunch of fresh basil leaves. Tie the fish closed with kitchen string, then grill over direct medium heat for 14–18 minutes until done.

Stuff Fish with Herbs

Grill Fish

- If you don't have a fish basket, you can sandwich the fish between 2 cooling racks. Tie with twine and use gloves to flip it.

- Use 100 percent cotton twine to tie the fish closed. Don't tie too tightly; the fish will expand when heated.

- If you'd like to serve a sauce with the fish, make a variation of tartar sauce flavored with the herbs you're using.

- Combine 1 cup sour cream, ½ cup mayonnaise, ¼ cup lemon juice, and chopped fresh thyme and rosemary.

- Delicate whole fish need to be cooked in a grill basket that is shaped like a whole fish. These baskets usually hold fish up to 2½ pounds.

- Meatier fish like trout, salmon, bass, or walleye can be cooked directly on the grill.

- Place the tail away from the heat as it will cook quickly. Build a two-layer fire and place the fish between the layers.

- When you flip the fish, turn it onto an unused portion of the grill.

SHRIMP AND SCALLOPS
The smoky flavor of grilled shrimp and scallops is delicious

Shrimp and scallops are such a treat. Cooking them on the grill adds a layer of smokiness and sweetness you can't get with any other cooking method.

This type of seafood cooks very quickly, especially on the grill. You have to watch these foods carefully. Don't move away from the grill, because they can go from perfectly grilled to charred in a matter of seconds.

There are two types of scallops: bay and sea. Bay scallops

are smaller and sweeter and harder to find. They need no preparation.

Shrimp are available in many sizes; the larger the better when it comes to grilling. Shell the shrimp before adding rubs and grilling to let the smoke flavor permeate. *Yield: 8 servings*

Ingredients

¼ cup olive oil

4 cloves garlic, minced

¼ cup minced red onion

1 (14-ounce) can diced tomatoes, drained

⅓ cup seafood cocktail sauce

2 tablespoons lemon juice

2 teaspoons chopped fresh oregano leaves

⅛ teaspoon pepper

⅛ teaspoon cayenne pepper

3 pounds peeled large shrimp

Marinated Grilled Shrimp

- Cook garlic, onion in olive oil until tender, 4 minutes.

- Pour into food processor; cool for 15 minutes. Add drained tomatoes, sauce, lemon juice, oregano, peppers; blend.

- Pour into large bowl; add shrimp. Cover; chill for 1

hour. Drain shrimp, reserving marinade. Double-skewer shrimp, pushing them close together.

- Grill shrimp over direct medium heat, brushing with marinade, for 5–6 minutes, turning once, until shrimp curl and turn pink. Boil marinade to serve with shrimp.

Prepare Sauce

- The sauce is cooled before it's processed because the hot ingredients will expand in the processor.

- This could force the material out of the food processor, possibly burning you.

- You can make the marinade ahead of time. It should be lukewarm or cooler before adding the shrimp.

- The shrimp only marinate for 1 hour. Any longer, and they will become tough. Scallops follow the same rule. Grill the shrimp or scallops right after marinating.

Skewer Shrimp

- The shrimp are pushed together so they form a larger mass, which helps protect them from the grill's intense heat.

- Add scallops to this recipe; marinate them for the same amount of time, and grill at the same time.

- You can add tender vegetables like cherry tomatoes or peppers to the skewers if you'd like. Pick vegetables that cook in the same amount of time.

- Serve this shrimp with some cocktail sauce jazzed up with red or green salsa.

SHELLFISH

Mussels, clams, and oysters are easily grilled with these delicious recipes

Shellfish is for a party! And shellfish cooked on the grill is very special. These mollusks have unique preparation methods.

Any shellfish has to be cooked while alive. All the shells should be tightly closed. Tap those that are open; if they don't close, discard them. Then after they are cooked, they must all be open; discard any that are still closed after cooking.

To prepare mussels, pull off the beards, which are the small wiry hairs that stick out from the shells. Use needlenose pliers to pull them off, and scrub under cold running water.

Scrub clams and oysters before cooking; you can soak them in salt water for a bit, which helps remove sand. *Yield: 4 servings*

Ingredients

½ cup butter

7 cloves garlic, minced

¼ cup lemon juice

1 cup grated Parmesan cheese

2 tablespoons chopped fresh thyme leaves

⅓ cup chopped flat-leaf parsley

4 pounds mussels

Grilled Cheese and Herb Mussels

- In small saucepan, melt butter with garlic over low heat. Let simmer until garlic is fragrant, about 4 minutes.

- Remove from heat and stir in lemon juice; set aside. Combine cheese, thyme, and parsley and place in several small bowls. Clean mussels and remove beards.

- Arrange mussels directly on the grate over direct high heat, or place on a grill mat. Cover the grill and cook until the shells open, about 3–5 minutes.

- Serve immediately with the butter sauce: Dip the mussels into sauce, then into the cheese herb mixture.

RECIPE VARIATION

Southwest Grilled Clams: Scrub clams clean and remove open or cracked clams; place on ice. Preheat grill to medium. In small skillet, cook 1 minced onion and 3 cloves garlic in ¼ cup butter. Add 1 tablespoon chili powder, ⅓ cup cilantro, and 1 cup salsa. Place clams on the grill, cover, and grill for 3–5 minutes until shells open. Serve with the onion sauce.

Prepare Mussels

- The shells should be smooth and hard, with no chips or cracks. Broken shells and open shells must be discarded immediately.

- The beards are small hairs called byssal threads, which help keep the mussels anchored to stones where they live.

- Pull toward the hinge end of the shell so you don't kill the mussel. Don't remove beards until you're ready to grill.

- Keep the shellfish cold until you're ready to cook them. Store them on ice or in ice water.

Grill Mussels

- It's very easy to grill bivalves like oysters, clams, and mussels; they just go directly on the grill.

- Place the mussels in a single layer on the grill. Just pour them on from the bowl and arrange with tongs.

- There's really no way to season the shellfish before they are grilled, so use flavorful sauces and dips.

- Enjoy the sweet, briny flavor of these shellfish, with the added tinge of smoky sweetness from the grill.

FISH PACKETS

For a one-dish dinner on the grill, these foil packets are a good way to feed a crowd

One-dish dinners are created by making packets of meat, vegetables, or fruits that are folded into an envelope and grilled. Sauces and cheeses can be added for flavor.

There are as many variations of these packets as there are fish! Think about complementary flavors when you compose your own packets. Be sure to choose ingredients that cook in about the same time, or precook harder vegetables like potatoes and carrots.

Packets are ideal for entertaining, too. You can prepare them ahead of time, or set up a packet buffet and let your guests assemble their own masterpieces. Those grill charms, again, will come in handy to identify packets. *Yield: 6 servings*

Ingredients

1½ pounds cod fillets

1 teaspoon salt

¼ teaspoon white pepper

1 teaspoon ground cumin

1 teaspoon smoked paprika

½ teaspoon cayenne pepper

1 red onion, sliced

1 summer squash, sliced

2 green bell peppers, sliced

¼ cup butter

2 tablespoons lime juice

Spiced Cod and Vegetable Packets

- Cut cod into 6 serving portions and pat dry. In small bowl, combine salt, white pepper, cumin, paprika, and cayenne pepper.

- Sprinkle spice mixture over both sides of fish and gently rub in.

- Tear off 6 18-inch x 12-inch sheets of heavy duty foil. Place onion in center, then top with fish. Add squash and bell pepper strips.

- Combine butter and lime juice and drizzle over all. Wrap up packets, then grill over direct medium heat for 15–20 minutes until fish flakes.

French Fish Packets

Use 1½ pounds orange roughy, cut into 6 serving pieces. Sprinkle with salt, pepper, dried basil, and herbes de Provence to taste. Top with 2 cups frozen baby peas, 1 minced red onion, and 2 cups sugar snap peas. Drizzle with ½ cup red wine vinaigrette and sprinkle with cubed Brie. Close packets, and grill as directed.

Honey Mustard Fish Packets

Use 1½ pounds trout fillets cut into 6 portions. Sprinkle with salt, pepper, and dried thyme leaves. Top with 1 pint cherry tomatoes, ½ cup chopped green onion, and 2 cups frozen hash brown potatoes. For sauce, combine ½ cup honey mustard dressing, ½ cup plain yogurt, and 2 tablespoons lemon juice. Spoon over food, close packets, and grill.

Layer Vegetables on Foil

- Heavy duty foil is necessary for these packets. If you don't have it, you can use doubled or tripled plain foil.

- Be sure that you season the fish well before you add the remaining ingredients.

- A sauce isn't necessary, but can add great flavor. Serve the packets with cooked hot rice or pasta.

- A double fold is made by folding the sides together once, then folding again. Do the long side first, then the two short sides.

Grill Packets

- Move the packets around on the grill so they cook evenly. Don't turn them upside down, however, or the sauce and juices may leak out.

- Use large spatulas to remove the packets from the grill to a serving platter.

- The foil won't hold heat as long as a metal dish would, but there's lots of steam in the packets.

- You can eat right from the packets, or remove the food from the foil to a serving platter.

ETHNIC FISH

Mild fish adapts very well to the flavors of any ethnic cuisine

As with the other ethnic recipes, fish takes very well to exotic flavors and ingredients. The only criteria is the type of fish you use.

Fatty, oily fish like salmon, tuna, and mackerel can take stronger flavors than the milder fish such as orange roughy, cod, and flounder. Stronger flavors include Tex-Mex seasonings, heavy spices like cumin and chili powder, teriyaki or hoisin sauce, and herbs such as rosemary and oregano.

The milder fish pair well with more delicate flavors like thyme, basil, lemon, nutmeg, chives, and vinegars.

Fruits and vegetables can be used with both; just think of your favorite recipes and flavor combinations and have fun.
Yield: 6 servings

Ingredients

⅔ cup crème fraîche

1 red bell pepper, diced

2½ teaspoon dried herbes de Provence

6 (6-ounce) salmon fillets

½ cup grainy Dijon mustard

3 tablespoons lemon juice

1 soaked cedar or maple plank

2 teaspoons salt

French Planked Salmon

- Mix crème fraîche, bell pepper, and ½ teaspoon herbes de Provence; refrigerate.

- In small bowl, combine mustard and lemon juice; spread over salmon and let stand at room temperature for 20 minutes.

- Prepare grill for direct medium-high heat. Place plank on grill, close cover, and grill for 10–12 minutes.

- Uncover, turn over, sprinkle 2 teaspoons herbes de Provence, salt on plank, and add salmon, skin side down. Cover; grill 10–14 minutes until salmon flakes. Serve with crème fraîche mixture.

Spanish Halibut

In small skillet, heat 2 tablespoons olive oil; brown 1 onion for 7–9 minutes. Add 2 cloves minced garlic, 1 chopped green bell pepper, 1 (8-ounce) can tomato sauce, ¼ cup white wine, ⅓ cup sliced green olives, and 1 teaspoon paprika. Simmer for 10 minutes. Sprinkle 6 (6-ounce) halibut fillets with salt and pepper; brush with oil. Grill over medium direct heat; serve with sauce.

Asian Grilled Salmon

In shallow casserole dish, combine ¼ cup low-sodium soy sauce, ¼ cup teriyaki sauce, 2 tablespoons lemon juice, 2 tablespoons honey, 1 teaspoon five-spice powder. Add 6 (6-ounce) salmon steaks; refrigerate for 3–4 hours. Grill salmon on medium direct heat until done, about 15–18 minutes.

Spread Mustard Mixture on Salmon

- For planking, it's best to choose fillets that have skin on, especially if you turn the plank to the burned side.

- Then you can just lift the salmon flesh off the skin when it's time to serve.

- Mustard and lemon juice make a pungent paste to put on the fish, although salmon can stand up to it.

- If you want something a little more subtle, add 3-4 tablespoons of honey or fish stock to the mustard mixture, along with herbs or spices.

Grill Fish on Plank

- The plank will crackle and pop as the moisture inside heats up.

- Try different types of wood for your planked recipes. Avoid resinous woods like pine because they're too strong.

- Have a selection of small planks available so your guests can choose the flavor they want.

- Always soak the plank each time it's used for at least 3–4 hours. And scrape off the burned part after cooking so it's ready to go.

SEAFOOD PASTA SALADS
Tender grilled seafood combined with pasta and other ingredients makes a delicious salad

Seafood and pasta are natural partners. The delicate flavor of seafood isn't overwhelmed by perfectly cooked pasta.

You can coat the salad with any type of dressing: creamy, vinaigrette, or dressings made with pureed fruit.

A pasta salad is an ideal way to use up leftover grilled seafood, or you can grill the seafood specifically for these recipes.

If you're using leftover seafood, go for make-ahead salads like pasta salads that need to be chilled before serving.

There are so many delicious bottled salad dressings on the market now, so you don't have to make them. You can jazz up the purchased ones with some fresh vegetables or herbs to make them your own. *Yield: 8 servings*

Ingredients

¼ cup olive oil

¼ cup lemon juice

½ teaspoon grated lemon zest

3 tablespoons mustard

⅓ cup heavy cream

1 teaspoon salt

¼ teaspoon pepper

½ teaspoon dried dill weed

½ cup plain yogurt

3 (6-ounce) salmon fillets

1 pound asparagus

1 (16-ounce) package orzo pasta

1 pint cherry tomatoes

⅓ cup crumbled feta cheese

⅓ cup toasted pine nuts

Orzo Salmon Salad

- Bring a large pot of salted water to a boil. Meanwhile, in large bowl combine olive oil, lemon juice and zest, mustard, heavy cream, salt, pepper, dill weed, and yogurt.

- Grill salmon, or use leftover grilled salmon; flake into large pieces. Grill asparagus

- or use leftover grilled asparagus; cut into 1-inch pieces.

- Cook pasta according to package directions. Drain and add to dressing in bowl; stir to coat.

- Add remaining ingredients and gently stir. Cover; chill 3–4 hours before serving.

Greek Shrimp Pasta Salad

Add 2 tablespoons Dijon mustard to ¾ cup purchased red wine vinaigrette. Slice 1 yellow summer squash, 2 orange bell peppers, and 1 red onion. Grill in grill basket for 7–8 minutes. Brush shrimp with some more vinaigrette and grill for 4–5 minutes. Combine all ingredients with 12 ounces cooked drained pasta, ½ cup crumbled feta, and ½ cup sliced olives.

Old Bay Seafood Salad

Combine ½ cup mayonnaise, ½ cup plain yogurt, 2 tablespoons lemon juice, and 1 teaspoon Old Bay Seasoning. Sprinkle 1 pound shrimp and 1 pound halibut fillets with Old Bay and grill. Add to dressing along with 12 ounces cooked seashell pasta, 1 chopped red bell pepper, 2 chopped green onions, and 2 cups baby peas.

Break Apart Salmon

- Salmon will break apart naturally; just use your fingers or a fork and gently push on the fish to flake it.

- If you're grilling salmon just for this recipe, let it stand for a few minutes when it comes off the grill before flaking it.

- In a pinch, you can use a 12-ounce pouch of salmon, drained, in place of the grilled salmon.

- The salmon and asparagus can be grilled in a dual contact indoor grill if you'd like.

Toss Salad

- Stir the salad very gently, with an over and under motion, almost like folding, so you don't break up the fish.

- The dressing has to be made before the pasta is cooked, so the pasta can be immediately added to the dressing.

- Use your favorite vegetables in this flavorful salad. Grill sliced bell peppers, mushrooms, or summer squash.

- When the salad has chilled, you'll notice that the pasta has absorbed the dressing. Stir it gently to break up the salad.

SEAFOOD SANDWICHES

Everything from French bread to pitas enclose flavorful fillings in these grilled sammies

Sandwiches are so easy to make, but they don't have to be boring. These sandwiches are fancy enough to eat with a knife and fork. It's easy to transform your favorite recipe into a sandwich. Just layer the ingredients on bread or in a pita half.

Sandwich spreads are a great way to use up leftover grilled seafood. Just combine the seafood with some chopped veg-

etables or fruit, your favorite salad dressing, or just some mayonnaise thinned with lemon juice, and place between bread slices. Grilled or not, these sandwiches are quite a treat.

Think about unusual breads for your seafood sandwiches. Flavored tortillas, croissants, cracker bread, and focaccia are good choices, as are hot dog buns. *Yield: 4 servings*

Ingredients

2 tablespoons olive oil

1 tablespoon lemon juice

1 tablespoon chili powder

1 teaspoon smoked paprika

¼ teaspoon pepper

1 teaspoon salt

1 pound large shrimp, shelled

1 large loaf French bread

¼ cup butter, softened

½ cup mayonnaise

⅓ cup mustard

2 cups baby spinach leaves

2 tomatoes, thickly sliced

Shrimp Po' Boy Sandwich

- In large bowl, combine oil, lemon juice, chili powder, paprika, pepper, and salt. Add shrimp; toss to coat; let stand for 20 minutes.

- Split French bread and spread cut sides with butter. Combine mayonnaise and mustard in large bowl.

- Drain shrimp, place in grill basket, and grill over direct medium heat for 3–4 minutes, until shrimp curl and turn pink. Grill bread on both sides for 4–5 minutes.

- Add shrimp to mayonnaise mixture; place on bread. Add spinach and tomato, then top of bread; gently press.

Salmon Croissants

Brush 1 (8-ounce) salmon fillet with olive oil; sprinkle with salt, pepper, and dill weed. Grill over medium direct heat for 8–9 minutes. Cool and flake. In bowl, combine ½ cup each sour cream and plain yogurt, ¼ cup Dijon mustard, 2 cups baby peas, 1 cup diced Havarti cheese, 1 cup shredded carrot. Add salmon. Chill in refrigerator. Use as sandwich spread.

Pesto Grilled Shrimp Sandwiches

Toss 1 pound raw medium peeled shrimp with ½ cup basil pesto. Thread on skewers with 2 sliced red bell peppers. Grill for 4-5 minutes over direct medium heat. Make sandwiches with 6 buttered and toasted Hoagie buns, shrimp and peppers, mixture of ¼ cup each mayo and pesto, and 12 spinach leaves.

Marinate and Grill Shrimp

Assemble Sandwich

- The shrimp should be peeled and deveined, and make sure that the tails are removed. They're easier to eat that way.

- Don't marinate shrimp longer than directed. Make the dressing ahead of time, then marinate the shrimp just before grilling.

- Or if you'd like, you can grill the shrimp ahead of time, then combine with the mayonnaise mixture and chill.

- Any grilled vegetables would be delicious in this sandwich. Try grilled bell peppers, onions, or mushrooms.

- You can grill the sandwich after it has been assembled; just wrap in foil and grill until hot.

- For a more traditional po' boy sandwich, you can serve the ingredients in sliced hot dog buns.

- For the classic style, buy unsliced buns and slice through the top, not the side, so the bread is sturdier.

- Line the buns with spinach, top with shrimp mixture, and add diced tomatoes. Or combine all filling ingredients to make a salad.

SEAFOOD OVER PASTA

With or without sauce, seafood and pasta are a winning combo

Go beyond spaghetti and meatballs with these elegant recipes that combine grilled seafood with pasta and sauces.

Not only can you grill seafood, you can grill vegetables and cook the pasta on the grill. And again, this is an ideal use for leftover grilled seafood and vegetables.

Smoky grilled tomatoes and onions really make a spectacular pasta sauce. You may want to grill a large quantity, then simmer them together to make a pasta sauce you can bottle or freeze for later use. Contact your extension service if you want to can sauces.

For the simplest grilled seafood pasta meal, grill seafood and toss with cooked pasta, ⅓ cup reserved pasta water, ¼ cup olive oil, salt, pepper, and fresh herbs. *Yield: 6 servings*

Ingredients

2 pounds tomatoes, halved

1 teaspoon salt, divided

1 onion, sliced

4 cloves garlic, peeled

2 tablespoons olive oil

1 tablespoon lemon juice

1 teaspoon paprika

½ teaspoon dried oregano leaves

½ teaspoon dried basil leaves

⅛ teaspoon cayenne pepper

1 pound medium raw shrimp, shelled

1 (12-ounce) package ridged spaghetti pasta

⅓ cup grated Romano cheese

Grilled Tomato and Shrimp Sauce

- Bring pot of salted water to a boil. Sprinkle tomatoes with ½ teaspoon salt. Skewer onion slices and garlic cloves.

- Mix olive oil, lemon juice, paprika, ½ teaspoon salt, oregano, basil, and cayenne pepper. Toss with shrimp; let stand for 15 minutes.

- Grill tomatoes, onion, and garlic. Remove tomato skins, chop, and add flesh to a large bowl. Chop onion and garlic.

- Grill shrimp for 4–6 minutes; add to bowl. Cook pasta, drain and add to bowl; toss. Sprinkle with cheese and serve.

Cajun Shrimp with Pasta

Combine 2 teaspoons Cajun seasoning with ¼ teaspoon pepper; sprinkle onto ¾ pound each shrimp and scallops. In pot, heat 2 tablespoons olive oil; sauté 1 chopped onion and 3 cloves garlic. Add 1 (26-ounce) jar pasta sauce and 1 cup chili sauce and simmer. Grill shrimp and scallops. Add to sauce with 1 pound cooked spaghetti. Top with Cotija cheese.

Scallops and Asparagus in Cream Sauce

Trim 1 pound asparagus. Skewer ½ pound button mushrooms with sliced onion. Sprinkle 1 pound scallops with salt and pepper; brush with oil. Grill for 4–6 minutes until cooked. Place in saucepan with 1 cup mascarpone cheese, 1 (10-ounce) container Alfredo sauce, 1 teaspoon dried basil, and 12 ounces cooked shell pasta. Cook until hot.

Grill Vegetables for Sauce

- For a nice change, use several different colors and varieties of tomatoes.

- Heirloom tomatoes are readily available these days, either in the supermarket or at a farmer's stand or farmers' market. You can also grow your own.

- You don't have to remove the tomato skins, but they may be tough.

- Watch the garlic carefully on the grill, as it will cook faster than the other ingredients.

Grill Shrimp

- You can grill the shrimp on skewers or in a grill basket, or even directly on the grill if they're large enough.

- Use fresh herbs in place of the dried, especially in the summer. Fresh basil and oregano have a milder flavor than dried.

- Scallops can be substituted for the shrimp, or grill fish fillets and flake them into the sauce.

- For another variation, prepare the vegetables, plate them, and top with the grilled seafood and some fresh herbs.

GRILLED SEAFOOD RECIPES

SEAFOOD VEGETABLE SALADS

Mixing grilled salmon and shrimp with grilled vegetables amplifies the smoky flavor

Freshly grilled seafood placed on a cold salad is a delicious taste experience and is a great idea for entertaining. Or you can make a completely cold salad, using fresh or grilled vegetables and leftover seafood.

Think about different combinations of seafood for your salad creations. You can mix shrimp with mussels, salmon with scallops, or fish fillets with clams.

Famous seafood dishes can easily be transformed into salads. Cioppino, the classic seafood stew, makes an excellent salad, as does shrimp scampi.

You can even grill greens for your salad; romaine, cabbage, and iceberg will grill well, for even more flavor. *Yield: 8 servings*

Ingredients

½ cup mayonnaise

¾ cup plain yogurt

5 tablespoons lemon juice, divided

1 tablespoon sugar

1 teaspoon salt, divided

7 teaspoons chopped fresh dill

3 tablespoons Dijon mustard

4 dashes Tabasco sauce

3 tablespoons olive oil

½ pound large raw shrimp, shelled

½ pound salmon fillet

1 head red cabbage, quartered

2 ears corn on the cob

1 red bell pepper, sliced

1 small red onion, sliced

Dilled Fish Coleslaw

- In large bowl, mix mayonnaise, yogurt, 3 tablespoons lemon juice, sugar, ½ teaspoon salt, 6 teaspoons dill, mustard, and Tabasco.

- Mix olive oil, lemon juice, salt, and dill. Drizzle over shrimp and salmon; rub in.

- Grill cabbage, corn, pepper, and onion over medium direct heat for 3–6 minutes until crisp tender. Grill shrimp and salmon on grill mat until done.

- Chop cabbage, cut corn from cob, chop pepper and onion, and add to dressing. Add shrimp and salmon and stir. Chill for 4–6 hours.

~ VARIATIONS ~

Cioppino Salad

Combine ¾ cup Italian seasoning with ½ cup sour cream and 1 teaspoon dried basil. Grill 1 pound shrimp and 2 sliced red bell peppers. Add to dressing along with 15-ounce can drained artichoke hearts, 1 cup cherry tomatoes, and 1 chopped red onion. Serve over mixed salad greens. Grill 2 pounds mussels and place on salad.

Shrimp Scampi Salad

Melt 3 tablespoons butter; cook 3 cloves minced garlic. Brush on 1½ pounds large shrimp; grill shrimp 4–6 minutes. Combine ¼ cup Dijon mustard, ¼ cup lemon juice, and 1 cup plain yogurt. Add shrimp, 1 pint cherry tomatoes, 1 chopped red onion, and 2 cups baby peas. Serve on salad greens.

Grill Vegetables

Shred Cabbage; Chop Vegetables

- Grilling cabbage is unusual, but the tight heads stand up well to the heat of the grill.

- You can use red or green cabbage for this recipe. It's a bit easier to tell when green cabbage is perfectly grilled.

- Corn should be shucked, with the silk removed. Grill until the kernels turn brown, turning frequently.

- If you put the pepper and onion in a grill basket it will be easier to handle all of these veggies at the same time.

- Quarter the cabbage so more of the vegetable is exposed to the heat of the grill.

- To shred the cabbage, place it cut side down on work surface. Cut across the cabbage with a chef's knife into slivers.

- You can leave the slivers whole, or cut across them to make smaller pieces.

- To remove corn from the cob, hold it in the center of a bundt pan and cut down along the kernels, which will fall into the pan.

SEAFOOD PIZZA, FAJITAS, & MORE

Corn and flour tortillas make delicious pizzas, quesadillas, and fajitas with grilled seafood

Quesadillas, pizzas, and fajitas can all be made from tortillas. Don't limit yourself to plain flour or corn tortillas; there are many different varieties.

Red tortillas are flavored with red pepper and blue corn tortillas are made from blue corn, while green tortillas are usually flavored with spinach. The flavor is subtle, but it's there.

Any pizza recipe can be turned into a fajita and vice versa. The difference is the way the food is presented. Quesadillas are flat sandwiches; fajitas are wrap sandwiches;.

To soften tortillas for fajitas, wrap them in foil and grill for 3–5 minutes, turning once. Tortillas used for quesadillas and pizzas don't need softening. *Yield: 4 servings*

Ingredients

1 peach, halved

2 slices pineapple

1 tablespoon lemon juice

2 tablespoons brown sugar

½ pound medium raw shrimp, shelled

1 teaspoon paprika

½ teaspoon salt

⅛ teaspoon pepper

⅛ teaspoon cayenne pepper

8 (10-inch) flour tortillas

½ cup diced Brie cheese

2 tablespoons olive oil

Shrimp and Fruit Quesadillas

- Brush peach and pineapple with lemon juice; sprinkle with brown sugar; set aside.

- Mix shrimp with paprika, salt, pepper, and cayenne pepper; toss.

- Grill fruit over direct medium heat until grill marks appear, turning once. Grill shrimp in grill basket until it curls and turns pink. Chop fruit.

- Place 4 tortillas on work surface. Top with fruit, shrimp, and cheese; top with remaining tortillas. Brush with oil and grill for 2–3 minutes on each side until cheese melts; cut into quarters and serve.

Mini Hawaiian Pizzas

Shape pizza dough from page 95 into 6-inch rounds. Grill for 2–3 minutes, turning once, then top with your favorite pizza sauce, grilled medium shrimp, and drained pineapple tidbits. Sprinkle with Gouda and mozzarella cheeses and grill again until cheese is melted and pizzas are hot, about 4–5 minutes.

Salmon Fajitas

Sprinkle 1 pound salmon fillets with 1 tablespoon chili powder and ½ teaspoon cumin. Slice 2 red bell peppers and 1 onion and place in grill basket. Grill salmon and vegetables until done. Flake salmon and combine in bowl with 15-ounce can drained cannellini beans. Serve in softened tortillas with salsa, shredded Monterey Jack cheese, and chopped tomatoes.

Assemble Quesadillas

- Don't overfill the tortillas. If you have leftover filling, just make more quesadillas!

- It's okay to push down on the quesadillas when they're on the grill. In fact, that will help the cheese melt and hold the whole thing together.

- If you use scallops instead of shrimp, cut them into quarters before filling the quesadillas.

- Grilled salmon, tuna, or any fish can be used in place of the shrimp; rub with the same seasoning mixture.

Grill Quesadillas

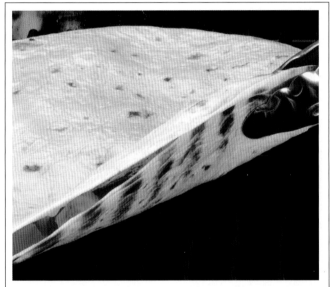

- Use the largest spatula you have to turn the quesadillas. The bottom tortilla will be crisp and should be sturdy enough to hold the filling.

- You can also slide a cookie sheet under them, flip them over, and slide onto the grill.

- Let the quesadillas stand for a minute, then with a sharp chef's knife or pizza cutter, cut them into quarters.

- Serve the quesadillas with a dip made from sour cream and any herbs or seasonings from the recipe.

SEAFOOD SOUPS

Hot and cold soups benefit from the wonderful flavor and texture of grilled seafood

Soups don't have to be simmered for hours. With the advent of boxed stocks, you can get a great homemade soup with old-fashioned taste in less than ½ hour.

Cold soups do need to be made ahead of time. Topped with hot grilled seafood, they are perfect for summer entertaining.

Rather than cooking onion, garlic, and vegetables in oil for the soup base, grill them instead, then combine in the stock to simmer for a few minutes.

Top soups with fun ingredients to add flavor, texture, and temperature contrast. Croutons are an obvious choice, but little crackers, fresh herbs, grated cheese, sour cream, popcorn, gremolata, or salsa are excellent options. *Yield: 6 servings*

Ingredients

- 3 potatoes, sliced
- 4 ears of corn, shucked
- 2 tablespoons olive oil
- 32 small clams, scrubbed
- 4 slices bacon
- 2 tablespoons butter
- 2 onions, chopped
- 3 cloves garlic, minced
- ¼ cup flour
- ½ teaspoon salt
- ⅛ teaspoon pepper
- 2 cups chicken or clam broth
- 2½ cups milk
- ½ cup heavy cream

Corn and Clam Chowder

- Brush potatoes and corn with olive oil; grill over direct medium heat until tender.

- Grill clams, covered, for 5–7 minutes until clams open. Remove clams from shell and chop; save liquor in small bowl.

- In large pot, cook bacon until crisp; drain and set aside. Add butter to pot; cook onion and garlic until tender. Add flour, salt, pepper; cook until bubbly.

- Add broth, milk, and cream; bring to a simmer. Cube potatoes, cut corn off cob, add with bacon, clams, liquor to pot; simmer 10 minutes.

Salmon Vichyssoise
Cut 4 potatoes in half lengthwise; brush with oil and grill along with 1 sliced leek. Remove potato skins and chop. Chop leek and combine in food processor along with potatoes, 4 cups chicken broth and 1 cup sour cream, salt, and pepper. Chill. When ready to eat, grill 1 pound salmon brushed with Italian dressing. Flake hot fish onto cold soup.

Italian Shrimp Soup
Sprinkle 1½ pounds large shrimp with 1 teaspoon celery salt, ¼ teaspoon pepper, and 1 teaspoon dried Italian seasoning, then grill until done. In large soup pot, melt ¼ cup butter; sauté 1 onion and 3 cloves garlic. Add ¼ cup tomato paste and let brown slightly. Add 4 cups chicken stock; simmer for 15 minutes. Add shrimp and heat through.

Grill Clams, Potatoes, and Corn

- The clam liquor is the liquid the clams give off when they are cooked.

- The liquor may be gritty if the clams have retained sand. You may want to strain it before adding to the soup.

- Remove the clams from the heat as they open. They will cook and finish at slightly different times.

- Turn the corn frequently so the kernels don't burn, and watch the potatoes carefully on the grill. Remove when brown and tender.

Prepare Corn, Finish Dish

- You can find utensils that will help you cut the kernels from the corncobs.

- After the kernels are cut off, scrape the cobs with the back of a knife to get the corn liquid and pulp; that adds lots of flavor.

- You can cook the bacon and finish this dish on the grill, or do it over medium-high heat on the stove indoors.

- This soup freezes well if there's any left over. Cool it, then pack into hard sided containers; freeze up to 1 month.

PLAIN VEGETABLES

Delicate vegetables can be quickly grilled to add smoky flavor and bring out their natural sweetness

Grilled vegetables can be delicious side dishes, or they can be the main course for a vegetarian feast. Vegetables grill very well; they take on a slight smoky flavor and their sweetness is intensified.

Vegetables are easier to grill than fruits, mostly because they are not as soft and delicate. The more delicate vegetables, like tomatoes, do better when cooked on a grill mat or in a grill basket. Pick the freshest vegetables you can find; they should be firm, with no dark or soft spots, and brightly colored. You can brush vegetables with just about anything when they're on the grill. Plain or seasoned butter, olive oil, salad dressings, or simple marinades are all delicious. *Yield: 6 servings*

Ingredients

1 tablespoon olive oil

1 onion, minced

3 cloves garlic, minced

2 tablespoons olive oil

2 tablespoons lemon juice

1 teaspoon salt

¼ teaspoon pepper

½ teaspoon dried basil leaves

1 teaspoon dried Italian seasoning

1 large zucchini

2 (8-ounce) packages whole mushrooms or 6 portobello mushrooms

Grilled Zucchini and Mushrooms

- In small bowl, combine all ingredients except zucchini and mushrooms; mix well.

- Slice zucchini ¼-inch slices. Trim edges from mushrooms stems; wipe mushrooms with damp cloth.

- Place vegetables in glass dish; marinade over. Let stand for 20 minutes. Heat grill medium-high heat.

- Place zucchini directly on grill, and place mushrooms in grill basket or on grill mat. Grill, turning zucchini once, and moving mushrooms around, brushing with marinade, until tender, about 5–7 minutes.

Portobello mushrooms are actually cremini mushrooms that are allowed to grow until large. The mushrooms have a tender, meaty texture and taste. They grill beautifully, either directly on the grill or on a grill rack or mat. The mushrooms will keep, wrapped in paper towel, in the refrigerator for 5–6 days.

•••• **RECIPE VARIATION** ••••

Grilled Flavored Corn on the Cob: Shuck 6–8 ears of corn; pull back but don't remove the green leaves. Remove corn silk; discard. Mix 1/3 cup softened butter with 1/4 cup grated Parmesan cheese and 1 tablespoon fresh thyme leaves. Brush this mixture over the kernels, then smooth leaves back over ears. Tie with kitchen twine; grill, turning frequently, for 8–11 minutes.

Grill Zucchini

Grill Mushrooms

- Don't peel the zucchini before grilling; it helps hold the flesh together and looks pretty, too.

- You could use just plain olive oil, flavored with salt and pepper, to brush on the vegetables as they are grilling.

- Tie fresh herb sprigs together and use those to brush the marinade on the vegetables.

- The marinade can be boiled and served with the vegetables as a sauce over hot cooked rice or couscous for a nice vegetarian main dish.

- Mushrooms have a high water content, which makes them delicate, but also good candidates for grilling.

- As the mushrooms grill, moisture evaporates and the flavor of the vegetable intensifies.

- Small mushrooms should

be cooked skewered on bamboo or metal skewers, in a grill basket, or on a grill mat.

- Larger mushrooms, like portobellos, can be cooked directly on the grill. Grill stem side down, then turn to finish; about 5–7 minutes total.

PEPPERS ON THE GRILL
Sweet bell peppers and hot jalapeños all benefit from the grill

Bell peppers, Italian peppers, and hot peppers, including jalapeños and habaneros, are all delicious grilled. These naturally sweet (and hot) vegetables only get better when grilled. Their flesh becomes meltingly tender, and they pick up a delicious smoky flavor.

You can peel grilled peppers or not. There are quite a few recipes that ask you to peel the grilled peppers, as the skins can interfere with the dish's texture.

If you do peel, never rinse the grilled peppers; you'll rinse away all the flavor! You can serve them as is without peeling, for even more smoky flavor.

Watch the peppers carefully. If you are going to peel them, the skins should blacken. If not, the skins should just be deep brown. *Yield: 6 servings*

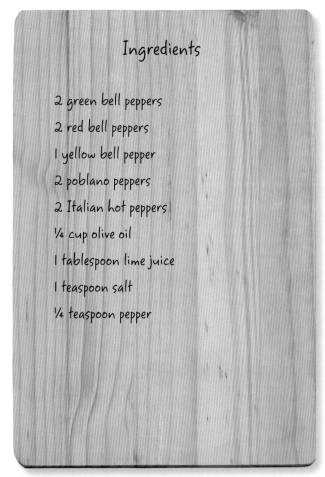

Ingredients

2 green bell peppers

2 red bell peppers

1 yellow bell pepper

2 poblano peppers

2 Italian hot peppers

¼ cup olive oil

1 tablespoon lime juice

1 teaspoon salt

¼ teaspoon pepper

Mixed Grilled Peppers

- Cut all the peppers in half; remove stems, tops, and seeds. In small bowl, combine remaining ingredients.

- Combine peppers in 2 large resealable plastic bags, Pour half of the oil mixture into each bag.

- Seal bag and gently knead to coat the peppers with the oil mixture. Let stand for 10 minutes.

- Prepare grill for medium direct heat. Grill peppers, skin side down, turning occasionally, until skin is blistered and brown. Remove peppers from grill. You can remove the skin, or leave it on.

218

Cheese Stuffed Peppers: Hold 5 large bell peppers upright and cut down each side, avoiding the core; cut 4 pieces from each pepper. Place peppers in dish and drizzle with 3 tablespoons olive oil and 2 tablespoons lemon juice. Grill peppers, skin side up, on direct medium heat. Turn peppers and fill with grated cheese. Cover; grill for 2–3 minutes until cheese melts.

ZOOM

Think about coordinating your cooking utensils based on whether they will be used on cooked or uncooked foods. Tongs, platters, and spatulas can be purchased in many different colors. You could designate all the red utensils to be used on uncooked food, such as for putting raw meats on the grill, and green utensils for food coming off the grill.

Grill Peppers

- If you cut the peppers in half or grill them whole, you'll need to turn them more often to get all the sides exposed to the grill.

- Pepper slices are easier to grill. You can grill them skin side down only, but if you want to stuff them, grill skin side up first.

- Sweet peppers, such as bell peppers, will become sweeter when grilled.

- The heat of hot peppers like habaneros will decrease slightly, but they will still be very spicy.

Peel Peppers

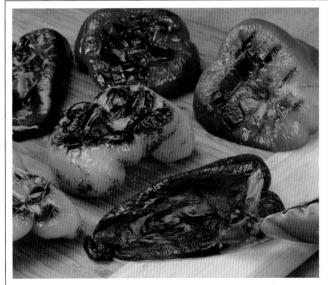

- If you want to peel the peppers, grill until the skins are blackened and blistered.

- Place the peppers in a paper bag and close it; let stand for 5–7 minutes. The peppers will steam, loosening the skins, so they'll be easy to peel.

- The skin will come off easily. Discard it, and serve the peppers as is, or use them in any recipe.

- Grilled peppers will be quite soft, so if you've stuffed them, let them cool a bit before serving.

MARINATED VEGETABLES
Lots of grilled vegetables benefit from marinades

Marinated vegetables are different from marinated meats. You aren't trying to tenderize these vegetables; you are just adding flavor and some moisture.

Some vegetables, like eggplant or cucumber, taste better after marinating. The marinades can remove some of the bitter liquid present in those raw vegetables.

You can use the marinade as a sauce to finish the vegetables if you boil it until slightly reduced. And topping the hot vegetables with fresh herbs or grated cheese adds more layers of flavor.

These vegetables are also excellent in salads. Chop them after they've cooled for a bit, then combine them with grilled meats, chicken, or seafood for an easy and healthy main dish. *Yield: 4–6 servings*

Ingredients

¼ cup olive oil

3 tablespoons lemon juice

½ teaspoon dried thyme leaves

½ teaspoon salt

⅛ teaspoon pepper

1 eggplant, peeled and sliced

1 onion, sliced

1 sweet red onion, sliced

2 red tomatoes, halved

1 tablespoon minced fresh mint

1 tablespoon minced cilantro leaves

3 tablespoons crumbled blue cheese

Marinated Eggplant with Onion Tomato Salsa

- In small bowl, combine oil, lemon juice, thyme, salt, pepper. Pour into 13-inch x 9-inch glass baking dish.

- Slice eggplant into rounds; add to dish. Skewer onions and add to dish. Cover; marinate for 30–40 minutes. Prepare grill for medium-high direct heat.

- Remove vegetables from marinade; reserve marinade. Grill vegetables, turning once, until tender, about 5–7 minutes.

- Place eggplant on platter. Chop onions, tomatoes; mix with reserved marinade, mint, cilantro, blue cheese; spoon over eggplant.

Marinated Mushroom Kabobs

Combine ½ cup zesty Italian salad dressing with 1 (8-ounce) package of cremini mushrooms, 1 onion cut into 12 wedges, and 1 sliced yellow summer squash. Marinate for 1–2 hours in the fridge. Thread onto soaked bamboo skewers and grill on direct medium heat for 2–4 minutes, turning once.

Marinated Mixed Vegetables

Combine ¼ cup olive oil, 3 tablespoons red wine vinegar, 1 teaspoon dried basil leaves, and salt and pepper to taste. Cut 2 red and 2 green bell peppers into chunks and add to marinade along with 2 sliced zucchini and ½ pound frozen green beans, thawed. Marinate for 15 minutes, then drain; grill on grill mat over direct medium heat for 5–7 minutes, stirring frequently.

Marinate Vegetables

- If the eggplant is very large, you may want to salt it before adding to the marinade.

- Just sprinkle the eggplant slices with salt and let stand for 15–20 minutes. Rinse off the liquid and salt and pat dry, then marinate.

- You can use any vinaigrette or oil and vinegar salad dressing instead of the olive oil mixture.

- Instead of skewering the onions, you can slice them and cook in a grill basket, or chop and grill on a mat.

Combine Salsa Ingredients

- All of the grilling can be done ahead of time. Assemble the recipe as directed, adding the cheese just before serving.

- You can leave the food at room temperature for a few hours, or chill it before serving.

- Other fresh herbs will also complement these flavors. Try fresh chopped basil, chives, oregano, or thyme leaves.

- And other cheeses will work well too. Feta cheese, diced Monterey Jack cheese, or grated Parmesan would be delicious.

GRILLED VEGETABLES

PRECOOKED VEGETABLES

Most hard vegetables, including root vegetables, need to be precooked before being grilled

Hard root vegetables should be precooked before grilling for best results. This also cuts down on the time spent on the grill, so the veggies will be moist and tender inside and crisp outside.

You can cut the potatoes any shape you'd like. Slices are easy to turn on the grill, but you can cut potatoes into chunks or wedges; they just need to be manipulated more often.

You can grill baby root vegetables. A combination of baby carrots, parsnips, and tiny red potatoes would be delicious.

Mix and match different types of root vegetables for a flavorful side dish. Most root vegetables grill at about the same time, especially if they are cut to the same size. *Yield: 6 servings*

Ingredients

4 Yukon Gold potatoes

3 russet potatoes

1 sweet potato

3 tablespoons white wine vinegar

1½ teaspoons salt

¼ teaspoon pepper

2 tablespoons olive oil

2 tablespoons mayonnaise

2 tablespoons Dijon mustard

1 tablespoon chopped fresh thyme leaves

Grilled Potato Medley

- Leave skins on potatoes; scrub, rinse, and dry. Cut potatoes into ½-inch-thick slices and place in large pot.

- Cover with cold water and bring to a boil; simmer for 4–5 minutes until potatoes are tender around the edges. Remove to wire rack. Sprinkle with vinegar and let cool for 15 minutes.

- Combine remaining ingredients and brush on both sides of potatoes.

- Grill potatoes over direct medium heat, until tender. This should take 4–5 minutes per side. Pile potatoes in serving dish.

Grilled Curried Cauliflower

Cut 1 large cauliflower into florets. Cook in simmering water for 3–4 minutes until crisp-tender; drain. In bowl, combine cauliflower with 2 tablespoons olive oil, 1 chopped red onion, and salt and pepper to taste. Grill mixture on grill mat, stirring, until tender, about 4–5 minutes. Sprinkle with 1 tablespoon curry powder; grill for another minute, then serve.

Grilled Baby Vegetables

Bring a large pot of water to a boil. Add 12 baby potatoes; cook for 3–4 minutes and remove. Add 1 pound baby carrots; cook for 4 minutes, then remove carrots from water. Add 12 baby beets; cook for 5–6 minutes and remove. Skewer vegetables, brush with vinaigrette, and grill for 5–6 minutes.

Simmer Potatoes

Grill Potatoes

- It's important to precook the vegetables until they give a bit when pressed, but are still firm.

- If overcooked, the vegetables will fall apart on the grill. If they do precook too long, just grill them on a grill mat.

- When you're precooking root vegetables, start with the least colorful so the vegetables retain their individual colors.

- For example, beets will stain the cooking water and color the vegetables cooked after them.

- Make sure that the grill is well oiled before you add vegetables. They do not contain fat, so will stick more easily than meats.

- When the vegetables are ready to be turned, they will release from the grill. Don't move them if they resist.

- You can create crosshatch grill marks on sturdy root vegetables; just turn them 90 degrees.

- Not all precooked vegetables will grill for the same amount of time; watch carefully.

GRILLED VEGETABLES

223

VEGETABLE SALADS
Grilled vegetables add wonderful flavor to hot or cold salads

Vegetable salads are delicious and so good for you. Add the flavor of the grill to bring these recipes to a new level.

Vegetables can be marinated before being put on the grill, or you can toss them with a salad dressing when they come off. The vegetables will absorb the dressing when added to it hot.

Think about your favorite vegetable side dishes and recreate them on the grill. Grilled potato salad can be made with

cheeses and vegetables from your favorite potato casserole, or an Asian stir-fry can be converted into a salad.

And if you add protein—whether it be cheese, grilled chicken, leftover steak, or ham—to these salads, you've created another main dish salad. *Yield: 6 servings*

Ingredients

1 small head green cabbage

1 head red cabbage

1 onion, sliced

7 tablespoons olive oil, divided

1 teaspoon salt, divided

¼ teaspoon pepper, divided

1 cup plain yogurt

⅓ cup lime juice

2 tablespoons grated fresh ginger root

1 tablespoon sugar

1–2 teaspoons ground five-spice powder

1 red bell pepper

1 bunch green onions, chopped

1 pint cherry tomatoes

Five-Spice Grilled Coleslaw

- Remove outer leaves from cabbages. Cut each head into 6 wedges. Skewer onion slices. Sprinkle with 3 tablespoons olive oil and ½ of the salt and pepper.

- Grill over medium direct heat, until vegetables are marked about 3 minutes on each side.

- Mix ¼ cup olive oil, yogurt, remaining salt and pepper, lime juice, ginger, sugar, five-spice powder in bowl.

- Chop cabbage, grilled onion, and bell pepper; add to dressing with green onion and tomatoes. Toss gently to coat, then serve or chill for 3–4 hours.

Grilled Romaine Salad

Slice 2 heads romaine lettuce into quarters. Drizzle with 3 tablespoons olive oil and salt and pepper. Grill lettuce on medium direct heat for 7–9 minutes, turning occasionally, until slightly charred. Remove, cool, and chop. Toss in bowl with 1 pint grape tomatoes, 1 chopped red onion, and ½ cup ranch salad dressing.

Grilled Tex-Mex Salad

Combine 1 sliced yellow summer squash, 2 red bell peppers, 1 green bell pepper, and 1 sliced zucchini. Sprinkle with 2 tablespoons each olive oil and lime juice, 1 tablespoon chili powder, Place in grill basket; grill until tender. Grill 4 ears corn, then cut kernels off cob. Combine all in large bowl with 1 cup salsa and 2 tablespoons olive oil.

Grill Cabbage

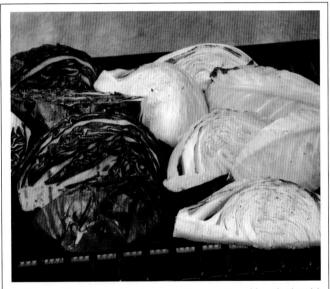

Mix Dressing

- Cabbage has a sweet and slightly spicy flavor that is enhanced by cooking on the grill.

- Choose heavy and firm cabbage with tight leaves and a smooth surface. You can cut out the core after grilling if you'd like.

- The quartered heads should stay together on the grill, but you may want to pierce them with a metal skewer to hold things together.

- For a change, you could grill 1 head iceberg lettuce instead of the green cabbage.

- Five-spice powder is a combination of pepper, anise, cloves, cinnamon, and fennel. Combine those spices yourself if you can't find it.

- For a non-creamy dressing, omit the yogurt and add ⅓ cup olive oil.

- You can add other grilled vegetables to this spicy cole slaw. Adding vegetables that haven't been grilled makes a nice texture contrast.

- Chopped mushrooms, grilled corn, grilled summer squash, or frozen baby peas are good choices for additions to this side dish.

GRILLED VEGETABLES

VEGETABLE PACKETS

To add a sauce, grill your vegetables wrapped up in foil packets for individual presentation

Foil packets don't have to be a full meal; they can contain the side dish when you are grilling a steak or hamburgers. Delicate vegetables work well in packets; the foil protects them from the grill's intense heat, and it holds in all the flavor.

The only thing better than well-flavored, tender grilled vegetables is to serve them with a contrasting sauce. You can serve vegetables spiced with jalapeños and chili powder with cold salsa. Grilled corn and bell peppers can be served with a sour cream and cheese mixture.

Hard vegetables do need to be precooked before adding them to packets. Delicate vegetables are perfect as is. Enjoy creating your own combinations. *Yield: 6 servings*

Ingredients

½ cup Greek yogurt

½ cup sour cream

1 cucumber, peeled, seeded, and chopped

2 tablespoons minced fresh mint

1 pound green beans, trimmed

3 red bell peppers, sliced

8 small red potatoes, quartered

2 red onions, chopped

8 cloves garlic, minced

3 tablespoons olive oil

3 tablespoons red wine vinegar

1 tablespoon sugar

1 teaspoon salt

1 teaspoon dried oregano leaves

¼ teaspoon pepper

Greek Grilled Vegetable Packets

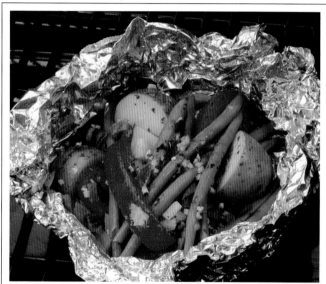

- In small bowl, mix yogurt, sour cream, cucumber and mint; refrigerate.

- Prepare vegetables. Tear off 6 sheets of 18-inch x 12-inch heavy duty foil. Place vegetables in center of each sheet.

- In small bowl, combine remaining ingredients and drizzle over each vegetable packet. Fold foil around vegetables, making a double fold.

- Grill vegetables over direct medium heat, turning and moving around the grill, until vegetables are tender, about 20–30 minutes. Serve with yogurt sauce.

Caramelized Onions and Garlic

Peel and chop 5 large onions and 6 garlic cloves. Place on 2 18-inch x 12-inch sheets heavy duty foil. In small saucepan, melt 2 tablespoons butter with ¼ cup olive oil, 2 tablespoons white wine vinegar, salt, and pepper; pour over onions. Fold packets closed, using a double fold. Grill over direct medium heat for 50–60 minutes, stirring after 25 minutes, until onions are caramelized.

All-American Grilled Vegetable Packets

In large bowl, combine 20-ounce package refrigerated potato wedges, drained, 15 frozen 2-inch pieces corn on the cob, thawed, 1 pound frozen green beans, thawed, and 1 chopped onion. Divide among six foil pieces; top with ½ cup purchased herb vinaigrette. Grill as directed, turning frequently, until vegetables are hot and tender.

Prepare Packets

- If you're pouring a sauce or marinade on the vegetables, bend the foil around them so the sauce is contained.

- The packets should have some room inside for heat expansion when on the grill.

- Place the vegetables with the most moisture on the bottom, so they steam as they cook.

- This will help cook the harder vegetables, while the moisture-rich vegetables caramelize. And make sure that any sauce reaches to the bottom of the packets.

Grill Vegetable Packets

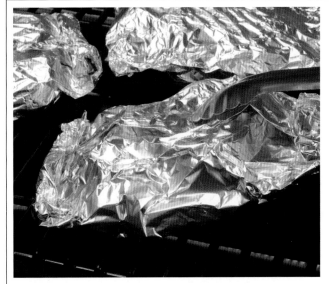

- Even though packets are easier to grill than vegetables straight on the grill, you still have to pay attention.

- Move the packets around, from direct heat to indirect heat, so the vegetables don't burn on the bottom.

- Move the packets with a large spatula or tongs. Don't pierce the foil.

- The packets will be very hot, as will the sauce inside. Let the packets stand for 5–15 minutes after grilling to cool off a little.

GRILLED VEGETABLES

227

MANUFACTURERS, HOTLINES, & MORE

Where to find information for your grilling needs

RESOURCES

When you grill, you're never alone. There are hundreds of books, videos, television shows, and information from manufacturers to help you. Invest in a few books and browse the Internet to find many more recipes for food on the grill. When you have questions, you can turn to grilling hotlines and Web sites.

Other people can be a great source of information. Join in on some online message boards and ask questions. There will probably be some questions you can answer too!

And don't forget about the store where you purchased your grill. There are often experts on hand who can answer questions and repair the grill.

Grilling Manufacturers

Big Green Egg
www.biggreenegg.com
- The Big Green Egg is a heavy duty cast-iron grill and smoker that will, literally, last a lifetime. It uses much less fuel than traditional grills.

Coleman Grills
www.coleman.com
- The Coleman Company makes equipment for outdoor living; not just grills, but camping equipment too.

Fiesta Grills
www.fiestagasgrills.com
- Fiesta offers four lines of grills, ranging from simple gas grills to complete built-in kitchens.

GrillSearch
www.grillsearch.com
- This website lists just about all of the grill manufacturers in the world. Links to websites and equipment information.

Hearth, Patio & Barbecue Association
www.hpba.org
- This association offers product information, news about new products and recalls, recipes, and service locators.

Holland Grills
www.hollandgrill.com
- Holland grills are designed to prevent flare-ups, because a drip pan is permanently installed between the food and the burners.

Jenn-Air
www.jennair.com
- Jenn-Air specializes in large, well-equipped gas grills. They also offer equipment and tools to complement the grills.

Viking Grills
www.vikingrange.com
- These premium, high-end grills are all meant to be built into a custom outdoor kitchen.

Weber Grills

www.weber.com
- Weber grills are classic. The makers of the original kettle grill also make sophisticated gas grills and lots of tools.

Grilling Hotline Numbers

Hedlund Hotline

1-866-HEDLUND
- This hotline is for ordering and questions about Holland Classic Grills.

National Fire Protection Association

www.nfpa.org
- All you need to know about grilling safety.

US Consumer Product Safety Commission

888-638-2772 (CPSC)
- This hotline is for questions and concerns about products manufactured and/or sold in the US.

Weber-Stephens' Hotline

1-800-GRILL-OUT
- You can also send an email to: grillout@ weber.com for questions about their grills and grilling in general.

WEB SITES, TV SHOWS, & VIDEOS
Find more recipes and join in on the conversation

RESOURCES

Grilling Web sites

Barbecue at About.com
www.bbq.about.com
- Site offers everything from grill reviews and recommendations to tips on cleaning and maintaining the grill, how to get the most out of your grill or smoker, and hundreds of recipes.

BBQ Bible.com
www.barbecuebible.com
- Steven Raichlen shares techniques and recipes. Also, a forum, newsletter, and store.

BBQ Central
www.nbbqa.org

- Join this organization for a members-only forum, lots of tips, recipes and events.

The BBQ Forum
http://rbjb.com/rbjb/rbjbboard
- Lots of forums for different types of barbecues and grills. Ask questions and get answers.

The Big Green Egg Forum
www.biggreenegg.com/forums
- Ask questions and get answers from other Big Green Egg aficionados.

Grilling Recipes.com
www.grilling-recipes.com
- Over a thousand recipes for your grill.

Kansas City Barbecue Society
www.kcbs.us
- Kansas City is famous for its barbecue. Join the society and attend events, meet other members, and take classes on grilling and BBQ.

USDA Food Safety (show photo of food thermometer)
www.fsis.usda.gov
- Look here for information about food safety and grilling safety from the U.S. Government.

Grilling TV Shows

BBQU on PBS
www.bbqu.net
- Steven Raichlen's show features a 'grill-cam' that is a camera built right into the grill. This show has lots of recipes and tips.

Boy Meets Grill on the Food Network

www.foodtv.com
- Chef Bobby Flay grills everything from appetizers to desserts at his New York loft.

License to Grill on The Food Network

www.foodtv.ca
- Chef Rob Rainford shows you how to grill for entertaining.

Road Grill on the Food Network

www.foodtv.ca
- Matt Dunigan sets up a grilling event at different locations every week.

Grilling Competitions

American Royal BBQ

www.americanroyal.com
- Enjoy this annual competition where competitors have to grill 10 pounds of meat. Set in Kansas City's stockyard district.

Cattlemen's BBQ Grand World Championship

www.cattlemensbbqsauce.com
- World-wide competition held every spring in Memphis, Tennessee.

Grilling videos

AllRecipes.com Outdoor Cooking

http://allrecipes.com/Info/Videos/Outdoor-Cooking/Main.aspx
- Choose from videos showing you how to roast marshmallows, make pizza on the grill, and campfire foods.

Epicurious

http://video.epicurious.com
- Lots of videos on every kind of cooking. Scroll down the 'Channels' to find videos teaching you how to grill.

Food Lion Videos

www.foodliongrilling.com/videos
- The grocery chain offers videos from experts on methods, fire building, and recipes.

Grilling Safety

http://video.epicurious.com
- Video showing food and fire safety tips.

MeFeedia

www.mefeedia.com/tags/grilling
- Hundreds of videos showing you how to grill everything from pineapple to lobster tail to stuffed bread.

RV Cooking Show

www.rvcookingshow.com
- Grill in your RV! Fun video showing how to grill with limited equipment and space.

GLOSSARY

Ash: Carbon compounds and other compounds left behind when charcoal or wood burn completely.

Baste: To cover food with a sauce or marinade while cooking.

Briquette: Fuel for the grill, made from coal dust and charcoal, shaped to look like a piece of coal.

Butterflying: To cut a piece of meat in half, then spread it open to increase surface area.

Caramelize: A chemical reaction catalyzed by heat that combines sugars and proteins to form complex flavors and colors in grilled food.

Charcoal: Real charcoal is made by burning solid wood in a controlled atmosphere without carbon; it becomes almost pure carbon.

Chimney Starter: A metal container with a handle that is used to start briquettes or lump charcoal before adding to grill pan.

Direct Grilling: To cook food directly over a heat source, whether a burner, coals, or burning wood.

Drip Pan: A pan, usually made of aluminum, placed in the coal bed under the food to catch drips as food cooks over indirect heat.

Flare-Ups: When melted fat drips onto the fire, a flame will shoot up from the coals or burners. Controlled by moving food on the grill grate.

Grill Marks: The deep brown marks on food that indicate where it was in contact with the grate while grilling.

Indirect Grilling: To cook food over an area on the grill where there are no coals, usually over a drip pan.

Marinade: A mixture of an acid like citrus, oil, and seasonings used to flavor meat, fruits, and vegetables before grilling.

Mop: Both a thin mixture placed on food as it is grilling, and a tool like a floor mop, used to apply marinades and glazes.

Quadrillage: A way of placing food on the grill to create crosshatch marks.

Rub: A mixture of dry ingredients, usually spices, pepper, and salt, that is rubbed on food to season before grilling.

Sear: To grill food, usually meat, over hot direct flame so the surface browns and caramelizes.

Skewer: As a noun, a sharp metal or wooden stick threaded with food. As a verb, to place food on a skewer to make ka-bobs.

Vents: Openings in the grill, both above and below the food, which can be used to regulate heat and temperature.

Wood Chips: Chips of real wood, sometimes flavored, soaked and added to the fire to add flavor to grilled food.

BOOKS AND MAGAZINES

Grilling Books

America's Test Kitchen (May 30, 2005). *The Cook's Illustrated Guide To Grilling And Barbecue: A Practical Guide for the Outdoor Cook.* America's Test Kitchen, 2005.
- Step-by-step guide to each recipe, with lots of detailed information. Huge product guide with reviews.

Better Homes and Gardens. *Biggest Book of Grilling.* Better Homes and Gardens, 2004.
- This huge book has more than 400 recipes, and lots of grilling help and information.

Guillen, D., M. Everly, M. Lowrey, and G. Brensdorff. *The Plank Grilling Cookbook.* Sasquatch Books, 2006.
- Lots of recipes and advice on how to grill food on a plank, including safety tips and different types of wood.

Mauer, Don. *The Complete Idiot's Guide to Grilling.* Alpha, 2006.
- Great book for novices, and step-by-step instructions plus more than 200 recipes.

Purviance, Jamie, and Tim Turner. *Weber's Real Grilling.* Sunset Publishing Corporation, 2005.
- Recipes with detailed instructions and lots of advice on how to choose the best grill for you.

Raichlen, Steven. *How to Grill.* Workman Publishing Company, 2001.
- Creative techniques, lots of recipes, and photos will help you become a grill master in no time.

Rama, Marie, and John Mariani. *Grilling for Dummies.* For Dummies, 1998.
- Book covers every step of the grilling process and offers more than a hundred recipes. Basic information and tips on grilling skills.

Schlesinger, Christopher, *The Thrill of the Grill.* William Morrow Cookbooks, 2002.
- Bold and highly flavored recipes are featured in this book. Lots of hot peppers and unusual foods.

Schloss, Andrew, David Joachim, and Alison Miksch. *Mastering the Grill.* Chronicle Books, 2007.
- Book focuses on the science of grilling. Lots of recipes and step-by-step illustrations.

Grilling Magazines

Backyard Living Magazine
www.backyardlivingmagazine.com
- This magazine (and companion web site) offers lots of grilling how-tos, information, and recipes.

Grilling Magazine
www.grillingmag.com
- Both a magazine and a web site, this tome features great recipes and grilling tips.

RESOURCES

METRIC CONVERSION TABLES

Approximate U.S. Metric Equivalents

Liquid Ingredients

U.S. MEASURES	METRIC	U.S. MEASURES	METRIC
1/4 TSP.	1.23 ML	2 TBSP.	29.57 ML
1/2 TSP.	2.36 ML	3 TBSP.	44.36 ML
3/4 TSP.	3.70 ML	1/4 CUP	59.15 ML
1 TSP.	4.93 ML	1/2 CUP	118.30 ML
1 1/4 TSP.	6.16 ML	1 CUP	236.59 ML
1 1/2 TSP.	7.39 ML	2 CUPS OR 1 PT.	473.18 ML
1 3/4 TSP.	8.63 ML	3 CUPS	709.77 ML
2 TSP.	9.86 ML	4 CUPS OR 1 QT.	946.36 ML
1 TBSP.	14.79 ML	4 QTS. OR 1 GAL.	3.79 LT

Dry Ingredients

U.S. MEASURES		METRIC	U.S. MEASURES	METRIC
17 3/5 OZ.	1 LIVRE	500 G	2 OZ.	60 (56.6) G
16 OZ.	1 LB.	454 G	1 3/4 OZ.	50 G
8 7/8 OZ.		250 G	1 OZ.	30 (28.3) G
5 1/4 OZ.		150 G	7/8 OZ.	25 G
4 1/2 OZ.		125 G	3/4 OZ.	21 (21.3) G
4 OZ.		115 (113.2) G	1/2 OZ.	15 (14.2) G
3 1/2 OZ.		100 G	1/4 OZ.	7 (7.1) G
3 OZ.		85 (84.9) G	1/8 OZ.	3 1/2 (3.5) G
2 4/5 OZ.		80 G	1/16 OZ.	2 (1.8) G

RESOURCES

FIND GRILLS AND ACCESSORIES

Where to Buy Grills

Ace Hardware
www.acehardware.com
- Ace Hardware carries many lines of grills, and they have a complete line of grilling tools and accessories. Grill repair available.

Barbecues.com
www.barbecues.com
- Online store with free shipping lets you choose grills, stoves, and accessories.

BBQ Depot
www.thebbqdepot.com
- Huge online store offers everything from grills to outdoor kitchens, fireplaces, fryers, smokers, and gifts.

Grill Showroom
www.grillshowroom.com
- This online store offers hundreds of grills, divided into categories of price and type.

Home Depot
www.homedepot.com
- Large national retailer offers a good selection of all grill brands and accessories.

Lowes
www.lowes.com
- This national chain offers all of the major grill brands along with all the accessories and tools you'll need.

Sears
www.sears.com/
- Sears offers Kenmore grills and accessories, along with Weber and Coleman grills. Lots of smokers, including BBQ Pro Deluxe.

SpitJack.com
www.spitjack.com
- Motto is 'for men who cook.' Lots of tools and accessories, including firepits, wood, grills, and knives.

True Value
www.truevalue.com
- Nationwide chain has good collection of all grill brands and accessories.

Grilling Catalogs and Websites

Cooking.com
www.cooking.com

- Web site offers cooking tools, cookbooks, and accessories for the grill and outdoor kitchen.

Frontgate

www.frontgate.com

- Another upscale catalog and website with high end grills and tools.

Grandin Road

www.grandinroad.com

- Upscale catalog has lots of top-of-the-line grills, accessories, and equipment for outdoor kitchens.

Solutions

www.solutions.com

- Fun catalog has an array of grilling and cooking accessories and toys.

Sur La Table

www.surlatable.com

- Catalog and website has extensive lines of cookware and tableware.

FIND INGREDIENTS

Farmers' markets

Always Brilliant.com
www.alwaysbrilliant.com
- Online source for grilling toys and equipment like flavored wood chips.

Charcoal Store.com
www.charcoalstore.com
- Online store offers grills, source for lump charcoal, flavored woods, and accessories.

Farmer's Markets
www.farmersmarketla.com
- Los Angeles Farmer's Market website; the original farmer's market.

Farmer's Market Search
http://apps.ams.usda.gov/FarmersMarkets
- The U.S. government's website with listings of farmer's markets in cities and states.

Island Seafoods.com
www.islandseafoods.com
- Online store offers door-to-door delivery of fresh seafood at market prices.

La Cense Beef
www.lacensebeef.com
- Source for organic and grass-fed beef from Montana.

National Directory of Farmer's Markets
www.farmersmarket.com
- Site has an index of U.S. Farmer's Markets listed by state.

Peapod
www.peapod.com
- Online grocery store serving some areas of the United States.

Schwans
www.schwans.com
- Home delivery of fresh and frozen ingredients.

Grilling enthusiast and paleontologist Christopher A. Norris videotaped the roasting of a whole lamb as part of a birthday celebration. The lamb recipe is listed below. For the video and more cooking information, please visit www.knackbooks.com.

Grill Roast Whole Lamb

The whole lamb will weigh 25-30 pounds. Some of the bones need to be sawed so the lamb will lie flat. Using an electric saw, cut through the pelvic bone, then cut on either side of the breastbone. Press down firmly so lamb lies flat.

Combine 3 tablespoons ground mixed peppercorns, 2 tablespoons kosher salt, five cloves of peeled garlic and mash together with a mortar and pestle to make a rub. Rub this mixture over the lamb, cover, and refrigerate while you prepare the rack and firepit.

For the basting sauce, combine 1 cup olive oil, ¾ cup balsamic vinegar, 3 tablespoons fresh rosemary leaves, 3 tablespoons fresh thyme leaves, 2 tablespoons fresh oregano leaves, and 1 tablespoon minced fresh sage leaves. Add 1 tablespoon whole black peppercorns, 4 crushed cloves of garlic, the juice of two lemons, and the lemon rinds. Mix and refrigerate along with the lamb.

Make your own racks using rebar, which are strong steel rods held together with wire. Be sure the racks are large enough to hold the lamb, with some rods going beyond the lamb so the rack can be suspended in the grill.

Now build your own firepit, using thirty-six concrete blocks placed on bare ground or a concrete slab (not asphalt!) Use four blocks to make the long sides of the rectangle, and two, inset into the rectangle, for the ends. Lay four to five sheets of heavy-duty aluminum foil over the blocks and into the pit, making sure the foil extends past the blocks. Lay a second layer of blocks on top of the first to hold the foil in place, then top with third layer.

Add 20 pounds of charcoal to several chimney starters and light. When the coals are covered with ash, pour into the firepit, divide them into several sections all around the edge of the pit, and clear a space for the drip pan or pans. Add water and rosemary and thyme sprigs to drip pan(s). Place the lamb 9-12 inches from the coals, sliding the rods between the concrete blocks to hold the lamb level and in place.

Brush thoroughly with the basting sauce, cover with a large sheet of aluminum foil held down with wood blocks or more concrete blocks, and start grilling the lamb. Baste the lamb every 3 hours; keep the basting sauce in the refrigerator in between. Grill the lamb for 7 to 9 hours or until for medium; a meat thermometer should read 155°F.

INDEX